THE GREAT BRIDGE SCANDAL

ALAN TRUSCOTT

MASTER POINT PRESS • TORONTO, ONTARIO

Master Point Press
331 Douglas Ave.
Toronto, Ontario, Canada
M5M 1H2
(416) 781-0351
Website: http://www.masterpointpress.com
Email: info@masterpointpress.com

National Library of Canada Cataloguing in Publication

Truscott, Alan
        The great bridge scandal : the most famous cheating case in the history of the game / Alan Truscott. -- 2nd ed.

ISBN 1-894154-67-3

        1. Reese, Terence. 2. Schapiro, Boris, 1909-2002 3. Cardsharping. 4. Bermuda Bowl Championships (11th: 1965: Buenos Aires, Argentina) I. Title.

GV1282.3.T78 2004   795.41'5'0922   C2003-906623-1

Editor   Ray Lee
Cover and interior design   Olena S. Sullivan/New Mediatrix
Interior format and copy editing Luise Lee

Printed in Canada by Webcom Ltd.

1 2 3 4 5 6 7   09 08 07 06 05 04

The king of hearts a broadsword bears,
The queen of hearts a rose.
Though why, not every gambler cares
Or cartomancer knows.
Be beauty yours, be honor mine,
Yet sword and rose are one:
Great emblems that in love combine
Until the dealing's done.
For no card, whether small or face,
Shall overtrump our two
Except the heart of hearts, the ace,
To which their title's due.

ROBERT GRAVES
(Reprinted by permission of the author.)

ACKNOWLEDGEMENTS

I SHOULD like to express my thanks to the numerous bridge personalities who contributed their own stories or otherwise supplied me with information, and also to the late Victor Mollo. He acted most ably as devil's advocate in two important areas, the technical evidence and the general arguments for the defense.

CONTENTS

PREFACE to the Second Edition

In May, 1965, headlines throughout the world proclaimed that Terence Reese and Boris Schapiro, Britain's greatest bridge partnership, had been accused of cheating in the World Championship tournament in Buenos Aires, Argentina. They were said to be using finger signals to convey to each other the number of cards held in the heart suit.

Some time later it became known that the World Bridge Federation (W.B.F.) had found the players guilty. But this was only the start. A British inquiry examined the evidence at great length and eventually found the players not guilty on the basis of 'reasonable doubt'.

In December, 1966, Reese published his own version of the affair in a persuasive book, *Story of an Accusation*. As part of his attempt to discredit his opponents Reese claimed that he and Schapiro had never been the object of suspicion. By contrast, *The Great Bridge Scandal* reveals a checkered past history, and cites documentary evidence demonstrating clearly that the heart code was in use five years before Buenos Aires. Reese implied that I and other witnesses for the prosecution manufactured evidence against him. The facts show that if he was innocent he must have been the victim of a gigantic international conspiracy. This book was my reply on behalf of the 'conspirators.'

This new edition, published thirty-nine years after the Buenos Aires affair, provides some corrections and updates. It also offers views of the case from two top players who are also lawyers.

ALAN TRUSCOTT
New York
February 2004

INTRODUCTION

BRIDGE is without question the queen of card games. It presents a challenge to players on all levels, from beginners to experts, from ages nine to ninety-nine.

But it has three substantial drawbacks lacking in chess, which is the other great intellectual game.

It provokes displays of bad manners and bad temper, simply because it is a partnership game. Husbands and wives rail at each other in domestic foursomes, and sometimes divorce is the result. National champions squabble acrimoniously at the table and indulge in bridge divorces without need for legal formalities. The game tests character, and it is perhaps unfair to blame the game because some players fail to pass the test.

The second drawback is that there is a luck factor, although some would regard this as a plus rather than a minus. The luck factor is a substantial element in rubber bridge, the form of the game normally played in homes and clubs, but good players will do better than bad players in the long run. In the tournament game the luck of the deal is eliminated. Each partnership and team is trying to do better than other players holding the same cards. Some luck remains: good contracts and good plays sometimes fail, bad contracts and bad plays sometimes succeed. Some decisions are strictly guesses, so the spinning of a mental coin can influence the result considerably.

This luck is at a minimum in a long team match, for the side that plays better almost always wins. Luck is about as likely to decide such a match as it would be in a close golf or tennis match between high-class performers. These head-to-head matches are the norm in world competition. Each team consists of six players, four of whom play in each session according to the instructions of the non-playing captain. Each deal is played twice, and the team that holds the North-South cards on the first occasion will hold the East-West cards when the hand is replayed. The two results are eventually compared, and if one team has an advantage it gains a certain number of "international match points" (IMPs) according to a sliding scale. The international matchpoint scores finally decide the result of the match.

The World Championship in 1965 was a four-cornered contest between Italy, the defending champions, Great Britain, North America, and Argentina. It was played in a nine-day period in Buenos Aires, and during that time each team played a match of 144 deals against each other team. Carl' Alberto Perroux led his great Italian Blue Team — Pietro Forquet, Benito Garozzo, Giorgio Belladonna, Walter Avarelli, Massimo D'Alelio, and Camillo Pabis-Ticci — to victory for the eighth time. In each session the spectators had a choice. They could watch a designated match in comfort in the Bridge-O-Rama theater, following the play card by card on a giant electric board and listening to an expert commentary. Or they could watch the other match "live" in less comfort by sitting on a wooden staging surrounding a playing table and peering down at the proceedings. This table, in the Open Room, was the only one at which the players could be seen by spectators, a fact that became significant later in the week.

The third drawback of bridge is generally assumed not to exist, and the assumption is an entirely reasonable one.

It is possible to cheat.

LIST OF CHARACTERS

BECKER, B. JAY, of New York (died 1987). Member of the U.S. team in Buenos Aires. See Chapter 1.

BOURNE, GENERAL LORD, of London (died 1982). Co-chairman in the London inquiry.

BUTLER, GEOFFREY, of London (died 1985). The British delegate to the World Bridge Federation in Buenos Aires. See Chapter 5.

CAPLAN, LEONARD, of London. Q.C. Counsel for the defense in the London inquiry.

ERDOS, IVAN, of Los Angeles (died 1967). Member of the U.S. team in Buenos Aires.

FELL, GEOFFREY, of Skipton, England (died 1979). Nonplaying captain of the British team in 1952.

FLINT, JEREMY, of London (died 1990). Member of the British team in Buenos Aires.

FORQUET, PIETRO, of Naples. Member of the Italian team in Buenos Aires.

FOSTER, SIR JOHN, Q.C., M.P., of London (died 1982). Chairman in the London inquiry.

FRANKLIN, HAROLD, of Leeds (died 1998). British tournament director.

FREY, RICHARD, of New York (died 1988). A.C.B.L. director of public relations.

GAROZZO, BENITO, of Rome. Member of the Italian team in Buenos Aires.

GERBER, JOHN, of Houston, Texas (died 1981). Nonplaying captain of the U.S. team in Buenos Aires. See Chapter 3.

GOLDBLATT, SIMON, of London. Counsel for the prosecution in the London inquiry.

GRIEVE, WILLIAM, of New York. Member of U.S. team in Turin, 1960.

GRUENTHER, GENERAL ALFRED, of Washington, D.C. (died 1983). Honorary President of the W.B.F.

HARRISON-GRAY, MAURICE, of London (died 1968) . Member of the British team in Buenos Aires.

HAYDEN, DOROTHY (now Truscott), of Hastings-on-Hudson, New York. Member of the U.S. team in Buenos Aires. See Chapter 2.

HÉRÉDIA, IRÉNÉE DE BAJOS, of Paris (died 1998). French tournament director.

HIRON, ALAN, of London, later of Malaga, Spain (died 1999). An assessor at the London inquiry.

HIRSCH, TANNAH, of Stamford, Connecticut. Assistant editor of A.C.B.L. Bulletin.

JAQUES, ARTURO, of Buenos Aires (died 1991). Chief commentator in Buenos Aires.

KEHELA, SAMMY, of Toronto. Coach of U.S. team in Buenos Aires. See Chapter 6.

KEMPSON, EWART, of Gainford, England (died 1966) . Nonplaying captain of British women's team in 1952.

KONSTAM, KENNETH, of London (died 1968). Member of British team in Buenos Aires.

LANDY, ALVIN, of New York (died 1967). A.C.B.L. executive secretary and former W.B.F. secretary.

LERENA, RAOUL, of Buenos Aires. Chief tournament director at Buenos Aires.

LEVENTRITT, PETER, of New York (died 1998). Member of U.S. team in Buenos Aires.

MACNAB, ROBIN, of Bozeman, Montana (died 1984). A.C.B.L. president and U.S. delegate to W.B.F. in Buenos Aires.

MARKUS, RIXI, of London (died 1992). Member of British women's team in Dublin, 1952.

MARQUARDT, EDUARDO, of Buenos Aires. Nonplaying captain of Argentine team in Buenos Aires.

MARX, JACK, of London (died 1991). Member of British team in 1950.

MATHE, LEW of Los Angeles (died 1986). Member of U.S. team in 1955.

MEREDITH, ADAM, of New York (died 1976). Member of British team in 1955.

MOBBS, SIR A. NOEL, of London (died 1959). Chairman of B.B.L. in 1950.

MOLLO, VICTOR, of London (died 1987). English bridge writer.

MURRAY, ERIC, of Toronto. Member of Canadian team in Turin, 1960.

OAKIE, DON, of San Jose, California (died 1983). Member of U.S. team in Turin, 1960. See Chapter 13.

PERROUX, CARL ALBERTO, of Modena, Italy (died 1977). Nonplaying captain of Italian team in Buenos Aires.

PETTERSON, KELSEY, of Los Angeles (died 1983). Member of U.S. team in Buenos Aires.

PRESTON, RICHARD of London (died 1978). Partner of Ralph Swimer.

PRIDAY, TONY, of London. An assessor at the London inquiry.

RAPEE, GEORGE, of New York (died 1999). Member of U.S. team in Turin, 1960.

REESE, TERENCE, of London, later of Hove (died 1996). Member of British team in Buenos Aires and one of the accused players.

ROSE, ALBERT, of London (died 1970). Member of British team in Buenos Aires.

RUBIN, IRA, of Paramus, New Jersey. Member of U.S. team in Turin, 1960.

SANTAMARINA, AGUSTIN, of Buenos Aires (died 1995). Member of Argentine team in Buenos Aires.

SCHAPIRO, BORIS, of London (died 2002). Member of British team in Buenos Aires and one of the accused players.

SILODOR, SIDNEY, of Philadelphia (died 1963). Member of U.S. team in Turin, 1960.

SOLOMON, CHARLES, of Philadelphia (died 1975). W.B.F. President.

SWIMER, RALPH, of London (died 1997). Nonplaying captain of British team in Buenos Aires. See Chapter 4.

TARLO, LOUIS, of London (died 1997). Nonplaying captain of British team in Turin, 1960.

THE BECKER STORY: OBSERVATION   1

B. JAY BECKER, of Flushing, New York, born 1904, was one of the world's greatest players. He was world champion in 1951 and 1953 and represented the United States on four other occasions. He had the rare distinction of winning a national championship in his first year of tournament play, and his thirty-one titles include twenty-one in major team events. He had the best record of any player in the Masters Individual Championship, an event no longer played.

His syndicated bridge column was published in more news papers throughout the world than any other, and he was a member of the National Laws Commission, which deals with matters of laws and ethics in bridge for North America.

He could field a Becker bridge team, including two sons, a brother, and two nephews, at the time the strongest family team of six in the world. (In 2003 this can be challenged by the Moss family group: Mike Moss, Sylvia Moss, Gail Greenberg, Jack Greenberg, Brad Moss, Andrew Moss and Jill Levin.)

It all began innocently enough. Dorothy Hayden and I were playing against Reese and Schapiro on the first day of our match against Great Britain, and we were about one-third through the evening session's play when I happened to look over at Reese on my right and noticed that he was holding his cards with two fingers spread in V style in front of his cards.

It meant very little to me at the time, but it struck me subconsciously that this was an uncomfortable way to hold cards. At least 99 per cent of all players grip their cards with thumb and four fingers; you would have to search far and wide for players who do not hold their cards this way.

I will never know whether this fleeting observation of how Reese was holding his cards would have made a lasting impression on me except that when I looked at Schapiro to my left on the very same deal I observed that he was also holding his cards with the same two fingers (the index and middle fingers) in a V formation.

Again what I saw caused only a subconscious ripple in my thoughts, since I was concentrating deeply on the bidding and play of the hand. At the time I had no reason to think that this extraordinary way of holding cards was more than a strange coincidence, since I had played against Reese and Schapiro on a number of occasions and had always found their behavior and their ethics at the bridge table beyond reproach.

However, as the evening wore on, I could not fail to notice that the number of fingers used by Reese and Schapiro in holding their cards varied from hand to hand. Usually there were three or four fingers showing, less often one or two, but the pattern, whatever it was, kept changing from one deal to the next.

While I did not permit my observations to interfere with my play, the gnawing feeling that something improper was going on and that finger signals of one kind or another were being exchanged could not fail to assert itself in the back of my mind. In a dull sort of way it seemed to me that the changing pattern of fingers with each deal could not be accidental, but I did not have time really to think about the matter because my first obligation, obviously, was to play each hand for all it was worth and not to allow myself to be diverted by anything else.

We finished the evening session without incident, and it turned out that Britain gained 10 IMPs on the 20 boards we had just played. With one-third of the 144-board match now over, the American team was 22 IMPs behind.

As usual, we met after the session with our teammates and went over the hands played. Peter Leventritt was greatly in need of cheering up; he had had a disastrous hand against M. Harrison-Gray and Albert Rose in which he had claimed the balance of the tricks in a slam contract and then proceeded to go down because he was not allowed to draw a missing trump he had forgotten about. The oversight cost us 17 IMPs; without it we would have been 5 IMPs behind instead of 22. It was not until nearly two hours after the session was over that I finally had a chance to speak to Mrs. Hayden privately about what I had observed.

As I expected, she had seen nothing irregular in the behavior of Reese and Schapiro at the table, and I remember that I even had had some doubts at the time about the advisability of telling her about the finger signals. As the session and the evening had worn on I had become more and more convinced that we were being cheated in some unknown way, and by the time I decided to tell Mrs. Hayden of my suspicions, my doubts were almost entirely dissolved.

What I said to Mrs. Hayden was: "Dorothy, I'm very sorry to have to tell you this, but I think we were cheated tonight."

Mrs. Hayden reacted to this quiet bombshell very calmly. She did not tell me that I was either crazy or mistaken but merely asked what had happened that made me think so. I then related what I had seen in the course of the evening. We had a deck of cards handy, and I demonstrated how the cards had been held by

Reese and Schapiro. I could not tell her how many fingers were shown on each particular hand because I had not noted either in writing or mentally the number of fingers associated with each hand.

As the conversation progressed Mrs. Hayden expressed strong doubts that Reese and Schapiro would be signaling in such a blatant and obvious manner, but when I pointed out that she had not observed the finger movements herself and that apparently no one else had noticed anything strange in the way they held their cards, she realized that there might be something to what I was saying. I said to her several times that she did not have to rely on what I had told her I had seen but that she could observe for herself the next time we played against Reese and Schapiro and then make up her own mind about whether they were signaling to each other.

There were two other matters I took up with Mrs. Hayden. One was that I asked her not to tell anyone else about our conversation or my suspicions, and to this she readily agreed. We were both well aware of the seriousness of a cheating accusation, and neither of us was inclined by nature to go off halfcocked on such a vital matter.

The other was a plea on my part, which I repeated time and again, that regardless of what she observed the next time we played against Reese and Schapiro, she was not to allow her game to be affected. I realized only too well that seeing the changing fingers might interfere with her concentration, and all I could do was stress the importance of playing her best game when we met them again.

We were not scheduled to play again against the British before Thursday, and during the interval Mrs. Hayden and I did not refer to the Reese-Schapiro problem in more than a very cursory way. We were busily engaged in playing against Argentina and Italy on Tuesday and Wednesday, and there was not much time to think about anything else. Furthermore, we did not know whether we would play against Reese and Schapiro again, or against some other British pair. The nonplaying captains —Ralph Swimer for Britain and John Gerber for the U.S. — primarily were responsible for the pairings, and there was a great deal of jockeying going on in this regard.

As it happened, Mrs. Hayden and I were pitted against Reese and Schapiro in the opening session on Thursday. I do not know whether this was accidental or by design, but there we were, carrying on where we had left off Monday night.

The fingers went into operation immediately. From the first board we played to the last one fourteen boards later, the ever-changing pattern of fingers continued. There was no need for me to ask Mrs. Hayden whether she saw what was going on: it was all too obvious.

My point had been proved, regrettably, but it was no cause for satisfaction. I knew that messages were going back and forth between Reese and Schapiro, and not knowing what the messages meant gave me a feeling of eeriness and futility, but there was nothing I felt I could do at this point except grin and bear it.

On top of that, Mrs. Hayden was playing badly, and I knew that the finger business had affected her game. It was a disastrous session for us — our team was outscored 63 IMPs to 2 — and most of these points were lost at our table.

When the session was over, we had only a few minutes left before the next session was scheduled to start. I had very little opportunity to talk privately to Mrs. Hayden, but I spent it pleading with her again to play to the best of her ability and stop allowing herself to be diverted by the march of the fingers. We were scheduled to play Reese and Schapiro again, this time on Bridge-O-Rama.

Apparently my words were more successful this time, because Mrs. Hayden recovered her poise and played well in this session. The finger changes continued as usual, but Reese and Schapiro had several bad hands, and we managed to have the best of them. Actually we lost IMPs on the session, but this was due primarily to poor results by our teammates in the Closed Room.

As soon as possible after the session was over, I had a long talk with Mrs. Hayden. There was no question about whether Reese and Schapiro were using finger signals; the question was what to do about it. Neither of us had ever encountered a situation like this before, and it was difficult to know what to do. To go directly to Reese and Schapiro and tell them that we knew they were cheating was bound to bring a vigorous and indignant denial. It seemed likely that they would immediately stop the finger movements if we told them what we had observed, but with the match more than half over and the British 101 IMPs ahead, this course of action would be equivalent to conceding the match to Britain. We had no way of knowing how many IMPs we had lost as a result of the signals, but it seemed to us that these losses were probably substantial.

I suggested that we ought to bring someone else into the picture to help us solve the dilemma, and Mrs. Hayden immediately named Alan Truscott. This struck me as a good idea for many reasons. Truscott was bridge editor of *The New York Times*, was known as a fair-minded person, and furthermore had lived nearly all his life in England. Also, he had been a member of the British international team in 1962 and undoubtedly knew Reese and Schapiro very well. On all counts, therefore, he seemed to be an ideal person to turn to, not only for advice but to have as one more witness to buttress our suspicions.

We sought out Truscott in the pressroom and told him that we had an important matter to talk to him about. He was busy at the time and still had a lot of work to do, so we made a date with him for 2 A.M., when he expected to be free. Mrs. Hayden and I had the evening off while our teammates were locked in battle for the third session of the day. We were pleasantly surprised to find at the end of the evening that our team had recovered 52 IMPs in twenty boards against the lineup of Reese-Jeremy Flint and Rose-Gray.

At about 2 A.M., Truscott, Mrs. Hayden, and I went up to my room for what seemed to me at the time a very important conference. As we entered the room I closed the transom over my door so that our conversation could not be overheard by outsiders. I began immediately by saying to Truscott that what I was about to tell him was highly confidential and that he was not to repeat what we said without our prior approval. Truscott readily agreed to this condition, and I started out by telling him that in my opinion and Mrs. Hayden's Reese and Schapiro were unquestionably using a code of signals and were transmitting illegal information to each other.

His spontaneous reply was that he had frequently heard such accusations against Reese-Schapiro in the past, but that no one had ever been able to prove anything. I now told Truscott what I had observed on Monday evening, and what both Mrs. Hayden and I had seen in the two sessions we had played Thursday afternoon against Reese and Schapiro. I also demonstrated with playing cards the various finger positions that had been employed against us, and Mrs. Hayden also described in detail what had occurred during our twenty-eight boards of play that afternoon.

Much to my surprise, Truscott did not take a very serious view of the matter. Apparently he did not think that Reese and Schapiro would engage in such a childish method of signaling as we had described; he seemed to think that such signals would be much too obvious and that Reese and Schapiro would not indulge in anything so foolish. I told him that he did not have to take my word for it, or Mrs. Hayden's, that finger signals were being exchanged; that all we wanted him to do was to watch Reese and Schapiro the next time they played together; and that he could then see for himself whether or not our accusation was well founded. As the conversation wore on, Truscott's original attitude of incredulity was somewhat dissipated, and by the time we had finished threshing the matter out, he had promised to watch Reese and Schapiro at the next opportunity. We discussed what could be done if it turned out that our suspicions were confirmed by him, but we got nowhere in this matter and decided that it would be best to postpone any action until after Truscott had had a chance to observe for himself.

Before going to sleep early that morning, I arrived at the conclusion that having Truscott as both a witness and an adviser would still not put us on solid enough ground. I decided we needed one more witness, someone not too high up in the hierarchy of bridge — since such a person might not be able to keep a confidence of this sort — but nevertheless someone with prestige in the world of bridge. It naturally occurred to me that I could go to Swimer or to Geoffrey Butler, the chairman of the British Bridge League (B.B.L.) and its most important official, and tell them what I had observed, but I barely knew either of them and did not know what type of reaction I would get.

In the end, the only one I could think of who fitted the need of the occasion was Gerber. I have since thought a great deal about whom I could have turned to for assistance in this very delicate matter, and I am satisfied that I made the best possible choice under the circumstances.

Later that morning I consulted Mrs. Hayden about informing Gerber, and she promptly agreed to the proposal. Accordingly, I telephoned Gerber and set up a date for the two of us to talk to him that afternoon in his room.

I began the conversation by informing Gerber that the matter I was about to discuss was important and I needed his assurance that he would treat it as highly confidential and not tell anyone else about it without my prior approval. This assurance was immediately forthcoming, and we then proceeded to tell Gerber everything that had transpired to that moment. Gerber was obviously impressed by what we told him and wasted no time telling us we might be mistaken. He promised to watch Reese and Schapiro if and when they played against Italy that afternoon. Gerber closed the conversation by assuring us again that he would treat the matter as confidential and not repeat it without first consulting us.

That afternoon Mrs. Hayden and I had both sessions off while our teammates were playing against Argentina. I had some letters to write and other work to do and did not appear in the playing area until about a half-hour after Reese and Schapiro had started to play against Pietro Forquet and Benito Garozzo in the Open Room in the second session of the afternoon. It had not occurred to me earlier that I should have been there at the start of play to observe in a leisurely manner exactly what Reese and Schapiro were doing on each hand.

As soon as I entered the Open Room Mrs. Hayden accosted me and said that Gerber had watched the first few hands and was completely convinced that something was "going on, all right". He had seen the finger signals for himself and needed no more proof on top of what we had told him earlier that afternoon. I also saw Gerber and he repeated what he had said to Mrs. Hayden.[1]

At the same time, Mrs. Hayden showed me the back of a scorecard on which she had entered the board number and the number of fingers shown by Schapiro on each hand she had watched. She had been standing in the grandstand behind Reese and could easily see the number of fingers Schapiro used each deal to hold his cards. She asked me to go to the opposite side of the grandstand and stand

---

1. See footnote, page 35. — A.T.

behind Schapiro so that I could see how many fingers Reese displayed each deal.

Accordingly, I posted myself behind Schapiro, and as soon as the bidding of each deal was over I descended from the tier of steps and met with Mrs. Hayden outside the playing area and behind the grandstand and told her the number of fingers shown by Reese on that deal. Mrs. Hayden in each case had already written down the board number and the number of fingers shown by Schapiro. In this way Mrs. Hayden compiled a complete record of all the hands both of us watched, and in addition she made jottings here and there of Reese's holdings in some of the suits.

In several cases, because of the height from which I was watching, I could not be sure whether Reese's little finger was holding the cards or was curled back out of sight, and in each of these cases, for the sake of complete accuracy, I asked Mrs. Hayden to record the finger showing as 3d, that is, three fingers showing with a drooping fourth. I knew that at some time or other in the future an attempt would be made to decode the meaning of the finger positions, and I wanted to be sure that my data would reflect not only what I clearly saw but also what was indistinct that I saw. It was my feeling at the time that whatever the code was, unraveling the solution might take months.

There was one other thing that I verified while watching, about which I had previously been unsure. I noticed that soon after the bidding was over and play commenced, Reese and Schapiro both went back to the normal way of holding cards, that is, with four fingers. This struck me at the time as highly significant. In addition, I now had the opportunity to study more carefully how Reese held his cards. There was one hand (Board No. 114) in which he held his cards in a most extraordinary manner. He was using the thumb and all four fingers in gripping the cards, but the four fingers were very widely spread, making three Vs and, furthermore, extended almost the full length of the cards. This posture struck me as rather crude, and of all the observations I made during the three sessions I played against him and the one I was watching, I thought this posture was the most awkward. Hands in which Reese held the cards with only one finger showing were likewise striking, but these occurred only rarely. It was only later, after the code had been broken, that we learned why the frequency was uneven.

I must confess that while Mrs. Hayden and I were recording the number of fingers shown on each hand, I did not have much faith in our ability to crack the code before the tournament was over. I thought the code would be much too complicated to solve quickly, and I very much doubted that the comparatively few deals we would be able to record and diagnose would provide the answer.

However, Mrs. Hayden, who is highly gifted when it comes to solving challenging problems, was much more sanguine about our prospects. Even during the bidding and when we met behind the grandstand after each deal she was busy theorizing about the possible meanings of the various signals. Her instinct told her that the fingers referred to distribution rather than high-card strength, while my instinct was just the opposite.

When the session was over, Mrs. Hayden, Truscott, and I had a brief conference. Truscott, as a newspaperman, had sat right at the table between Reese and Forquet and had had an even better view than we had of the proceedings. However, he had taken no notes. He had seen the changing fingers on each deal and was convinced that a code of some sort was being used by Reese and Schapiro, but he had no idea what the signals meant.

Mrs. Hayden and I were scheduled to play that night against Argentina, so we gave Truscott a copy of the notes we had made and asked him to take a shot at trying to break the code. We knew he would have access to the official records of the hands played that afternoon and that a comparison of the notes with the hands might prove fruitful. He willingly undertook to do this and spent most of the time, while we were playing against Argentina, trying to solve the code. We made a date to meet again after the session was over.

There was an unexpected development late that afternoon. Gerber came to me and again stated that having watched Reese and Schapiro in action, he was completely convinced that they were transmitting illegal signals to each other. He also said that under the circumstances he had felt obliged to inform both Robin MacNab, president of the American Contract Bridge League, and Waldemar von Zedtwitz, president emeritus of the A.C.B.L., of what he had seen. He apologized profusely for having broken his promise to us and said he hoped I would not mind what he had done.

There was very little I could do or say when Gerber told me this, since I could not undo what he had done. Actually, I said nothing. At the time I was greatly annoyed that he could see fit to break a confidence so soon after he had promised he wouldn't, but I now realize that in view of his position as captain of the American team he could not afford to be silent in the matter. Perhaps he should have come to me first, as a matter of protocol, but it is only fair to add that the urgency of the situation demanded action and bare formalities could excusably be brushed aside.

Of course I knew that with six people[2] now aware of what was going on, the matter was slipping out of control. In some respects this was a favorable development because I was actively engaged playing in a world championship and did not

---

2. Becker did not appreciate, even at this point, that Perroux had been told by Gerber —
   A.T.

really have the time to pursue the matter and give it the proper attention. Mrs. Hayden and I had been told by Gerber that we would play all three sessions in the crucial match against Italy the next day, and I could hardly be expected to take the time required to push the Reese-Schapiro problem to a conclusion. Besides, I did not know what to do because much as I wanted to save Reese and Schapiro from a public exposure, which would almost certainly ruin them, I could think of no way of saving them while protecting the rights of the American team.

From this point on, the matter was actually out of my control. The circle of officials who learned of the affair kept widening, and Gerber on two or three occasions posted me on developments, but from the time that MacNab and Von Zedtwitz were informed, I had nothing to do with the steps taken by the World Bridge Federation.

Shortly after 2 A.M., Mrs. Hayden, Truscott, and I went out to an all-night restaurant some two or three miles from the Plaza Hotel. Truscott brought with him the officially recorded set of hands that corresponded to the boards noted by Mrs. Hayden that afternoon. He informed us that he had studied not only the Reese-Schapiro hands of the Friday afternoon session against Italy but also others they had played against different opponents earlier in the week. He had found some hands that he felt Reese and Schapiro had bid in an odd manner, but he had made no real progress in trying to solve the finger code. Throughout Truscott's discussion of what he had found and failed to find, which took nearly half an hour, Mrs. Hayden insisted that the best way of trying to solve the problem was to take all one-finger signals and compare them with the corresponding hands, and so on.

Eventually Mrs. Hayden had her way. There was only one hand (No. 120) that afternoon which had a one-finger signal, and when we examined it, we found that Schapiro, who had held his cards with one finger, had a singleton heart. It was at this point that Mrs. Hayden was struck by a brilliant thought. She recalled a hand (No. 51) we had played against Reese-Schapiro on Thursday in which Reese had held the cards with one finger and it turned out he had the singleton ace of hearts. They had bid six spades and easily made it, and I had no trouble remembering the hand.

"Wouldn't it be strange," Mrs. Hayden now said, "if it turned out that one finger meant one heart, two fingers two hearts, three fingers three hearts, and so on?"

Breathlessly we examined the hands in which two fingers had been shown. By the time we had examined them and found the number of fingers to correspond to the number of hearts, we were fairly well convinced, and when we went to the three- and four-finger hands we found the correlation to be exactly correct. There was now no doubt that we had broken the code. The three of us each had some knowledge of probabilities, and the chance that all these correlations (there were nineteen of them) were accidental was bound to be billions or more to one.

There was one stumbling block we encountered as we went over the hands, but it was quickly surmounted. On the fourth board (No. 121) we compared, Mrs. Hayden's notes showed that Schapiro held his cards with two fingers while the official hand record showed him to have five hearts. We concluded that two fingers represented either two or five hearts and I suggested that in this respect the ambiguity was similar to the Roman Blackwood convention where a response of five clubs indicates either no aces or three aces and a response of five diamonds indicates one ace or four aces. Shortly after this, when we came to the four-finger hands, the theory was more precisely pinned down. On deal No. 114, the hand previously referred to in which Reese had four fingers very widely spread, he had seven hearts. Since it was reasonable to assume there was an arrangement by which a holding of more than four hearts could be represented with only four fingers, we all more or less simultaneously reached the conclusion that two fingers together meant two hearts and two fingers spread apart meant five hearts; that three fingers together meant three hearts and three fingers spread apart meant six hearts; that four fingers together meant four hearts and four fingers spread apart meant seven hearts. There were no six-card heart suits held by Reese or Schapiro that afternoon, so we were unable to confirm the theory in full, but the two-finger signal with five hearts on No. 121 and the spread four-finger signal on No. 114 made it seem highly likely that we had solved the question of how five, six, or seven hearts were represented.

There was one other case in which the comparison was not precisely correct. As mentioned before, I had been uncertain several times whether Reese was holding his cards with three or four fingers. I was watching him from a height in the grandstand where my eyes were about ten feet above his hands, and it was difficult to tell whether his little finger was touching the cards or was curled out of sight. In four cases I told Mrs. Hayden to mark my observations as 3d. It turned out, as we compared, that in three of the cases Reese actually held three hearts, and that in the fourth case (No. 115) he had four hearts.

Mrs. Hayden, Truscott, and I were of course pleased to have solved the code, and I, especially, because I had thought there was little chance of finding the solution before the tournament was over. It was now 4 A.M., but despite the hour, we agreed to notify Gerber at once of the newest development. Truscott tried to reach him by telephone at the Plaza Hotel, but his room did not answer. As Mrs. Hayden and I were due to play against Italy that day (Saturday) and needed the sleep, Truscott undertook to inform Gerber in the morning.

Most of the developments on Saturday and Sunday are covered elsewhere in this book, but I can summarize them briefly. Truscott notified Gerber at 9 A.M. on Saturday that the code had been broken. Swimer and Butler were then brought into the picture and watched Reese and Schapiro play that night against Argentina. They took notes on the finger signals and found them to conform to the code. On Sunday morning, the last day of the tournament, I testified before the Appeals Committee of the World Bridge Federation and told them what I knew of the affair. Later in the day, after Reese and Schapiro had appeared before the Executive Committee, they were unanimously convicted of cheating. Swimer told the committee that he would not permit Reese or Schapiro to play any sessions that day against North America and that at some point before the tournament was finished Britain would concede its matches. (I did not learn most of the details of what had happened on Saturday and Sunday until many weeks later.)

There was one incident that occurred Sunday evening which struck me at the time as very peculiar. Mrs. Hayden and I had played both afternoon sessions against Great Britain and were also scheduled to play the evening session on Bridge-O-Rama. We arrived ten minutes early and were in the foyer on our way to the Bridge-O-Rama playing room when we were accosted by Sam Kehela, the coach and deputy captain of the American team.

Even before the tournament started, Kehela had expressed to us his admiration for Reese both as a bridge player and as a person: He told us that he enjoyed the way Reese spoke and thought, that in his opinion Reese was the best player in the world, and that Reese and Schapiro were easily the outstanding pair on defense in the entire bridge world. I agreed heartily with his ranking of Reese and Schapiro on defense, since I had had a similar opinion for many years. I did not realize at the time that this conversation in which Kehela expressed what amounted to hero worship would later on be supplemented by an extraordinary loyalty on his part after Reese and Schapiro had been found guilty of cheating by the World Bridge Federation.

Now, as Kehela spoke to us in the foyer, he was obviously in an upset state. His eyes were red, apparently from lack of sleep. I was aware that Gerber had told him on Saturday of the code that Reese and Schapiro were using and that Kehela had witnessed the finger signals for himself and was fully convinced. I knew that he had said as much to Mrs. Hayden the night before.

Kehela asked me to withdraw my insistence, which I had voiced to Gerber from the start, that the United States could not lose its match to Great Britain. (At the time of this conversation, Britain was leading the United States by 46 IMPS.) Kehela said something to this effect: "If they were cheating, what difference does it make to you whether you finish second or third? You have won so many championships that it cannot matter to you whether you are second or third, but it will mean a great deal if Britain does not have to forfeit the match to the U.S. and we can avoid a public scandal."

I told him that so far as I was concerned I still wanted to keep the matter as quiet as possible but that I could not subscribe to the thought of losing a match in which I thought we were lagging behind chiefly because of unfair means used by Reese and Schapiro. It was up to the rest of the British team, I said, to forestall a forfeiture if they chose.[3]

Kehela urged me to relent, but again I told him that I could not see my way clear to accepting defeat and that furthermore the matter was really out of my hands. (At that point I did not know that lengthy hearings and meetings had been held all day long and that many final decisions had already been reached by the World Bridge Federation. Mrs. Hayden and I had been busy all afternoon playing against the British.)

The conversation ended unsatisfactorily, with Kehela still greatly disturbed and unhappy. Mrs. Hayden and I went to the Bridge-O-Rama playing room, and there we played for a while against Rose and Gray until Swimer came into the room to tell us there was no use continuing to play because Britain was forfeiting the match to the United States.

The British Bridge League did not find it expedient to accept the verdict of the World Bridge Federation, and shortly after the scandal became public, the League decided to conduct hearings of its own to determine the guilt or innocence of Reese and Schapiro. They appointed Sir John Foster, a Member of Parliament and a Queen's Counsel, but with no ranking as a bridge player, to look into the matter. In August, 1966, more than fifteen months after the World Championship had been concluded, and having heard fourteen witnesses, he came forth with the astonishing conclusion that Reese and Schapiro did not cheat in Buenos Aires.

I testified at length before Sir John in London in September, 1965, telling essentially the same story that I have outlined here. I was cross-examined by Leonard Caplan, the highly competent attorney who represented Reese and Schapiro, but he found himself utterly unable to change the facts of what had occurred in Buenos Aires. Mrs. Hayden and Truscott also testified before Sir John, and their stories likewise stood up under Caplan's cross-examination.

In addition the tribunal heard Butler's and Swimer's testimony of what they had seen in Buenos Aires, but apparently Sir John arrived at the conclusion that the three American witnesses and two British witnesses for the prosecution had

---

3. Becker means that the British could have deliberately and unobtrusively played badly at the end to lose the match — a possibility that they considered before playing the final abortive session Sunday night —A.T.

not seen what they saw. In his report to the British Bridge League, Sir John paid scant attention to the testimony of eyewitnesses but gave a great deal of weight to the bidding and play of hands in which Reese and Schapiro were involved. This was rather an odd way of attempting to determine whether or not a pair actually used finger signals. Obviously if a pair uses illegal signals — all nine eyewitnesses in Buenos Aires agreed that the number of fingers shown by Reese and Schapiro changed from one deal to the next — it does not matter whether the signals are successful or not or whether they are used in the most effective manner possible. The one-sided testimony offered by the defense and swallowed by Sir John, that if a pair cheats, an examination of the hands is bound to reveal it, is palpably absurd. Surely a pair such as Reese and Schapiro, who were smart enough for twenty years to have ranked among the best pairs in the world, would also be smart enough to apply illegally acquired information in a manner that would defy 100 per cent proof in postanalysis. In my view, the hands strongly confirm a knowledge of the heart suit, although I would not regard them as conclusive in the absence of other evidence.

Sir John's naive acceptance of the contention by the defense that the hands must prove a pair is cheating is a broad license for any pair to cheat provided they do not carry it to the extent where the hands prove they are cheating. Obviously, the World Bridge Federation cannot possibly accept such a code of ethics, even if the British Bridge League is willing to subscribe to such a standard of conduct in order to protect its leading pair.

THE HAYDEN STORY: DETECTION

Dorothy Hayden, *then of Hastings-on-Hudson, NY, and now of Riverdale, NY, is now Dorothy Hayden Truscott. For many years she headed the world rankings for women, and has represented the United States in four categories, the Bermuda Bowl, the World Open Pairs, the World Women's Teams and the World Women's Pairs, a unique record. She owns four world titles and thirty national titles. She is a mathematician by training, and has three children and nine grandchildren.*

Her book Bid Better, Play Better *was the bridge best-seller of 1966. Originally, the book was to include a chapter on international bridge, and with this in mind Mrs. Hayden kept a day-to-day diary of events in Buenos Aires. As it turned out, the contents of the diary were too exciting, and she decided to omit the entire chapter.*

When the Reese-Schapiro matter first arose, Mrs. Hayden was very conscious of the need for secrecy, and her original notes contained only a few guarded references to the affair. For the two crucial days they were as follows:

THURSDAY ... (B. is right about S. & R.) ... Talked to Truscott.

FRIDAY ... talked to Johnny, who talked to McNab, Von Z & Peroux. Took notes and cracked it at 4 A.M. with Truscott and B.[1]

> *It will be seen that in moments of stress Mrs. Hayden has trouble spelling proper names, and she was therefore quite right not to attempt Von Zedtwitz in full.*
>
> *After the affair reached official levels and before leaving South America, Mrs. Hayden expanded her notes so that they provided a complete and readable story. The following extracts are partly from the original notes and partly from the expanded version.*

---

1. Leading characters are referred to by initials. The other members of the American team were S., Howard Schenken; L., Peter Leventritt; P., Kelsey Petterson; and E., Ivan Erdos. — A.T.

SUNDAY MAY 9   We took off at 9 A.M. It was supposed to be 10 hours nonstop to B.A., but we are making a nonscheduled stop in Caracas. It seems the Shah of Persia and his wife are due in B.A. tomorrow and Pan Am is stopping to pick up Venezuelan dignitaries. B. says that in '46 when he and [Sidney] Silodor and Helen [Sobel] and Charlie [Goren] went to Brazil for an invitational match it was a thirty-three-hour flight.

MONDAY MAY 10   Shah staying at the Plaza too. Police all over . . . . Had another good session of slam-bidding practice.[2]

TUESDAY MAY 11   Practice with Gerber and Sammy [Kehela], mostly against Roman. My biggest worry is that I will get a Roman bid and a Neapolitan bid mixed up. Am not worried about the Little M [Little Major] because it is so different.[3] Dinner at Joe Niemad's apartment. Everything in gorgeous taste. Sterling dinner plates! Menu Near Eastern. Delicious.

WEDNESDAY MAY 12   Practice all afternoon. Dinner at a Hungarian restaurant with [Kelsey] Petterson, [Ivan] Erdos, and Becker. Ivan sang Hungarian songs.

THURSDAY MAY 13   Shah left. (Thank heavens.) At five-thirty the U.S. team drove to the chess club for dinner and a thirty-six-board match against a young Argentine team who played very well. These fellows are not on the official Argentine team but almost made it. We won by 16 IMPs. Afterwards they presented us with lovely alligator wallets.

---

2. Mrs. Hayden and Becker practiced with a deck from which about half of the low cards had been removed. Six years of this made them one of the best slam-bidding pairs in the world. — A.T.

3. The Roman system was used by Giorgio Belladonna and Walter Avarelli, and in a modified form by Massimo D'Alelio and Camillo Pabis Ticci. One club usually showed a weak, balanced hand. Other one-bids were forcing also and showed unbalanced hands: a short suit was bid first, sometimes of three cards, and a second suit always had at least five cards. One notrump was very strong (17-20 points). Two clubs and two diamonds showed weak and strong three-suited hands respectively. Two spades and two hearts showed a five-card suit with at least four clubs.

   The Neapolitan system used by Forquet and Garozzo was more natural. It was based on a strong one-club bid (17 points or more) with control-showing responses, and resembled the Schenken Club system.

   The Little Major was a highly artificial creation of Reese and Flint, now apparently abandoned. One club indicated a heart suit, and one diamond a spade suit or a strong notrump type. One heart showed a hand that was either enormously powerful or nearly worthless, and one spade showed minor-suit length. — A.T.

FRIDAY MAY 14 There was a captains' meeting at noon. Gerber got us a good draw. We play Argentina, then Italy, then G.B. Perroux succeeded in getting a private dining room for the Italian team. Wonder why he wanted this? The British and the Americans will eat together in what is called the players' dining room.

Reception at home of U.S. Ambassador and his wife, Mr. and Mrs. Martin. They will be over to watch the tournament.

LATER Went to a party at [Agustin] Santamarina's house [member of the Argentine team]. Got into quite a discussion with Flint and Schapiro about the Little Major. Schapiro refuses to play the Little M and never misses an opportunity to poke fun at it. He has a terrific sense of humor.

Perroux and the Argentine captain [Eduardo Marquardt] voted to bar the LM, but Gerber voted to allow it. Very smart of Gerber. Our best chance to beat Reese is the Little M (the Little Corporal as Schapiro calls it). In the first place, Flint is not as good a player as Schapiro[4], but he is the only one Reese can play the LM with. I am afraid, however, that the LM will be abandoned before we meet G.B. on Monday. Have already heard that England is not playing the LM against Italy tomorrow.

After the party there was a meeting to allow players to ask questions about the Little Major. Think both Reese and Flint answered very well and calmly considering some of the ridiculous questions put to them.

Went out for supper about 2 A.M. with Becker, Garozzo, Forquet, and Sammy. How can anyone so handsome as Forquet play such good bridge? Becker made me do a few percentages for Garozzo. He didn't believe that the proper play with K-9-x opposite A-10-x-x is to lead small to the nine.

SATURDAY MAY 15 Players' meeting at noon. Reese started off by asking questions about the Italian spot cards. They play odd-even discards. Reese asked if your partner led the king and you held 10-7-3 and wanted to *discourage* what would you play. [Massimo] D'Alelio answered the ten because it is even. Erdos almost created an incident by asking if the speed of the play mattered! Gerber shut him up promptly, and Erdos later apologized to the Italians.

Too bad the waiters can't speak English. Petterson can speak a little Spanish.

3.30 P.M. [Howard] Schenken and Leventritt poor on Rama. Erdos and P. good. We lost 4 IMPs to Argentina.

---

4. Not an opinion I share. Mrs. Hayden was judging by the past international record of Reese and Schapiro, which in retrospect may not be a true index of ability — A.T.

6.30 P.M.(LATE STARTING) B. & I on Rama. We were only fair. Finished session at 10 P.M.Word came over the intercom that we had lost 2 IMPs. No time to compare boards. Dashed upstairs to get dressed. All the men have to wear tux for the ten-thirty session. Got to the dining room at ten-fifteen in time to swallow some tea and cold meat and arrive in the Closed Room by ten-thirty. B. & I had a good game. We picked up 27 IMPs and now lead by 21. Out for supper afterwards with Dimmie [Mrs. Fleming of the British press], Garozzo, Forquet, and Becker. Tomorrow B. & I start in the pit against Italy.

SUNDAY MAY 16, 1:30 P.M. Sammy briefed us on the Little Roman[5] as we ate. Chunks of lamb floating in gravy is not my idea of breakfast. Gerber is going to arrange for us to get a menu starting tomorrow.

3:30 P.M. Into the pit against D'Alelio and Pabis Ticci. Schenken and Leventritt in the Closed Room. Both pairs on both teams played very well. We won 7 IMPs.

6:30 P.M. Petterson and Erdos on Rama ... we had the best of the luck and won 10 more IMPS.

10:30 P.M. Back into the pit this time against Garozzo and Forquet. B & I played very well, and we won 9 more IMPs. Before we began, Gerber met Garozzo and kiddingly said: "Remember Mrs. Hayden is a lady, and I don't want you to make her cry." After the session he couldn't resist going up to Garozzo again and asking: "Well, did you make Mrs. Hayden cry?"

"No," answered Garozzo in his broken English, "she make cry mel" Garozzo and Forquet joined us for drinks in the Schenkens' room afterward.

MONDAY MAY 17, 3:30 P.M. B. and I on Rama against Reese and Flint playing the Little Major. Great Britain and North America tied, but the Little Major lost, and I doubt if we see it again unless England gets way ahead of us.

6:30 P.M. B. & I in the Closed Room against Schapiro and [Kenneth] Konstam playing Acol[6]. Petterson and Erdos in open. We lost 12 IMPs.

10:30 P.M. On Rama against Reese and Schapiro. Played well and were surprised to hear that we had lost 10 IMPs. Gerber came in at the finish to tell us about Peter's accident. It seems they bid six hearts and Peter had it made, but he made a claim, forgetting there was still a trump out .... The director ruled he was one down, and the board cost 17 IMPs. Poor Peter is sick. We are all doing our best to

---

5. The modified Roman System employed by D'Alelio and Pabis Ticci. — A.T.
6. The normal British system, which is a natural style embodying many nonforcing limited bids. — A.T.

cheer him up. Thank God it didn't happen to me. If I had an accident like that everyone would say, "Isn't that just like a woman!"

Becker brought up an earlier hand on which Reese claimed against us without stating that he would play Becker for the club queen[7]. At the time neither of us seriously considered calling the director. It would have been very sharp practice to do so. When we now told Gerber he was furious that we did not call the director...

The difference, I believe, is this. When Peter claimed, he had obviously forgotten that there was another trump out. When Reese claimed he simply forgot to say that he was going to play B. for the club queen. We both knew that his intention was to do so, and it would have been ungentlemanly to call the director. Am sure if the positions had been reversed Reese would not have called the director...

After the session Becker took me aside. He thinks we have been cheated by Reese and Schapiro. I believe B. is mistaken, but he is very convinced. It seems just by coincidence he happened to notice R's fingers on about the fifth board of the session. He was holding his cards with only two fingers showing. Very odd position. He glanced at S., and to B.'s horror S. was also holding his cards with only two fingers showing. On succeeding boards he saw different numbers of fingers. He is convinced they have a finger signal going. I will watch Thursday, but I doubt that this can be true. In the first place R. is a very superior person. Not only the best bridge player in the world but apparently one of the most ethical. No intonation and very good tempo. We will tell no one and watch Thursday.

TUESDAY MAY 18   Nothing very exciting today. B. & I had two sessions off because we are playing Argentina.

WEDNESDAY MAY 19   Fireworks today. Started off the day 26 up over Italy. We were off the first session and our teammates lost 18.

6:30 P.M.   B. and I in the pit against Avarelli and Belladonna. They played beautifully. We were all right but not inspired. Neither were Schenken and Leventritt in the other room, and we lost 24 more IMPs. So we are now 16 IMPs behind Italy .... Only half an hour to dress and eat as B. and I have to start early in the Closed Room.

10:30 P.M.   In the Closed Room against Garozzo and Forquet. We played well and were lucky to boot. Could easily have picked up 50 IMPs against par. Our teammates were below par on Rama however, but we still picked up 21. So we now lead Italy by 5 IMPs. Johnny came to us after the session and told B. and myself that we

---

7. See page 31. — A.T

would go all the way from here — that is, play every session except against Argentina.

Word leaked out from the Italians that Forquet and Garozzo have asked their captain not to put them against Hayden and Becker as they feel they are unlucky against us.

And so ended a swingy day.

THURSDAY MAY 20, 3:30 P.M. Went into the pit against Reese and Schapiro. B. was right. Something terrible is going on. I could not believe my eyes. I watched every hand. The movements are very natural and graceful-looking. The fingers do not register unless you know what to look for. How can they do this in front of a whole grandstand of people?

Sometimes two fingers show. Occasionally one finger, usually three or four fingers. R. and S. sometimes have the same number showing and sometimes different numbers.

What can it be? The fingers only last during the bidding. Once play begins they hold their cards normally. One time R. had two fingers going. He even scratched his neck with two fingers. He put his hand on the arm of his chair with two fingers extended.[8] It is hypnotic.

It can't be point-count. Fingers would be impractical for this. It has to be either controls or distribution. Perhaps one stands for spades, two for hearts, etc., and they signal their short suit. Obviously no one would invent a signal for the long suit. The bidding should take care of that.

But why does one finger appear so much less frequently than the others? God, this is nerve-racking. I am not concentrating on my game. Will go wash my face...

Only one bid that sounded odd to me. Becker opened three spades, and Reese, vulnerable, doubled, holding:

$$\spadesuit K x \quad \heartsuit K 10 x x \quad \diamondsuit K \quad \clubsuit A Q x x x x$$

Surely a pass or even four clubs is more normal. How did R. have the nerve to double? What was he going to do if S. responded in diamonds? Does he know the distribution? If he knew that S. was short in diamonds he could safely double. S. held:

$$\spadesuit A x x \quad \heartsuit J 8 x x \quad \diamondsuit Q J \quad \clubsuit K x x x$$

---

8. Richard Frey, editor of the American Bridge Contract League Bulletin, saw something similar. During the same session he noticed Schapiro holding two fingers on the edge of the table and thought (innocently): "That's a silly thing to do. Somebody might think he was cheating." — A.T.

They played it in four hearts doubled, down one for a tied board.

After the session we had only ten minutes before we were due on Bridge-O-Rama at six-thirty. No time to talk to B. No privacy anyway. He knows from my eyes that I know. But what can it be? My mind keeps racing as I try to swallow a cup of hot tea .... To top it off we had had our first bad session of the tournament. It was mostly my fault. P. & E. in the Closed Room were awful too, and we lost 63-2.

6:30 P.M.   Into Rama. Now we are alone with R. & S. Alone except for an announcer and a scorer. If they did it in the pit it will be worse here. The announcer and scorer are Argentinian. I don't think they speak much English. R. & S. are fearless. How naive do they think we are? The very first board on Rama I picked up a big hand. Was thinking about a slam before the bidding had even begun.

Then I glanced at R. He had two fingers showing. How eerie! Can he have two aces? I had to smile to think I could consider myself off two aces before anyone had made a bid. We bid a shaky six clubs and made it. R. had only one ace. He held:

$$♠ K Q J x x \quad ♡ x x \quad ♢ x x x \quad ♣ A J x$$

We did not play badly this session, but we lost 18 more and this put us down 101 IMPs. Johnny decided to give us a rest, for which I was very grateful. Think he had given up on the match.

The British got a bit cocksure and decided they were far enough ahead to try the Little Major again. Our teammates picked up 53 IMPs and now we only trail by 48.

THURSDAY NIGHT   Now comes the problem. What to do about R. & S.? We don't meet England again until Sunday. Can we break the code by then? Even if we do break it, what can we do by ourselves? If we confront R. & S. they will simply laugh at us and change their code.

Furthermore it may be very difficult to do anything. Tomorrow England plays Italy. The English are so far behind they may have given up on the match, in which case they may put the Little Major back in and break up Reese and Schapiro. Our original thought was to tell no one, but it has become apparent that we need at least one reliable witness.

I suggested Truscott. He is a person of integrity, and his position as bridge editor of *The New York Times* will give his evidence the necessary weight. I edit Truscott's columns and am very friendly with him. So is B. More important, if he gives his word not to tell anyone, he will keep it.

So we found Truscott in the pressroom, and the three of us went to Becker's hotel room, shutting the transom in best detective style. T. was shaken but not convinced. He pointed out that similar accusations had been made against R. & S. in Turin in 1960. He thinks we are wrong but has agreed to watch tomorrow.

If they play together tomorrow, R. & S. will be in the Rama room. T. thinks he can get the job of announcer in the Rama room as he is friendly with [Arturo] Jaques, the leading Argentine commentator.

FRIDAY MAY 21   We must get at least one more reliable witness, but whom? I would like to go to Swimer, but neither of us knows him well. We can't go to Charlie Solomon or Von Zedtwitz or General [Alfred] Gruenther. Their positions in the World Bridge Federation are too high,[9] and we couldn't very well ask them to conceal this. What are we trying to accomplish? Nobody wants a scandal. God knows we don't want to crucify Reese and Schapiro, but if this gets out they will be crucified. But they must be prevented from playing together again.

And what about the points they have stolen from the U.S. in this match? England is leading us by 48 IMPs at this moment. If you don't count the sessions that R. & S. played as partners, the U.S. would be leading by 41 IMPs.

Here is a possible solution. With the help of Truscott and one other reliable witness we will collect enough evidence to crack the code. Becker will then go to Reese with an ultimatum. R. & S. can quietly retire from bridge and a worldwide scandal will be averted.

Decided to tell Gerber, our captain, and went up to his room. B. said he had a matter he wished to discuss but he would have to insist on Gerber's word that it go no further without our permission. G. agreed and we told him all.

Gerber is no fool, and he did not waste time telling us we were imagining things.

There has been a switch in plans, and England is going to be playing Italy in the pit this afternoon, not on Rama. If R. & S. are in the pit, Gerber will watch...

I left to find Truscott. If he does not know about the switch in plans he may find himself locked in the Rama room watching the U.S.A.-Argentina match by mistake... Arrived just in time to find T. arguing with Jaques. It seems T. was trying to get the job of announcer in the Rama room, and J. was claiming his accent was too bad.

I agreed promptly with Jaques that T.'s accent was atrocious and told T. on the side about the change in plans. T. left quickly for the pit, where he grabbed Sammy's ringside seat. Sammy was furious: he idolizes Reese, and a ringside seat to watch Reese-Schapiro play Forquet-Garozzo would be a lifetime ambition.

---

9.   President, Executive Committee member, and honorary president, respectively. — A.T.

Becker and I have the first two sessions off as we are playing Argentina. I looked into the pit. T. is sitting right beside R. Why doesn't he sit behind one of the Italians where he can see both R. and S.? From where he is he can see only Schapiro's fingers.

Gerber is up on top of the bleachers behind Schapiro. I hope they are both taking notes. Maybe I had better make a safety play and take notes myself.

As I climbed up to the top of the bleachers the announcer was calling "Mano numero 119." Schapiro had four fingers showing. I could not see Reese's fingers. I wrote down "119 S 4" and continued to keep a record.

After a few boards I noticed that Gerber was leaving. Climbed down and intercepted him. He took his cigar out of his mouth as he passed me and muttered, "Something is going on, all right."

"Aren't you taking notes?" I asked. But he was gone...

Becker arrived just then, and I asked him to climb up the other side of the grandstand and check Reese's fingers. We were not close enough to see the cards, but I knew T. could get the hand records later...

After the session, met T. in the pressroom. Found he had taken no notes! Believe it or not, he had forgotten to take a pencil. I gave him a copy of my notes, and he will work on them tonight while B. and I are playing Argentina. Made a date for 2 A.M. after the session. (Time is running out.)

SATURDAY MAY 22, 2 A.M.   Becker, Truscott, and I took a cab to an all-night restaurant. T. reported that he had gotten nowhere during the evening. He spent hours on the records and has eliminated several possibilities but has found nothing positive.

After presenting his findings, T. said: "All right, Dorothy, you try it your way."

I said the way to do it was to lay out all the one-finger boards side by side, then all the two-finger boards, etc., and I was sure we would see something similar in the distribution.

There was only one one-finger hand in my notes. It was Board 120, and Schapiro held:

♠ K Q 8 3   ♡ K   ◇ J 8 3   ♣ Q 10 7 6 5

Rather nondescript. From Thursday's session in the pit, however, I remembered a one-finger hand where Reese bid six spades holding:

♠ K Q J x x x x   ♡ A   ◇ K x x   ♣ Q x

As I was convinced the signals were distributional, the two singleton hearts stuck out like sore thumbs.

Quickly we looked at the two-finger boards. Doubleton heart! Doubleton heart! Doubleton heart! Then we struck a two-finger board with five hearts.

Could two fingers stand for two or five hearts? Every two-finger board had two or five hearts! Every three-finger board had three or six hearts! (As it happened, there were no six-card heart suits.) Every four-finger board had four or seven hearts!

The code was broken![10]

Two fingers together meant two hearts; spread apart, five hearts. Three fingers together meant three hearts; spread apart, six hearts. Four fingers together meant four hearts; spread apart, seven hearts. One finger was used only for a singleton heart, which is why the one-finger signal appeared so seldom.

It is now 4.30 A.M. Can't raise Gerber by phone. T. is going to take charge of informing Gerber first thing in the morning . . . . I dread tomorrow.

SATURDAY MAY 22. Italy won. B. & I on Rama, S. & L. in Closed Room. We had two disasters but several good hands and thought we were up a little. Down 33 IMPs.

We sat out the second session, and our teammates picked up 12 IMPs. Sixteen IMPS behind and one session to play. After this pickup, Johnny decided to keep them in for the evening session.[11]

Disaster struck. P. and E. collapsed on Rama. We lost 74-16.

Swimer and Butler watched Reese and Schapiro in the pit against Argentina. Imagine Swimer's feelings as he sat across from S. knowing from S.'s fingers how many hearts he had each hand.

Later the notes that Swimer and Butler took were compared with the hand records of the session. In every case the finger signals corresponded with the hearts held.[12]

Too many people know. Gerber has even told Sammy. He is crushed. Reese is his idol...

There is nothing we can do. There is nothing anyone can do now. Tomorrow the whole world will know. God have mercy on Reese and Schapiro.

---

10. There was no indication about the method of signaling a void, which did not occur during the period observed. See page 148 — A.T

11. A somewhat surprising decision. Most observers thought that Becker-Hayden played the best of the three American pairs. — A.T.

12. Not quite in every case, as it turned out. But this was Mrs. Hayden's understanding at the time. — A.T.

THE HANDS AND THE FINGERS

(For reference purposes the cards held and the notes made are shown below.)

119 Schapiro (4 fingers showing)
♠ J 10 5 3
♡ K 10 5 3
♢ J 5
♣ A K 5

120 Schapiro (1 finger)
♠ K Q 8 3
♡ K
♢ J 8 3
♣ Q 10 7 6 5

121 Schapiro (2 fingers)
♠ 10 9
♡ J 9 7 6 5
♢ 10 6 5 3
♣ K 3

123 Schapiro (4 fingers)
♠ K Q 5 2
♡ J 9 7 5
♢ J 7 2
♣ K J

Reese (2 fingers)
♠ A 10 4
♡ A 2
♢ Q 10 6
♣ 10 8 7 4 2

124 Schapiro (3 fingers)
♠ 10 8 5 4 3
♡ 9 8 6
♢ 6 5
♣ 10 8 5

Reese (3 drooping)
♠ A J 9
♡ A J 7
♢ 10 8 7 2
♣ A K Q

111 Schapiro (4 fingers)
♠ A K 3
♡ A 9 3 2
♢ 9 5
♣ K Q 10 4

Reese (2 fingers)
♠ 7 6 4 2
♡ K 6
♢ K 4 2
♣ 7 5 3 2

112 Schapiro (2 fingers)   Reese (4 fingers)
     ♠ K   ♠ Q 7 3
     ♡ J 3   ♡ 9 8 4 2
     ◇ J 9 7 3   ◇ Q 10 6 5
     ♣ Q 10 9 6 5 3   ♣ A 4

113 Schapiro (3 fingers)   Reese (3 drooping)
     ♠ A 10 7 4 3 2   ♠ Q 8
     ♡ K 10 2   ♡ Q J 7
     ◇ Q   ◇ A K J 6 4
     ♣ 8 5 3   ♣ A J 6

114 Schapiro (3 fingers)   Reese (4 wide fingers)
     ♠ J 10 8 6 3   ♠ 9 7 5
     ♡ 5 4 2   ♡ K Q J 9 8 7 3
     ◇ —   ◇ Q J 2
     ♣ A K Q 7 3   ♣ —

115 Schapiro (3? fingers)   Reese (3 drooping)
     ♠ A 3   ♠ 9 4
     ♡ 10 3 2   ♡ 8 7 5 4
     ◇ A 10 9 5   ◇ J 4 2
     ♣ A 10 9 5   ♣ K Q J 3

116 Schapiro (4 fingers)   Reese (3 drooping)
     ♠ Q 10 7   ♠ J 9 3 2
     ♡ A 10 8 2   ♡ J 5 3
     ◇ A J 7   ◇ 9 5 4 2
     ♣ 8 4 3   ♣ 10 2

NOTES ON THE NOTES

The original notes were made in pencil on the back of a scorecard. They were never out of my possession until they were turned over to the Foster Inquiry in London.

The original was mislaid while in the possession of the tribunal, and no photocopies were ever made. The following is a facsimile of a typed copy made from the original notes:

	S	R
119	4	
120	1	
121	2	
123	4	2
124	3	3d
111	4	2 hearts
112	2	4 short clubs
113	3 (later 4)	3d
114	3 (void D)	4 (void C) wide 4
115	3?	3d 2 spades
116	4 (4333)	3d 2 clubs

When I began to take notes at Board 119 I could see only Schapiro's fingers. The notations under the column marked "S" mean that on boards 119, 120, and 121 Schapiro was showing 4, 1, and 2 fingers respectively. I missed Board 122 when I left to speak to Gerber and Becker.

Starting with Board 123 Becker was able to see the fingers displayed by Reese from the other side of the grandstand. During the play of the hand, Becker and I met behind the grandstand. He told me the number of fingers he had seen, and I wrote them down under the column marked "R."

On boards 124, 113, 115 and 116 Becker was not sure from his angle on top of the stand whether three or four fingers were meant to be showing. It looked like three with `a "drooping fourth." Accordingly I marked 3d in my notes.[13]

Starting with Board 111, I made an effort to look into Reese's hand after I had noted Schapiro's fingers. I knew this was not important as the hand records would be available later.

---

13. See photo section. — A.T.

I thought at the time that the fingers might stand for the shortest suit. This accounts for the notations beside the "R" column on boards 111, 112, 114, 115, and 116. On 114 and 116 Becker was able to see Schapiro's distribution, which accounts for the note that S. was void in diamonds on 114 and had 4-3-3-3 distribution on 116.

On Board 114 Becker was very insistent that Reese's fingers had been spread far apart and were most unusual looking. I did not think this important at the time, but as Becker was so impressed I jotted "wide 4" beside the "R" column.

I cannot now recall how we came to miss Board 117, which must have been the last of the session.

POSTSCRIPT

I first met Reese and Schapiro in Turin in 1960, and we were on friendly terms at international events during the following years. I had never heard of any previous accusations against them, and when Becker first told me about the finger signals on May 17 my first thought was that he must be mistaken. Neither of us did anything about the matter, nor did we speak to anyone else until after I had seen the signals for myself on May 20.

The breaking of the code was the end of my direct involvement with the affair in Buenos Aires. I was still hoping that the affair would be handled quietly, and neither of us told even our teammates because it seemed obvious that the fewer people that knew, the better.

The only other person with whom I discussed the cheating was Sammy Kehela, who told me that he had been told by Gerber. Sammy had watched a few hands knowing the code and was obviously very upset. He told me he would never have believed it if he hadn't seen it with his own eyes. We discussed the terrible consequences if word of this should ever leak out. Sammy said if he were ever asked about it he would deny that there was enough evidence.[14] At the time I thought it was a great mistake for Gerber to have told Sammy. I could see no reason why he should ever have to know.

Later I was told by more than one person in Buenos Aires that they had seen Swimer and Schapiro together in tears, and I assumed at the time that Schapiro had broken down and confessed when confronted by Swimer's evidence.

I saw Swimer in London shortly before I testified at the inquiry and asked him if it was true that Schapiro had confessed.

---

14. Kehela denies having said this.

"Please don't ask me anything about that," he replied and added that he would appreciate it if I wouldn't mention the matter to the inquiry.

Oddly enough, my first question from Reese's attorney, Caplan, in cross-examination was: "Mrs. Hayden, you are aware, are you not, that Mr. Reese and Mr. Schapiro have denied these charges since the beginning?"

This was a stumper. I finally replied: "I am aware that Mr. Reese has denied these charges since the beginning."

Caplan was annoyed. "I said, Mrs. Hayden, that you are aware, are you not, that Mr. Reese and Mr. Schapiro have denied these charges from the beginning."

I repeated my previous answer, and the whole exchange was repeated four or five times, with Caplan becoming more irritated each time. I realized that he had gotten started on a very unfortunate tack but that he felt that he would lose face if he gave up. Finally I asked permission not to answer this particular question again. Sir John readily agreed, and everyone seemed relieved to get off *that* merry-go-round.

Caplan started on a new tack. "Mrs. Hayden, I hope you will not mind if I now attempt to point out to this court that everything you have testified is a complete fabrication from beginning to end."

I assured him that I would not mind and that I understood that this was his job and that his only defense was to prove that all the witnesses were lying.

That was not the response he had hoped for. "Oh, that is not my *only* defense, Mrs. Hayden."

I agreed but couldn't resist adding: "I'm sure it's your *best* defense, Mr. Caplan." '

I had never been cross-examined before, but my impression was that Caplan was being purposely rude in an effort to get me to lose my temper. The fact that I answered all his questions as pleasantly as possible seemed to irritate him more than ever.

I don't remember most of the questions he asked. I do know that he studiously avoided the subject of the notes, which were of course the most important part of the evidence. He preferred to tackle details.

A typical exchange went something like this:

"You testified, did you not, Mrs. Hayden, that Mr. Becker told you that he first noticed these signals by coincidence."

"Yes, sir."

"Do you still feel this was a coincidence?"

"Yes, sir.'"

He then rephrased the question. in several different ways, in a tone of mounting incredulity.

"Do you still maintain, Mrs. Hayden, that it was just a coincidence that . . ." and so on.

At the time I had no idea what he was driving at. It seemed like a ridiculous quarrel over semantics. Finally I volunteered that it was possible to take exception to the word "coincidence" if he chose, because it was after all not a coincidence that Becker just happened to be playing against Reese and Schapiro at that particular moment in Buenos Aires.

Sir John agreed that almost anything could be termed a coincidence or not a coincidence depending on how you defined the word, and Caplan finally passed on to something else.

Caplan had a difficult job, but he did make one rather good point. I had testified that on a particular hand I had been thinking of bidding a slam and that seeing that Reese had two fingers showing, I had been momentarily disconcerted by the thought that he might have two aces.

Caplan pointed out that if two fingers stood for two aces, then three and four fingers would probably stand for three or four aces.[15] And there had been many earlier hands on which each of my opponents had three or four fingers showing.

"Did you suppose," finished Caplan triumphantly, "that you were playing with a pack containing seven or eight aces?"

This was really quite funny and we all laughed. Of course he was right. It had been silly of me to think that two fingers could stand for two aces.

After about three hours Caplan finished his cross-examination and the hearing adjourned. Both Sir John and his collaborator, General Lord Bourne, independently apologized to me for Caplan's manners and wondered that I had been so patient with him.[16]

---

15. Not necessarily — there would be many possible variations. — A.T.
16. Mrs. Hayden had the reputation for being extremely good-tempered at the bridge table. After years of being patient with hundreds of rubber bridge partners, often incompetent and sometimes unbearable, being pleasant to Caplan was no problem. — A.T.

THE GERBER STORY: INVESTIGATION 3

JOHN GERBER, of Houston, Texas, born 1906, was one of America's leading players. He played on the North American team in the 1961 World Championship, and was the nonplaying captain of the team in 1962, 1963, and 1965. His many successes in American tournament play included five national championship wins.

He was the inventor of the Gerber Four-Club Convention, an ace-asking device that is widely used, especially after an opening bid of one notrump or two notrump.

A transatlantic telephone call in May, 1963, was my first contact with Terence Reese.

"Mr. Reese, this is John Gerber in New York. I would like to know whether you would be willing to act as the official coach of the North American team in next month's World Championship in St. Vincent, Italy. If you accept, the American Contract Bridge League will pay you $1000 to cover your expenses and fee."

The offer was declined with thanks, because Reese had other commitments. He suggested Jeremy Flint as a substitute, but he was unknown to me, and I chose to have Sammy Kehela of Toronto. We led against Italy for seven sessions out of nine but lost by a narrow margin of 19 international match points — a result quite unconnected with the identity of the coach.

My first face-to-face meeting with Reese was in the 1964 Team Olympiad in New York, where he thanked me briefly for having made him the offer the previous year.

Boris Schapiro proved much more conversational in New York, but our relationship was not entirely happy. He repeatedly bummed cigars from me, adopting a manner that he no doubt thought was jocular but that seemed to me both crude and rude. As he was a visitor in my country I suffered this behavior in silence. But I saw no reason to put up with it the following year in Buenos Aires, where we were on neutral ground. When Schapiro came up to me on the first day, accompanied by Konstam and Flint, and began the same nonsense, I permitted myself an eruption:

"Mr. Schapiro, as long as you can be civil you can talk to me at any time. But if you cannot keep a civil tongue in your head please do not talk to me except on official business."

That ended the conversation. Fifteen minutes later Harrison-Gray came up to me and offered an apology, which I of course accepted.

This trivial irritation was followed by the captains' meeting, which is usually a formality concerned with such matters as the schedule of play and the arrangements for Bridge-O-Rama. But this time there was a battle over the Little Major system, a highly artificial method of bidding invented by Reese and Flint, which they intended to play whenever possible.

The rules of the Championship required each team to submit outlines of systems well in advance, so that the players could study the methods they would have to meet and work out countermeasures. This was obviously of special importance in the case of the Little Major, but owing to some administrative confusion the Italians and the Argentinians had not received the system details until just before the Championship began. My team was not handicapped in the same way, because we had taken the trouble to write and ask for a copy well ahead of time.

Perroux proposed that the Little Major should be barred and was strongly supported by the Argentine captain. Swimer naturally opposed Perroux, and my vote became crucial.

I could see no reason why the British should be put at a major disadvantage because of a technical misdemeanor that was not the fault of the players. So I sided with Swimer, making the vote a 2-2 tie. This was held to defeat the motion, and the Little Major survived, thanks to American support.

This is surely sufficient proof that I was neither anti-British nor anti Reese-Schapiro, as alleged subsequently in England on the slender basis of the cigar incident.

The first day of play between my team and the British, on the third day of the Championship, produced an episode that suggested that our opponents were more eager than we were to enforce the letter of the law.

Leventritt made a claim in a slam contract and carelessly omitted to state that he intended to draw the missing trump. The opponents asked him to play on, without following the required procedure of calling the tournament director. One trick later they objected to a trump lead and were upheld by the tournament director. The lay-down slam was defeated, and the ruling cost my team 17 IMPs.

I lodged a protest, which was turned down by the Appeals Committee. As a gesture, I submitted a second protest relating to a hand played earlier in the day. Becker had led the club king from a K-Q-x combination against three notrump.

Reese held J-x-x of clubs in his hand and A-x-x in the dummy. He naturally allowed the king to hold and was eventually able to endplay Becker. He claimed the contract without bothering to state that he was playing for Becker to hold the club queen.

Becker said that he had no intention of calling the tournament director, but that if he did so Reese would be required to play the club ace on a low club lead.

My belated protest about this matter was rejected also — and rightly.

Protests on points of law, personality clashes, and maneuvers over ground rules are nothing new in world championship competition. I had met them in 1962 and 1963 when I had served as American captain.

But nothing in my previous experience had prepared me for Becker's bombshell on Friday afternoon.

After the end of the first session of play he told me that he and Dorothy Hayden wished to speak to me privately. We went up to my suite, and he stated that he had something of great importance to tell me. He first asked me not to pass on his information without consulting him, and I gave him this assurance.

Then came the story that is now familiar to all followers of the game. Earlier in the week Becker had seen a peculiar grip on the cards by Reese, matched by a similar grip by Schapiro. Alerted by this, he had watched on subsequent deals and seen a pattern of changing fingers, on both sides of the table, which seemed meaningful. Later in the week his partner had watched and had come to the same conclusion. If their story was accurate — and I had no reason to doubt it — there was a strong prima facie case of cheating.

As it happened there was an immediate opportunity to see for myself. In the second session of play, starting at 4 P.M., Reese and Schapiro were in action in the Open Room against Forquet and Garozzo of Italy. This clash between two of the world's most famous partnerships had attracted a big crowd, and I had to climb to the top of the wooden staging to get a good view of the play.

I was carrying my scorecard of the early afternoon session between my team and Argentina, and the back of the card was a convenient place to make notes. By the end of the session my scorecard looked like this:

118	3	
119	2	1-2
#120 Fold	4	Schapiro 1 (scribble)
#121	1	Shap 2
122	2	" 4
#117	2V[1]	

---

1. Gerber made this entry later than the others. See page 36. — A.T

The notes compared as follows with the hearts actually held.[2]

Board	Reese			Schapiro		
	I	II	III	I	II	III
	Hearts Actually Held	Code for I	Fingers noted	Hearts Actually Held	Code for I	Fingers Noted
118	4	4	3			
119	2	2	2			
120	4	4	4	1	1	1
121	1	1	1	5	2	2
122	5	2	2	4	4	4
117	5	2	2			

THE HANDS AND THE FINGERS

118 Reese (3 fingers)
♠ 8 6
♡ K J 9 5
♢ Q J 8 4
♣ Q 4 2

119 Reese (2 fingers)
♠ K 7 4
♡ 6 4
♢ Q 9 6 2
♣ Q 8 6 2

120 Reese (4 fingers)
♠ J 2
♡ J 7 6 3
♢ A 9 7 6 5 2
♣ 4

Schapiro (1 finger)
♠ K Q 8 3
♡ K
♢ J 8 3
♣ Q 10 7 6 5

2. The extent to which Gerber's notes corresponded to the heart code can be seen readily by comparing columns II and III. It is noteworthy that Gerber's one discrepancy, out of nine notations, was a 4-3 confusion, from which Becker also suffered, and was at the start of his observations. The impromptu observer, as in Oakie's case five years earlier, is liable to inaccuracy at the beginning, when he is organizing himself and making up his mind what to note. — A.T.

121   Reese (1 finger)   Schapiro (2 fingers)

     ♠ K Q 8 7 5   ♠ 10 9
     ♡ 3   ♡ J 9 7 6 5
     ◇ Q 9   ◇ 10 6 5 3
     ♣ A 9 7 5 4   ♣ K 3

122   Reese (2 fingers)   Schapiro (4 fingers)

     ♠ 5   ♠ 9 3 2
     ♡ J 8 4 3 2   ♡ A Q 6 5
     ◇ J 6 3   ◇ K 9 8 4
     ♣ 8 7 6 4   ♣ 10 5

117   Reese (2 fingers)

     ♠ K 9
     ♡ A J 10 9 5
     ◇ K 8 7
     ♣ A J 5

At first I could see only Reese's fingers, which I listed on the left of the card. But after two deals I moved along to a position in which I could see both players. To my right was Dorothy Hayden, who was also taking notes.

The 1-2 notation on Board 119 referred to a change of Reese's fingers during the play of the hand, but what I intended by the entry at the extreme right of Board 120 I cannot now remember.[3]

After five deals I was satisfied that Becker was right: the two British players were playing "piano," and such movements could not be accidental or coincidental.

I decided that I should talk to Perroux, who was not only captain of the Italian team but also vice president of the World Bridge Federation. When I climbed down from the grandstand Mrs. Hayden followed me.

---

3. This is the only suggestion by any observer that the fingers could have been meaningful during the play of the cards. The consensus was that the cards were held in an entirely natural manner after the play started. The "fold" notation against Deal 120 presumably means that Reese closed up his cards at some point, a normal action to which no significance should be attached.

"Aren't you going to stay and find out what it means?" she demanded, rather indignantly. I assured her that I had seen enough. Becker was standing nearby, and I told him I was going to talk to Perroux. He did not comment, and I felt that I had discharged my obligation to tell him about any action I might take.[4]

I quickly found my Italian opposite number and steered him into a small dining room, where we could have privacy. We have always had a frank and cordial relationship, only slightly restricted by the fact that his English is poor and my Italian nonexistent.

"Captain Perroux," I began, "my players and I feel that Reese and Schapiro are using a signaling method with the use of fingers."

"I know, I know, my players know," he replied immediately. "But we don't know whether it's aces or distribution." Some French pronunciation entered into this statement, but I had no trouble identifying "asses" and "distriboosyon."

Perroux is a very human and sympathetic personality, and he explained that an item of past history was worrying him.

"Unless you use cameras to get proof, I cannot vote 'guilty'. There was a player in the European Championship who was accused, and he afterward committed suicide. I do not want this to happen again." This consideration was no doubt in his mind when the World Bridge Federation Executive voted two days later.

"It's Friday afternoon in a foreign country," I answered. "I don't believe I can get photographic evidence at this late date. I will continue my investigation and keep you informed."

We parted amicably, and I considered the next step. I had a responsibility to the American Contract Bridge League, and it seemed right to advise Robin MacNab, the president of the League. I knew him to be a man who would approach such a delicate topic with intelligence, discretion, and common sense.

I discovered that MacNab was taking part in a World Bridge Federation committee meeting. For a matter of such importance I had no hesitation in interrupting the meeting and asking him to come outside. When he had heard the story he suggested informing Solomon. I pointed out that the president of the World Bridge Federation should not be made to appear to be taking sides in a major clash between Britain and America. We agreed instead to bring in Von Zedtwitz,

---

4. Becker did not recall that Gerber said he was going to see Perroux, the Italian non-playing captain. If Gerber said he was about to see Perroux but did not make it clear that he was intending to discuss the Reese-Schapiro matter, the statement would not have seemed significant to Becker. It would have seemed an unimportant explanation for Gerber's departure from the scene of action, and Becker would have no reason to remember it. See page 6. — A.T.

who left the meeting to join us and hear the story in his turn.

We returned to the Open Room in time to watch the last board, No. 117. The bidding had just ended, but we could see that Reese had two splayed fingers at the back of his cards. This reminded me of Churchill's Victory sign, and I added a final note in ink to my earlier observations.

Von Zedtwitz said that he would be able to watch the two British players that night, exercising his right as a member of the Appeals Committee to enter the Closed Rooms. He carried out this plan and later told me that he had seen the same pattern of finger variations as the other observers. Subsequently he was able to link a V signal by Reese with a hand in which five hearts were held.[5]

Later that evening, after the final session of play had begun, I came upon Alan Truscott sitting in one of the hotel corridors. He had a copy of the hand records from the session I had watched and a copy of the notes taken by Mrs. Hayden and Becker. He was trying to establish a correlation between the two but was having no success. I wished him luck.

The luck was eventually forthcoming, if luck is the right word. Next morning, about 9 A.M., Truscott called me from his hotel with the news that the code had been broken. Half an hour later, looking rather tired, he was in my room with the details. A few hours earlier, not long before dawn, he and Becker and Mrs. Hayden had attacked the problem afresh. A procedure suggested by the feminine investigator had produced the answer — the heart suit. Truscott showed me how accurately the heart hypothesis fitted the Hayden-Becker notes. I at once produced my notes, and fortunately I had observations of Reese on six deals and Schapiro on one deal which did not overlap with the other notes.

My first notation did not correspond to the heart code. But everything else fitted, and my note on Board 117, the V sign, confirmed the idea that spread fingers showed fingers plus 3 in the heart suit. I was now completely satisfied, and we quickly arranged a meeting with MacNab and Von Zedtwitz. They were brought up to date, and Truscott cited a few deals that seemed to offer some technical reason for supposing illegal knowledge of the heart suit — not that in my opinion any technical evidence was needed.

We agreed that the proper procedure was to advise Swimer, the British captain. He was not in his room, and it was more than an hour before we were able to find him. When he eventually arrived, Truscott told his story for the third time that morning.

---

5. Von Zedtwitz testified to this effect in an affidavit that was submitted to the British inquiry. It was not admitted as evidence because there was no opportunity for the defense to cross-examine him. — A.T.

Swimer was visibly shocked and naturally incredulous. But he realized that he would have to face the problem and chose to consult Butler, the chairman of the British Bridge League. The meeting broke up, and except for Truscott's explanation to Butler that afternoon, the two British officials carried the ball for the rest of the day.

Before play started that afternoon, Becker spoke to me, with rather less than his usual calmness. He was burned up by the thought that our team might wind up losing to Great Britain, who would profit from what we believed to be outright cheating. If the affair was going to be settled in any private way, he wanted an assurance that in some way our team would wind up winners over Britain.

A private deal between Britain and America, perhaps including the retirement of the two players and a deliberate stage-managed last-day collapse by the British against us, was not in the cards. For one thing, such an arrangement would certainly be incompatible with the responsibility and dignity of the officials concerned. For another, it would be quite unfair to the Argentinians, who played the British on Saturday and were heavily defeated.

After lunch I told Kehela what was going on. I felt that as my deputy he was entitled to know.

During Saturday afternoon I had many things to think about. My team was fighting a decisive battle against the Italians, a battle that swung against us only in the night session. This was shown on the Bridge-O-Rama screen in front of a large, tense audience, leaving the Great Britain-Argentina match to be played in the Open Room.

I tore myself away from the vital action and made several brief trips to the Open Room to satisfy myself about an important point. How did Reese and Schapiro hold their cards when playing with other partners?

I saw Reese playing with Flint, and subsequently Schapiro playing with Konstam. Each time I watched, *both partners held their cards in a normal, consistent, relaxed fashion.*

To my mind, this proved two things. First, that the other members of the British team had not been infected by the cheating disease. Second, that the Reese-Schapiro finger variations could not conceivably be an innocent mannerism — farfetched as such an assumption would be — because they disappeared when the partnership broke up.

When I visited the Open Room for the fifth or sixth time, Marquardt, the Argentine captain, became curious. My team was locked in a tense fight that would decide the world title, while his team was doomed to lose.

"Why are you so interested in our match?" he asked me.

"I cannot tell you today," I replied. "Tomorrow I promise you will know."

Then I had to forget about the British for a time and concentrate on my captaincy problems. We were due to start the final session against the Italians trailing by 18 IMPs. We still had a chance to become world champions, although the betting was 3-1 against us.

I had to make a crucial decision. Which two pairs should I rely on in this crisis? Becker and Hayden had been the most reliable pair earlier in the week, but I was not sure to what extent their detective activities might upset their concentration. What was more, the other two pairs had snatched back a few vital points in the late-afternoon session.

So, after much soul-searching, I left Becker and Hayden on the sidelines, a decision that turned out badly. The Italians produced the irresistible finish that they seem able to turn on at will, and my two pairs were rather below their best. The score went steadily against us, and the final margin in favor of Italy was 304-230.

In the middle of this Bridge-O-Rama agony I saw Swimer come in, looking grim, and beckon to Butler. Later, when the play was over, Butler asked me to appear at an Appeals Committee meeting the following morning.

The next day, Sunday, was a day of meetings so important that I was able to dismiss from my mind for a time the acute disappointment of losing yet again to the great Italian Blue Team.

I was present throughout the morning meeting of the Appeals Committee, although the official minutes fail to record the fact. Solomon heard the story for the first time, but the others present, Butler, MacNab, Von Zedtwitz, and Swimer, were already fully informed.

I now learned that Swimer and Butler had watched the play on Saturday night and taken notes. As far as they could judge at the time, their observations and notes corresponded with the code. The test did not come until later in the day, when the hand records became available.

The two accused players were called in separately. Schapiro appeared first and described the accusations as "ridiculous." He added that he intended never to touch a card again.

Reese also denied the charges. He was asked by Butler whether he intended to continue playing. "You have made it impossible for me to play with Boris," he replied. "I have not made up my mind."

When the Appeals Committee had decided to refer the matter to the full Executive of the W.B.F. and adjourned for lunch, I took the opportunity to advise the other four members of my team of the situation. Petterson lost color, and I thought he was about to be ill. But Schenken, Leventritt, and Erdos, all more accustomed to the eccentricities of the tournament world, were not unduly perturbed.

Many of the players and officials in such tournaments feel a need to escape from the stuffy playing rooms into the fresh air from time to time. A favorite strolling ground in Buenos Aires was a stretch of park immediately in front of the Plaza Hotel, where play took place. Wandering out there between meetings, I saw something that was as significant as it was astonishing: two middle-aged men in conversation and visibly in tears. It was Swimer and Schapiro, and it was not difficult to guess what they were talking about.[6]

A necessary preliminary step before the afternoon meeting was to secure the hand records of the previous night's play between Great Britain and Argentina. Some time invariably elapses before such records are available to the captains and the press, because the tournament staff must enter, on a master sheet for each deal, the bidding and play records from each room and the actual cards held by the four players. In Buenos Aires this work was done in person by the overworked Argentinian chief tournament director, Raoul Lerena.

On Butler's suggestion, Hammerich obtained these vital documents from Lerena. Neither of the two key British witnesses had had a chance to see them before we began the afternoon meeting, and the first step, after reporting the morning's proceedings, was to carry out a comparison.

The observations of Butler and Swimer, as compared with the actual cards held, fitted the code with close to 100 per cent accuracy. This evidence on its own was virtually sufficient to convince the four people present who were hearing the story for the first time: General Gruenther, Carl'Alberto Perroux of Italy, Dr. Alfredo Labougle[7] of Argentina, and Hammerich.

The meeting heard my evidence, and also testimony from Becker and Truscott. The latter had examined the hand records in search of internal evidence, but the members of the Executive clearly regarded this as of minor importance beside the direct evidence of observations.

Reese and Schapiro were brought in and were confronted with the evidence of Butler and Swimer. They repeated their denials, and Reese, maintaining his usual sang-froid, made some observations in his own defense.

At this stage, Reese, Schapiro, and Truscott were asked to leave. It was suggested that I should leave also, but as Swimer was remaining I requested and obtained permission to stay. My players were involved in the matter almost as much as Swimer's, and I felt I should be present in their interests.

---

6. Josh (Johannes) Hammerich, the assistant secretary of the W.B.F., was one of several people who observed this episode. — A.T.

7. The Argentinian delegate to the W.B.F. — A.T.

Each member of the Executive in turn then offered an individual opinion. Only one man had any doubts, and they were both slight and predictable.

"I am a criminal lawyer," declared Perroux, "and all my life I have insisted that 99 per cent proof is not enough. It must be 100 per cent."

This statement was in French, and when Hammerich had translated for the benefit of the Americans there was a prompt and dramatic answer.

"Gentlemen, they are not 100 per cent guilty," announced Swimer with tears in his eyes. "They are 110 percent guilty."

Remembering the meeting I had seen in the park earlier, I put in a question.

"Captain Swimer, are there any facts in your possession which are not in the possession of the committee which has made you come to this conclusion?"

"I cannot answer that question," replied Swimer, rather stiffly. From this moment I felt sure that Schapiro had confessed privately to Swimer, and I was therefore not surprised to hear, months later, that the story of such a confession had been put in evidence at the London inquiry.

I left the meeting at this point, leaving the committee to debate the next step. The debate went on and on, but eventually I was recalled to the meeting together with Swimer and Marquardt.

The verdict was read out: "The World Bridge Federation has found Terence Reese and Boris Schapiro guilty of conveying information illegally. Swimer has suspended them from play, has forfeited the match to Argentina, and will forfeit to the United States."

We were asked not to reveal this information, and the Argentine captain, who had known nothing about what was going on, staggered out of the room in a state of shock. A heavy defeat for his team had suddenly turned into a "victory" — the first victory for Argentina in the history of Bermuda Bowl competition.

Beside the action in the back rooms, the play on the final day fell rather flat. The Italian match against Argentina was a foregone conclusion, and our match against Britain was less interesting than it might have seemed to the spectators. Our opponents had a substantial, but not insuperable, lead, and we had to go through the motions of trying to win. I knew, of course, and my players no doubt suspected, that Swimer would eventually forfeit the match.

We had to continue play for the benefit of the Argentinian spectators, not to mention the tournament exchequer. But the general lack of interest in the proceedings infected the organizers and led to a farcical conclusion to the match.

When I went into the Bridge-O-Rama just after the start of the final session it seemed to me that my players were seated in the wrong direction. I had earlier had to submit my official lineup, and I felt sure that Leventritt and Schenken should be sitting East-West instead of North-South as the board indicated.

If they were seated wrong, no comparison of hands would be possible and the play would be entirely meaningless. Recalling that this same mishap had occurred when I had played in Buenos Aires in 1961, I spoke to the assistant director in charge, using my best Spanish, and asked him to check the seating. He departed, and came back shortly afterward to inform me happily that everything was in order.

An hour later it dawned on someone else that all was not well, and play had to be curtailed. It was now too late to require the players to begin again to no purpose, and Swimer made his speech conceding the match.

The 1965 World Championship was over.

But the Reese-Schapiro affair was not. Almost my last recollection of Buenos Aires was of seeing my deputy, Kehela, standing at the airport looking distinctly blue.

"Sammy," I asked him, "have I done anything to annoy you?" It had struck me that he had hardly spoken a word to me for more than forty-eight hours.

"Even if they were guilty," he burst out, "they were unfairly treated. And I shall say so."

I tried to explain that nothing else could have been done in view of the evidence and gave him a word of advice: "You're over twenty-one, Sammy. But don't do anything foolish."

Many of the players and officials were leaving at the same time. I happened to hear Solomon give voice to a sudden thought.

"Boy," he announced, "will I get it from Oakie now."

THE EVIDENCE OF SWIMER: CONFESSION 4

Ralph Swimer, of London, England, born 1914, was one of the leading British players. He partnered Jeremy Flint twice in international events, including the 1960 Turin Team Olympiad where they almost won the world title. In England he won the Gold Cup, and had an outstanding record in the Master Pairs; his four wins with Richard Preston have been exceeded only by Reese and Schapiro.

Swimer was an importer by profession, and bridge was simply a hobby — a fact which distinguished him from nearly all the British players of the top rank. His appointment as nonplaying captain of the British team in Buenos Aires was his first involvement in bridge politics.

As his earlier relations with Reese and Schapiro became an issue at the British Inquiry, his story begins two years before Buenos Aires. In the hope of throwing doubt upon his testimony, the defense suggested that he was nursing a grievance against the accused players — a topic which is discussed on page 182.

SOME PAST HISTORY

In 1960 Swimer played with Jeremy Flint in the World Team Olympiad in Turin as part of a British team which included Reese and Schapiro. Flint-Swimer was a new partnership, but a very effective one, and Great Britain almost won the world title.

Two years later Flint and Swimer played for Britain in the European Championship in Beirut; and Reese was the nonplaying captain. (For two years, 1961 and 1962, Reese refused to be a candidate for selection in Britain. His awareness of the Turin accusation described in Chapter 13 may have been a factor in this refusal.) The British team did less well than usual.

The following year Reese and Schapiro were back as candidates for international honors, and entered for the British Trials with Swimer and Flint.

This promising arrangement was upset when Reese announced that he did not want to play with Schapiro. He and Flint had developed a highly artificial system called the "Little Major," and wanted to play it together. Shortly before play started Swimer offered to play with Schapiro, an offer which suited the other two members of the team.

Schapiro lived up to his reputation as a difficult and intolerant partner, so although their team won the Trials it was clear that the Schapiro-Swimer partnership was not a success. The selectors chose Reese, Flint and Schapiro, together with three other players. Swimer had some reason to be annoyed by this discrimination, and was upset that his teammates were so ready to accept his exclusion from the team.

Swimer's annoyance soon evaporated. Within a year he was traveling to Switzerland with Reese and Schapiro as part of an unofficial British team.

SELECTION AND TENSION IN 1965

The 1965 Trials for the British team led to a similar disappointment for Swimer. He played with Albert Rose in a trial based on pairs, and finished third. But the selectors exercised their rights by selecting Rose with Harrison-Gray, again leaving Swimer on the sidelines. Rose protested this decision, and Swimer had to persuade him to accept the invitation to play.

But Swimer was to attend the 1965 world championships after all, not as a player but as nonplaying captain. The six selected players, who included Reese, Schapiro, Flint and Konstam, had the right to select their captain. At a team meeting five of the players voted for Swimer, with Konstam the only dissentient.

Swimer had to be persuaded, and Schapiro did most of the persuading — although he subsequently denied it. (See page 182.)

Finally Swimer agreed to accept a position which is normally one of dignity and prestige, combined with the straightforward task of determining the line-up of the team in each session of play. He did not know that this was a fateful decision which was to affect his whole life.

Swimer knew that he would have a difficult team to handle, and there was bickering and animosity from the start. Schapiro was furious that Reese openly expressed his preference for playing with Flint and using the Little Major. He criticised the other two players, and their system, openly and publicly. This led to a Reese-Schapiro storm at a team meeting one morning, but they left the room together and returned afterward announcing that they had made their peace.

THE ACCUSATION AND THE CORROBORATION

The next part of Swimer's story, described in detail in other chapters of this book, is a familiar one: how he was called to a meeting on Saturday morning and told of the accusations against the two members of his own team; how he consulted with Geoffrey Butler, the official representative of the British Bridge League; and how they decided, for better or worse, that they would have to see for themselves.

What Swimer saw that day can best be described by extracts from his testimony in the London inquiry. He realized, as Gerber had done independently, the importance of watching the accused players when they were not playing with each other. He arranged for Schapiro to play with Konstam, and watched. Later he testified that Schapiro held his cards "always in the same way, with four fingers showing, one thumb holding the inside of the cards."

The crucial test came that night when Swimer sat down to watch Reese and Schapiro play Argentina. At the end of the session he had recorded evidence of the highest importance. Out of 20 deals he took notes on 19. He missed board 125 because he left the room feeling nauseated. From that point Butler occupied the official seat, and Swimer watched from another position.

The following is a copy of Swimer's original notes. The original disappeared during the London inquiry, and this record is based on the evidence submitted to the inquiry.

	Reese	Schapiro
135	3	4
6	4	4
7	3	2
8	3	2
9	1	4
40	3	3
41	2	2
42	4	3
43	4	2
44	3	2
126	2	3
127	Hand drops	3
128	4	3
129	—	4
130	—	4
131	—	4
132	2	2
133	3	1
134	4	3

THE HANDS AND THE FINGERS

135 Reese (3 fingers)
♠ A Q 4 3
♡ 10 6 4
♢ A 7 6 5 2
♣ J

Schapiro (4 fingers)
♠ K 9 7 6 2
♡ 9 7 3 2
♢ —
♣ A K Q 10

136 Reese (4 fingers)
♠ A 2
♡ 10 4 3 2
♢ K 7 6 4
♣ 8 7 2

Schapiro (4 fingers)
♠ K Q 6 4
♡ K J 6 5
♢ Q
♣ K Q 5 3

137 Reese (3 fingers)
- ♠ 8 7 3 2
- ♡ A J 7
- ◇ J 6 3
- ♣ A K 3

Schapiro (2 fingers)
- ♠ A K Q 10 6 5
- ♡ K 10
- ◇ A 10 5 4 2
- ♣ —

138 Reese (3 fingers)
- ♠ A 9 2
- ♡ K 9 2
- ◇ Q 9 3
- ♣ J 9 4 3

Schapiro (2 fingers)
- ♠ 4 3
- ♡ Q J
- ◇ K 8 5
- ♣ A K 8 7 5 2

139 Reese (1 finger)
- ♠ Q 6 5 4 3
- ♡ 2
- ◇ A 9 5 2
- ♣ K 10 2

Schapiro (4 fingers)
- ♠ A 7 2
- ♡ A Q 9 3
- ◇ K 10
- ♣ J 9 5 4

140 Reese (3 fingers)
- ♠ A J 5 4
- ♡ K 7 3
- ◇ A 9 5 2
- ♣ 10 4

Schapiro (3 fingers)
- ♠ 10 8 6
- ♡ A J 9
- ◇ K Q 8 3
- ♣ J 9 2

141 Reese (2 fingers)
- ♠ K 9 3
- ♡ A J 9 8 6
- ◇ J 10 6 5
- ♣ 5

Schapiro (2 fingers)
- ♠ J 8
- ♡ K 7 5 4 3
- ◇ K Q 8 7
- ♣ 9 8

142 Reese (4 fingers)
- ♠ A K 7 6
- ♡ A Q J 3
- ◇ A 9 2
- ♣ 8 4

Schapiro (3 fingers)
- ♠ Q 5 2
- ♡ 10 9 8
- ◇ 8 6
- ♣ A 10 9 6 3

143 Reese (4 fingers)
- ♠ J 9 8 7
- ♡ A K J 8
- ◇ K 10 5
- ♣ 8 2

Schapiro (2 fingers)
- ♠ K 10
- ♡ Q 4
- ◇ A J 4 3 2
- ♣ K Q J 3

144 Reese (3 fingers)   Schapiro (2 fingers)

     ♠ A K   ♠ Q
     ♡ 10 5 4   ♡ A 9
     ◇ 8 5 2   ◇ Q J 10 9 3
     ♣ J 10 9 4 2   ♣ A Q 7 6 3

126 Reese (2 fingers)   Schapiro (3 fingers)

     ♠ 7   ♠ 6 3 2
     ♡ Q J 10 5 2   ♡ K 4 3
     ◇ Q 8 6 4   ◇ A K J 9
     ♣ K J 10   ♣ Q 6 3

127 Reese (no note)   Schapiro (3 fingers)

     ♠ A K Q 10   ♠ 9
     ♡ —   ♡ A J 10 8 4 2
     ◇ Q 7 6   ◇ A J 9 8
     ♣ K Q 10 8 5 2   ♣ J 3

128 Reese (4 fingers)   Schapiro (3 fingers)

     ♠ J   ♠ 8 4
     ♡ A J 10 5   ♡ 9 8 6
     ◇ K Q 10 5   ◇ 9 8 7 6 3 2
     ♣ A 8 7 6   ♣ 9 3

129 Reese (no note)   Schapiro (4 fingers)

     ♠ 4 3   ♠ Q J 7
     ♡ J 10 8 5 2   ♡ A 9 6 4
     ◇ K   ◇ 7 6 4
     ♣ J 10 9 7 2   ♣ K 8 5

130 Reese (no note)   Schapiro (4 fingers)

     ♠ K 6 4   ♠ J 9 3
     ♡ 5 2   ♡ J 10 7 6
     ◇ J 6 4 2   ◇ 7 5 3
     ♣ J 10 4 3   ♣ A Q 8

131 Reese (no note)   Schapiro (4 fingers)

     ♠ 10 7 6   ♠ K J 5
     ♡ —   ♡ A Q J 6
     ◇ A 9 6 4 3 2   ◇ Q 8 7
     ♣ Q 7 4 3   ♣ J 6 2

132	Reese (2 fingers)	Schapiro (2 fingers)
	♠ 6 5 2	♠ Q 3
	♡ Q J 10 3 2	♡ 8 7
	◇ 4 3	◇ Q 10 8 2
	♣ Q 4 2	♣ A K 7 6 5
133	Reese (3 fingers)	Schapiro (1 finger)
	♠ 8 7 6 5	♠ A 2
	♡ A 9 5	♡ 4
	◇ K 7 5 4	◇ J 10 9 6 3 2
	♣ 9 8	♣ 6 4 3 2
134	Reese (4 fingers)	Schapiro (3 fingers)
	♠ K Q 10 9 4	♠ A 8 6 3
	♡ A J 9 4	♡ Q 7 2
	◇ K 10	◇ A J 7 6
	♣ 9 4	♣ Q 3

This evidence was put before the World Bridge Federation on the following day and was compared with the hand records. It contributed substantially to the finding of "guilty."

By that time Swimer could have added some further evidence.

Torn by conflicting loyalties, he kept quiet about it for almost six months.

THE MEETING IN THE PARK

About noon on the final Sunday in Buenos Aires Swimer had been dismissed, together with Gerber, from the World Bridge Federation meeting. Feeling in need of air, he went for a stroll in the park opposite the Plaza Hotel with his wife and Albert Rose.

Schapiro called Swimer aside in the park, saying that he wanted to talk to him. The witnesses agree that the conversation was an emotional one, but the details remained a secret.

Swimer exploded a bombshell in the London Inquiry when he revealed belatedly that the conversation included a confession of guilt by Schapiro — a confession that Schapiro denied when it was his turn to give evidence.

Swimer was reluctant to reveal to the inquiry the details of the conversation, but when pressed he gave the following answer:

"He sort of began saying 'Ralphy' and I think he was about to say a lot of nonsense but he stopped there and I said 'Boris, don't waste your time; don't tell me this sort of thing. I saw everything for myself. I know exactly what happened.'

"He said, 'Well, let me tell you.' I said, 'Yes.' He said, 'Will you believe me, this is the first time it has ever happened?' Then he said, 'Will you forgive me?' By this time I had actually broken down. He said 'Will you forgive me?' I said to him, 'How could you do such a thing and how could you — I am supposed to be your friend — let me become a party to this?'

"He said, 'Will you believe me, it was that evil man, he made me do it. I wouldn't play the Little Major and he made me do it.' Then he kept saying, 'What shall I do now?' I said to him, 'I suppose you'd better deny it,' sort of thing."

Two minutes later Swimer added to the conversation: "I missed out something. Mr. Schapiro said to me, 'You won't tell anybody.' Several times he said, 'Promise me you won't tell anybody.' I did not promise and I did not say anything to that but I did not intend to tell anybody about it."

The immediate reaction of Reese's counsel in London was to suggest that Swimer had concocted the story of a confession in his own interests.

Caplan said, "I am going to suggest to you that this is all a lot of made-up rubbish. I am going to put to you why you have made it up... I suggest to you that you have seen the possibility that all might not go well with you in that libel action."

Caplan was referring to Swimer's libel case against Rixi Markus which is described on pp. 195-198. This provoked a legal argument about questioning which could affect a case which was *sub judice*.

On the following day Swimer offered to prove to the inquiry that the story of the confession was not one which he had just made up for his own legal purposes.

He produced for the consideration of the tribunal a letter he had written to himself from South America. His intention was to put on record his Buenos Aires evidence in case his plane should crash on the return journey. But both author and letter arrived safely, so the letter was put away unopened.

This unusual item of documentary evidence produced a legal storm. Caplan, for the defense, insisted that the letter could not be produced as evidence. Coldblatt, for the prosecution, insisted that it could be brought in to refute Caplan's suggestion that the confession story was a recent concoction by Swimer.

After a lengthy debate about the laws of evidence, Sir John Foster ruled that the letter would not be admitted as evidence if Caplan would withdraw his suggestion that Swimer's confession story had just been made up by him.

Caplan grudgingly agreed to this, and the letter remained unopened. More than two years later, however, it was opened in connection with the libel action, and the story in it closely paralleled Swimer's evidence to the inquiry six months after the event.

(Above) The envelope which Swimer addressed to himself from South America.
(Right) The letter which the Foster Inquiry refused to accept as evidence.

Sunday May 23rd 1965

During recess Boris pressed me to speak with him,

I said to him — how could you do this to me I felt emotional and broke down and he said to me

Ralph I swear to you this is the first time it has ever happened

'That evil man that swine forced it on me when I refused to play little Major.

(page 1)

Can you forgive me — Why are you crying I am the one who should be crying — Will you promise me not to tell anything to anybody — I said I cant forgive you the way I feel now why did you tell me all this, I wish you hadn't,

Boris said tell

(page 2)

③
me what to do, my life is finished, shall I commit suicide? what shall I do — tell me', tell me', I said I suppose you'll have to continue to deny it.

He continued to press me to stay with him repeating the same words he had already used specially that the

(page 3)

was the first time ever and will I forgive him.

I'm writing these words while, it is all fresh in my mind, I hope not ever to repeat them and am posting to London in case anything should happen to me before arriving home.

Ralph Swimer

(page 4)

But if Sir John Foster had looked at the letter he would have seen one significant variation — a variation which helps to explain why Swimer chose to remain silent about the confession until the pressure of events, a threat to his own reputation, forced him to disclose it.

Here is a reproduction of the letter. It is a record of a time of agony, written by a man who was still suffering from a severe emotional disturbance:

> Sunday May 23rd 1965.
>
> During recess Boris pressed me to speak with him. I said to him — how could you do this to me
>
> I felt emotional and broke down and he said to me
>
> Ralph I swear to you this is the first time it has ever happed That evil man that swine forced it on me when I refused to play Little Major.
>
> Can you forgive me — why are you crying I'm the one who should be crying — Will you promise me not to tell anything to anybody — I said I cant forgive you the way I feel now
>
> why did you tell me all this, I wish you had'nt.
>
> Boris said tell me what to do, my life is finished, shall I commit suicide? What shall I do — tell me? tell me? I said I suppose you'll have to continue to deny it.
>
> He continued to press me to stay with him repeating the same words he had already used
>
> specially that this was the first time ever and will I forgive him.
>
> I'm writing these words while it is all fresh in my mind. I hope not ever to repeat them and am posting to London in case anything should happen to me before arriving home.
>
> RALPH SWIMER

Perhaps subconsciously, Swimer did not reveal to Sir John Foster the element in the confession which made him so reluctant to talk about it.

Schapiro not only begged Swimer to keep silent about their conversation, but he threatened to commit suicide. Schapiro was in a distraught condition, and perhaps meant what he said.

Can one say that Swimer was wrong? Is it not understandable that he would hesitate to take an action that might drive an old friend, however guilty, into taking his own life?

THE EVIDENCE OF BUTLER: VERIFICATION 5

GEOFFREY BUTLER, of London, England, was one of the world's most experienced bridge administrators. His many official titles included chairman of the British Bridge League for fifteen years, and then president, a new office; member of the Executive committees of the European Bridge League (from 1951) and of the World Bridge Federation (from its foundation in 1955). He represented Europe in the long and difficult task of preparing the 1963 International Codes of Laws.

Butler played a major role in the Buenos Aires drama for a crowded twenty-four hours, and a minor role for a further twelve. However, he maintained silence on the affair apart from testifying to the two official bodies — the World Bridge Federation and the Foster inquiry. This chapter is therefore based on other sources.

A lunchtime encounter on Saturday outside the Plaza Hotel in Buenos Aires was the beginning of Butler's involvement in the crisis.

"We've been looking for you, Geoffrey," announced Alan Truscott, arresting his rush toward a long-overdue breakfast. "Ralph and I need to talk to you about something urgently."

A meeting was set up for 3 P.M. in Swimer's room, and Butler and Truscott arrived first. Truscott began, for the fourth time that day, to explain the code.

Butler listened in shocked amazement for about five minutes, when the explanation was interrupted by Swimer's arrival. This interruption was probably responsible for a good deal of subsequent confusion.

Butler did not later recall that be had been told about the "spread-finger" hypothesis, which at that time was not completely documented. Nor did he remember being told about the Hayden-Becker notes, a copy of which Truscott had been carrying around with him since the previous evening.

If Truscott had not completed his story when they were interrupted by the arrival of Swimer, who had heard it all before, Butler's later ignorance on two important points becomes explicable.

In any event, one might think it unlikely that an elderly man who has just received highly distressing news would absorb every detail of a complicated situation.

Butler took relatively little part in the conversation at this stage, because Swimer wanted to look at hands and had some records that had not been available to Truscott the previous night. Butler makes no claim to being an expert player, and he was willing to leave technical analysis to the others.

Swimer was, not unnaturally, serious and gloomy, but his gloom lifted somewhat when he discovered the deal on which Schapiro had played in one heart with a four-two trump fit. That was the only crumb of comfort he was able to extract from the records.

Truscott departed, leaving the two British officials to confer on what steps they should take. After much discussion they decided they would have to see the code in operation for themselves.

This decision has since been much criticized in England, on the ground that it was an unpatriotic action that represented a "betrayal" of the British players. But it is difficult to see how responsible officials could have taken any other course. They had an official duty, not only to themselves but to the British Bridge League and the World Bridge Federation, to test the validity of the allegations. To place the burden of investigation on others[1] who might be less competent or less trustworthy could be regarded as negligence. The suggestion in some British quarters that their observations constituted "spying" and that a proper course was to tip off the accused players is patriotism carried to the immoral point of chauvinism.

Butler and Swimer clearly hoped that the allegations were false, in which case the fewer people who knew about it, the better. "If I could prove it had not taken place," testified Butler in London, "I certainly would not have pursued the matter further. I did not want to tell other people, obviously."

It was agreed to play Reese and Schapiro in the Open Room that night against Argentina.

And to watch.

That night Butler observed nine deals and took written notes, sitting in the captain's seat next to Reese, which Swimer had vacated.

The actual notes are shown on the following page and represent Butler's record of the two accused players' finger positions.

The correspondence between the observations and the hearts actually held can be judged from the table given below the notes.

For example, on Board 129 the hand records show that Reese held five hearts. In the code, two fingers would be showing for five hearts. Butler noted two fingers. Schapiro held four hearts, for which the code would be four, and Butler noted four fingers.

---

1. See page 75.

The degree of correspondence between the observations and the code can be seen at a glance by comparing columns II and III for each player.

Butler's notes were:

	Reese	Schapiro
126	2?	3
127	4	3
128	4	3?
129	2=5	4
130	3?	4
131	4	4
132	2=5	2
133	3	
134	4	3

Below is a comparison of the notes with the hearts actually held:

	Reese			Schapiro		
	I	II	III	I	II	III
	Hearts Actually held	Code for I	Fingers noted	Hearts Actually held	Code for I	Fingers Noted
126	5	2	2?	3	3	3
127	0		4	6	3	3
128	4	4	4	3	3	3?
129	5	2	2	4	4	4
130	2	2	3?	4	4	4
131	0		4	4	4	4
132	5	2	2	2	2	2
133	3	3	3	1	1	
134	4	4	4	3	3	3

(The complete hands held by Reese and Schapiro for these deals are shown on pp. 47-48.)

There have been two published assessments of this vital matter, and the reader will be able to place his own value on the worth of these assessments.

At a late stage in a grueling cross-examination the defense counsel in London extracted from Butler a positive answer to the following question:

"There was only one hand, or at the most two hands, where both coincided?"

This passage from the transcript Reese has since quoted on several occasions. Sir John Foster in his report was a little more generous to Butler's notes.

"Mr. Butler's evidence, confined to watching 9 of the hands... was that there was correspondence in some 5 or 6 hands."

Both assessments are difficult to reconcile with the evidence.

It is easy to see that in only one case was there a discrepancy between the notes and the code. This was in Deal 130, on which Butler noted "3?" when Reese actually held two hearts. This was one of three observations that were queried, and the other two fitted.

Butler made seventeen separate finger notations, and they can be classified in this way:

Fitting the code and not queried	12
Fitting the code but queried	2
Not fitting the code but queried	1
Corresponding to a void, which was undecoded	2
	17

If one takes only the positive unqueried observations that matched the code, the correspondence is 100 per cent.

If the queried observations are included, the correspondence is 93 per cent.

How, then, was Foster able to conclude that the correspondence was about 60 per cent, and Caplan to imply that it was less than 20 per cent?

THE FALLACY OF HANDS

For the purposes of checking a code, there is no logical reason to relate the fingers of a player on a particular deal to the fingers of his partner on the same deal.

Caplan, Foster, and Reese, whether deliberately or not, repeatedly obscured the issue by referring to 'hands'. They professed to be impressed only if the code agreed with the fingers on *both* sides of the table on a particular deal.

If one accepts this artificial approach, it is possible to see how Caplan reached his remarkable conclusion. On three of the nine deals Butler had queries. On two of the deals, by an incredible chance, Reese held a heart void, for which no decoding had been put forward.[2] (A particular player should hold a heart void once in about eighty deals.) And on a sixth deal, Butler omitted to make a note of Schapiro's fingers. The reason for this he was unable to recall clearly. He eventually suggested an unconvincing explanation — that a spectator had got in his way — which afforded Reese an opportunity for a typical jibe.

Looking at it in this curious way, it is true that 'both coincided', in Caplan's phrase, rather seldom. 'One hand, or at the most two hands', was going rather far. But it is hardly surprising that a witness who had been battered for several hours by the cross-examination of an aggressive lawyer and had heard a bewildering exhibition of arithmetical conjuring that had reduced 100 per cent to less than 20 per cent, should have found it difficult to count up to three.

Goldblatt, the prosecution counsel, presented the evidence of the notes in a more scientific and accurate fashion. He tabulated them and classified them according to the extent to which they corresponded with the heart code.

Foster's summing-up was that there was correspondence in "some 5 or 6" hands. This rather vague conclusion suggests not only that he had accepted the defense classification by hands rather than by observations, but also that he was writing his report from memory: it would not have been difficult to state the precise degree of correspondence.

Butler's honesty and integrity have never been questioned, and his notes showed a correspondence with the code far beyond the reach of coincidence. Some people might think that this evidence by itself would be sufficient to prove the case.

---

2. See page 148.

THE EVIDENCE OF KEHELA: INDECISION

*Sammy Kehela of Toronto, one of North America's outstanding play-
ers, has played in five world team championships, twice represent-
ing North America in the Bermuda Bowl and thrice Canada in the
Olympiad. He has won six national championships, including the
Spingold twice and the Vanderbilt within a two-year period. Most of
these successes were with his regular partner, Eric Murray. In
Buenos Aires he was the official coach and deputy captain of the
American team.*

*This chapter is based on his personal recollection of the events
in Buenos Aires and his testimony in the London inquiry.*

Kehela visited his family in London shortly after the events in Buenos Aires and
was invited to testify for the defense. His evidence was one of the two factors that
influenced Sir John Foster in arriving at his "Not Guilty" verdict and is an important part of the story.

Kehela was told by Gerber about the allegations and code on Saturday afternoon "in case I die tomorrow." Late that night he watched the second half of the
session between Argentina and Britain, at the time when both Butler and Swimer
were observing and taking notes.

In one respect Kehela's testimony confirmed that of other observers: he noted
the changing finger pattern behind both Reese's and Schapiro's cards. He took no
notes of the finger change but looked for correspondence between fingers and the
code, which he had been given. He testified that in nine or ten deals, representing
eighteen or twenty separate hands, he saw a correspondence with the code on
between 40 per cent and 50 per cent of the maximum. On three or four deals the
correspondence was complete, and on one or two deals the fingers of one player
corresponded.

The remainder of Kehela's testimony was of a more general character: the
technical evidence of specific hands; the unimportance of the Argentine session
for the British players; and the poor form shown by Reese and Schapiro, particularly against Italy. (All these points are discussed elsewhere in the book.)

THE VALUE OF THE KEHELA OBSERVATIONS

Butler and Swimer were observing and taking notes at the same time that Kehela was watching. When compared with the hand records, Swimer's notes showed 100 per cent correlation with the code, and Butler was only slightly less accurate. Assuming that all the evidence was given in good faith, how could Kehela testify to a 50 per cent correspondence?

One possibility, of course, is that Kehela's memory played him false when he testified to the number of noncorrespondences. But there are three specific factors that could have contributed to "noncorrespondence."

Twice during this group of deals Reese held a heart void, for which no correspondence was possible.

Three or perhaps four times Reese held three or four hearts, a circumstance that had caused Becker a problem the day before when observing at a distance from the table.

Even more significantly, Kehela had to try to see the number of hearts held by each player. This is not nearly as easy to do as one might think when moving backward and forward, a task complicated by a wooden grandstand, a roped enclosure, and other spectators. The other observers, of course, were not subject to this possibility of error. Their finger observations were compared later with the official hand records, and it was not necessary for them to watch the hearts.

Two statements made by Kehela at the London inquiry deserve attention. One of them was highly ambiguous: "I am satisfied that Reese and Schapiro were not using signals throughout the session I watched." On the face of it this could mean that he was satisfied that no cheating took place while he was observing. But Kehela assures me that he meant it quite literally and that a suitable paraphrase would be: "I am satisfied that, if Reese and Schapiro were in fact signaling while I watched, they could only have done so for about half the time."

It would be tempting to suppose that the signals disappeared at some stage. About halfway through the session, Kehela shook his head at Reese, intending to imply that the last British hope had gone because the Italians were destroying their American opponents. This might have led Reese to conclude that the time for signaling had gone by, but such an explanation does not fit all the facts. All the observers, including Kehela, saw finger variations throughout the session.

Kehela made one other statement to the inquiry in London which Reese did not choose to quote in his book. He said, in effect, that he did not regard his own evidence as conclusive in either direction. This statement indicates that Sir John exaggerated somewhat in his report when he stated that "Mr. Kehela... came to the conclusion that the pair were[1] not cheating."

Kehela's evidence needed some explanation from the defense counsel and apparently did not get it. If Reese and Schapiro were innocent, the 40 or 50 percentage of correspondence noted by Kehela was remarkably high.

THE PERSONAL FACTOR

Sammy Kehela is, deservedly, one of the most popular personalities in the world of American bridge. He has remained almost magically free of the jealousies, backbiting, and feuds that pervade the narrow world of bridge champions. But he had one significant psychological quirk. He believed that Terence Reese was the world's greatest bridge player.

He was not alone in this — I thought so myself and so did many others — but he was certainly alone in the passionate conviction with which he held to this view. His feeling for Reese, verging on hero worship, dated back to 1956, when as a stripling of twenty-three Kehela made a big impression on the English tournament scene before emigrating to Canada.

In Buenos Aires the idol fell. From the moment Gerber broke the news to him on Saturday afternoon, Kehela was in a somewhat dazed state. He wandered sadly around the tournament rooms and hardly spoke to anyone. At the time, as he later stated in London, he believed that the two players were guilty and specifically said so to Becker and Mrs. Hayden. Subsequently, as he testified, he had doubts — not a complete change of heart, just doubts. His admitted uncertainty contrasts strangely with the emphasis placed on his evidence in the Foster report.

Kehela's decision to give evidence in London was clearly due to loyalty to a man for whom he had had the greatest respect. Loyalty is a virtue that one can always admire, even if it is sometimes misplaced.

---

1. A plural statement of a singular conclusion! — A.T

TWO OTHER WITNESSES: CORROBORATION 7

THE TESTIMONY of six witnesses has already been described. There were two more in addition to this writer, and they were both members of the World Bridge Federation Executive.

Waldemar von Zedtwitz, president emeritus of the American Contract Bridge League and an elder statesman of the bridge world equally renowned as a player and an administrator, was one of them. His first opportunity to watch occurred on Friday night before the code was broken but after the finger movements had been reported. He submitted an affidavit to the London inquiry, but it was rejected as evidence because he was not present to be cross-examined.

Reese dismissed this evidence as negligible. Whether this is an accurate assessment can be judged from the following quotation from von Zedtwitz's affidavit:

> Mr. John Gerber, captain of the North American team, requested me to watch Messrs. Reese and Schapiro in play to determine whether in my opinion they were exchanging finger signals and, if so, whether I could observe a correlation between any messages exchanged and the actual holdings.
>
> I had previously observed Messrs. Reese and Flint playing against Messrs. Belladonna and Avarelli at the request of the Italian captain, Mr. C. A. Perroux, for the purpose of forestalling any unpleasant incidents that might develop in connection with the use of the Little Major as employed by the British pair. Nothing untoward occurred at that time, nor was Mr. Reese seen to move his hands or fingers unnaturally.
>
> Availing myself of a privilege I enjoy as a member of the W.B.F. Executive Committee, I entered the Closed Room on the evening of May 21st and watched Messrs. Reese and Schapiro play boards 127-144 against Messrs. Forquet and Garozzo. Seating myself to the left and behind Mr. Schapiro, I had a full view of Mr. Reese but could not, because of my position, keep Mr. Schapiro under observation. In all but two of the hands I saw Mr. Reese execute complicated movements with his left hand (sometimes reinforced by fingers of his right hand).

The process invariably resulted in a final configuration of 2, 3, or 4 fingers,[1] usually held horizontally across the backs of the cards. As soon as the final position was reached, all motion ceased, the hand thereafter remaining immobile. On at least one occasion Mr. Reese dropped his right hand abruptly onto his knee.

One deal stands out in stark clarity, Board 131. Reese's holding on this deal was:

♠ 10 8 7 6 3   ♡ K 8 7 6 2   ◇ J   ♣ 7 4

He held his cards with the thumb of his left hand on the inside, while the index and the finger next to it were spread wide apart on the outside to form an upright V. To achieve and maintain this unnatural position requires considerable dexterity; I have never seen it before.

My observations took place before the signals allegedly used had been interpreted and I was therefore not able, at that time, to verify their precise significance. I consider it highly improbable, however, that the carefully executed movements could have been random, fortuitous, or based on mannerisms. They gave me the impression of being deliberately designed.

The eighth witness was Robin MacNab, President of the American Contract Bridge League in 1965 and also a member of the World Bridge Federation Executive. That he had significant evidence to give was not known to the London inquiry, simply because at the time no one thought to ask him. It occurred to me to ask him, nearly two years after the event, about the part he had played in Buenos Aires. I knew that he was told about the suspicion on Friday and about the code on Saturday, but I did not know that he had made observations of his own.

"I felt it was a mistake to watch first one, and then the other," he states, "and I happened to select Schapiro for the purpose. It was a most inconclusive test simply because I did not watch over fifteen or sixteen hands and made no notes of my own. Some hands were thrown in, and I did not have a continuous test for that reason. I probably got a thorough test on only four or five hands, but I was satisfied in my own mind that the players were cheating."

Inconclusive, perhaps, but no more and no less significant than the evidence of Kehela, who watched a smaller number of boards more intensively during the same session.

---

1. Von Zedtwitz should have seen one case of a one-finger signal to show a singleton heart. — A.T.

THE TRUSCOTT STORY: DISILLUSION

THE FIRST bridge tournament I ever attended was a memorable one for a player with some theoretical knowledge and little practical experience. It was at Harrogate, a resort town in the North of England; the year was 1946, and at twenty-one I was probably the youngest competitor.

I arrived partnerless and teamless but had a stroke of luck. An expert team was a player short for the first event, and I found myself, for the first and last time in my life, a teammate of Ralph Swimer. We did well in the qualifying session and eliminated a star-studded London team that included Albert Rose, but we scored poorly in the final — no doubt the result of my inexperience.

My naval officer's uniform caused Paul Stern, the captain of the Austrian team that won the World Championship in 1937, to christen me 'The Admiral', a slight exaggeration of my rank. He was kind enough to play with me in a one-session event and emitted one of his well-known bull-like roars when I removed a double that he had intended for penalties.

In the final of the pair championship, I played two deals against Terence Reese and Boris Schapiro. On one of them Schapiro bluffed me out of a game by opening vulnerable with a psychic bid, and I remember admiring his courage. The next day I shared a compartment with them for the three-hour train ride back to London and talked to Reese about chess — a game at which I was the expert and he was the amateur. Five years later, we three became teammates on an occasion of the greatest importance. This was the climax of my years at Oxford University, from which Reese had graduated before the war.

In 1951 the British Bridge League, for the first and last time, threw the trials for the British team open to all comers. It was to be a long grind, with three stages of pairs trials to be followed by two stages of team trials. I entered with my Oxford partner, Robert D'Unienville, who would surely have become one of the world's great players if he had not returned soon after to his native Mauritius. We needed the experience and hoped to get through a stage or two.

The result was beyond our wildest dreams. We were second in the first stage, from which the experts were exempted, won the second stage, and were second again in the third stage. At this point eight pairs survived, and we were the only unknowns.

Bob and Jim Sharples were the winners of Stage III, and we were surprised when they passed up a chance to pick Reese and Schapiro to complete their team for the final rounds. There were rumors of a feud in which these two pairs were on opposite sides. This gave D'Unienville and me the chance to pick Reese and Schapiro, but my partner was reluctant. He felt we might spoil their chances of qualifying for the team, but I talked him out of such excessive modesty.

Our famous teammates were very gracious about being stuck with the least experienced pair in the field, and we did very well. They were in top form, and we won all three semifinal matches and then the final. I greatly admired the intensity with which they played in the final, because the rules provided for one pair to be selected from the losing team and they could therefore expect to qualify for the team in any event. Looking back sixteen years later, I am not so sure. The Sharples brothers were on the opposing team, and if they had won, their views might have influenced the selection of the third pair.

The European Championships were played in Venice, and we finished in a tie for second position, behind the Italians. Our failure to win was due largely to a very bad start, to which my partner and I contributed substantially.

Seven years elapsed before I again qualified for a European Championship team, and an ill-assorted team it was. I played with Harrison-Gray, and as the result of a selection accident, the other two pairs were the Sharples brothers and Reese and Schapiro. The old animosities remained below the surface and the team did well, tying on victory points with the Italians but losing the title on match-point quotient. A different guess on one deal, shown for other reasons on page 107 of this book, would have given us a shot at the World Championship.

In the intervening years I had developed a taste for writing about bridge, and this led me into a cordial professional relationship with Reese, who edited the *British Bridge World*. I contributed to the magazine each month for almost seven years and also wrote a section of a book for him. When I finally succeeded in winning a European title in 1961 in Torquay, he served as the Bridge-O-Rama commentator and subsequently paid a kind tribute in print to my efforts as a player and an organizer. At that time I was secretary of the British Bridge League.

In 1962 I played in the World Championship in New York and accepted an invitation to move to America and write a bridge encyclopedia for the American Contract Bridge League. In my first few months of residence two West Coast experts independently asked me my opinion of Reese and Schapiro. I was happy to say that in my opinion they were the world's best pair and that Reese was the world's best player and writer. I was less happy to discover that my questioners wanted an opinion about their honesty, because in some American circles they were thought to be 'wired' — a popular colloquialism for having illicit understandings. I denied the innuendos with considerable indignation but thought no more about them.

I was therefore both astonished and disturbed when Becker and Mrs. Hayden took me into their confidence in Buenos Aires at 2 A.M. Friday, to be precise. I told them something they did not know: that there had been one or two unsubstantiated charges against the same players in the past. I told Becker that I could not believe it and that I was sure he was wrong, but I was privately appalled by the thought that he might be right. My informants were far removed in character from the tiny group of American experts who throw out accusations based more on envy and egotism than on evidence. I agreed to watch during the play that afternoon.

Reese and Schapiro were due to play on Bridge-O-Rama against Italy on Friday afternoon, which meant that only a scorer and an announcer would be able to watch them "live". I was trying to talk my way into the announcing job, which I had done once earlier in the week, when Mrs. Hayden arrived with the news that the two matches had been switched so that the local Argentine supporters could watch their own team play North America. I gave up arguing and rushed to the Open Room, where a large crowd had already gathered to watch Reese and Schapiro play Forquet and Garozzo. Sammy Kehela was occupying the privileged press seat within the ropes, but my claim was greater than his so I claimed, drawing a withering look, which would have had more impact if my mind had not been on more important things.

Becker had prepared me mentally, but nothing could have prepared me psychologically for what came next. Sitting next to Reese, I saw Schapiro's fingers vary from one hand to the next throughout the session of fourteen deals. The changes were clearly planned and purposeful. They bore no resemblance whatever to an accidental mannerism. Gradually my shocked amazement became slightly diluted with anger: for two players to cheat while representing a nation in a world championship constituted a complete betrayal of followers of the game everywhere.

In spite of what I had been told, I had not really believed that I was going to see anything. So I took no notes of what I saw, an omission that subsequently annoyed Mrs. Hayden. I offered her two trivial practical excuses, that I did not have a pencil and that I was afraid Reese would see what I was doing, but the real reason was quite different. I was still in Stage One, being convinced that something was happening. The need to take notes to discover what the finger signals meant did not occur to me, any more than it had occurred to Becker and Mrs. Hayden on the previous day. But they were now in Stage Two, taking records with a view to decoding signals.

Immediately the session was over I met Becker and Mrs. Hayden. She expressed herself on the subject of my recording abilities and showed me the notes that she had compiled on the back of an old scorecard with Becker's help. I copied them onto the back of some pressroom hand records that I was carrying and promised to study them that evening while Becker and Mrs. Hayden were in play against Argentina.

I spent more than an hour comparing the notes with the records of the session that we had watched. There were a number of possibilities to be tested, and I started with aces. The idea that one finger would show one ace and so on was not particularly plausible and was easily discarded. But there were many other possibilities. On the Blackwood principle, four fingers might mean four aces or none, three fingers might mean one ace, two fingers might mean two aces, and one finger three aces. A solution of this type would have accounted for the infrequency of the one-finger signal. Another possibility, which Mrs. Hayden had had in mind when taking the notes, was that the finger signal in some way indicated the short suit in the hand. The trouble with this hypothesis was that on many deals there would be two or even three equally short suits.

I devoted most of my time to the complex possibility that the fingers in some way showed the point-count in the hand. The signal might show that the hand belonged within a certain point-range. It might have an arithmetical base, with one signal showing four, eight, twelve, etc., another three, seven, eleven, etc.; another two, six, ten, etc., and another one, five, nine, etc. And it might be fully meaningful only in relation to some other signal we had not observed — such as the Turin hand-and-level combination considered on page 166. Another possibility was that the code might not be a consistent one. There could, for example, be one arrangement for odd-numbered boards and another arrangement for even-numbered boards.

At the inquiry in London, Caplan indicated that it should have been very easy for me to associate the fingers with the heart suit. No doubt he would have been smarter than I was, but it did not occur to me at the time that a signal that had apparently four positions could be utilized to show the number of cards in a suit.

I abandoned the decoding attempt and went off to write my story for *The New York Times* with mixed feelings. I would have liked to think that the problem was insoluble, but there was no sense in that. I could not credit that we had all been the victims of some delusion, or that Reese and Schapiro were transmitting meaningless signals as a species of intellectual joke.

Much later I met Becker and Mrs. Hayden, and we took a cab to an all-night restaurant. There we faced up to two problems. The first was how to say "well done" in Spanish, a coding operation for which my pocket dictionary proved unhelpful. The second was the decoding operation, which proved unexpectedly easy. After listening, somewhat impatiently, to the story of my earlier efforts, Mrs. Hayden suggested a procedure that made good sense. We would examine the hands on which similar signals had been given, and try to establish a correlation.

There was only one one-finger signal, but luckily Mrs. Hayden recalled a deal from Thursday's play in which Reese had given a one-finger signal. On both hands the player had a singleton heart, and we had to discover whether this was just a coincidence. It was lucky Mrs. Hayden recalled the earlier deal, which I did not know about, because it might not have been so easy to reach the solution by examining the two-finger signals. As Schapiro held five hearts and Reese held two hearts on Deal 123, we might perhaps have rejected the heart hypothesis prematurely.

As it was, everything fell into place. We could not be sure how five hearts was distinguished from two, but we had noticed that on several occasions the fingers had been spread apart. Becker's observation of four fingers spread apart on Board 114 was a clue. As Reese had seven hearts on that deal, it seemed reasonable to suppose that two fingers spread apart would mean five hearts and that three fingers spread apart would mean six. As the evidence for this was very limited, we did not feel completely confident about it, and I laid little emphasis upon this point during the meetings the following day. That Butler and Swimer did not take in this detail was probably my fault. I had to tell the same story four times the following day, in a tired state, and no doubt my narrative became more and more condensed as time went on.

When we had broken the code, we tried unsuccessfully to call Gerber, and I was left with the task of telling him at the earliest possible moment. Becker and Mrs. Hayden went back to their rooms, for as they had to face a final crucial day of play against Italy, their need of sleep was greater than mine.

When I got back to my room I spent an hour or so looking at the records of several sessions played by Reese and Schapiro during the week. I noted a number of bids that in themselves suggested illicit knowledge, a number of others that were consistent with illicit knowledge. I found none that pointed in the opposite direction.

As we had observations and a decoding, the hands themselves were of minor importance. But I wanted to satisfy myself that Reese and Schapiro had not made a series of blunders involving the heart suit.[1]

After three hours' sleep I called Gerber and told him that we had broken the code. I went to his room and explained everything to him. He got out his notes, and we found that all but one of his observations agreed with the code. In the next

1. As they had in 1955. See pp. 134-135.

six hours I had a lot more explaining to do, first to MacNab and Von Zedtwitz, then to Swimer, and finally to Butler.

Much of my meeting with Swimer and Butler was taken up by discussion of hands. After I had told the story of the observations and the decoding, we went through the twenty hands I had noted the night before. Butler, who was not an expert player, took little interest in this secondary evidence, but Swimer followed me closely. When I had finished he wanted to look at more hands and produced his captain's records. He had three sessions I did not have, and we went through them. He cheered up considerably when he found U.S. 74, the deal on which the contract was one heart with a 4-2 fit, but that was his only crumb of technical comfort.

I left the unhappy British officials to decide what step they should take next and went back to the playing area. Reese was playing with Flint in the Open Room, and I watched for two or three deals. As I expected, both players were holding their cards in a normal, relaxed fashion. There was no suggestion of the finger variation that had been so obvious on the previous day.

This observation had a double importance: it absolved Flint from any suspicion, and it ruled out the remote possibility that the finger variation was an innocent mannerism. Reese suggests, not unreasonably, that two deals would be too small a sample. It is perhaps worth pointing out that if my evidence were given dishonestly — as he implied at another point in his book — I would no doubt have testified, without any risk of contradiction, to some larger number of deals.

For the rest of the day the final stages of the North America-Italy match took all my attention. Until close to midnight it seemed possible that Italy might at long last be deprived of its world title. But the American collapse in the last session made it necessary for me to write a familiar story for my New York readers: a close and exciting fight, but the Blue Team had won again.

On the final Sunday I appeared before the Appeals Committee in the morning and the full W.B.F. Executive in the afternoon. Reese and Schapiro were called in to hear the charges and were given their opportunity to defend themselves. Reese did not say much, and Schapiro said practically nothing. I was asked to go through some of the hands that I had noted, and I had covered eight out of twenty when Solomon quite rightly called a halt. It was clear to him and to the other members of the Executive that argument about specific hands was not going to help.

The rest of the day was one of journalistic frustration. I had decided, perhaps wrongly, that it would be improper for me to cable the scandal story to my paper while it was still under consideration by the official body. I could, of course, have sent a full story on Saturday and hit the headlines before Reese and Schapiro even knew they had been accused.

On Sunday, rumors began to circulate in the pressroom. It was known that highly secret meetings were going on, that Reese and Schapiro had been called in, and that their captain had benched them. The World Bridge Federation asked the press to hold back any stories until they had reached a decision. This affected me far more than any other journalist, because I was the only one who knew what it was all about. We understood that an announcement would be made by dinner time, which suited me well enough for the purpose of a Monday deadline.

At dinner there was no announcement, and we were told that the Executive had adjourned its meetings. It seemed we would hear something about 10 P.M. or 11 P.M., in which case my story would still make the later editions. Later we discovered the reason for the delay. The "Guilty" verdict, with Perroux a lone abstainer, was taken halfway through the afternoon meeting, but the committee needed another seven hours to decide what to do about it.

Their first-draft statement — never released — was a clear statement that Reese and Schapiro had been found guilty of cheating by the World Bridge Federation. Two factors contributed to the watering-down process that resulted in a statement referring merely to "certain irregularities," the names of the four innocent players, the concession by the British captain, and the transfer of responsibility for further action to the British Bridge League. One was the nervousness of some of the lawyers on the Executive, who were unsure of the Federation's legal position. The other was an appeal by Reese. He pointed out to Solomon that Schapiro had aged parents and that the shock of a bald announcement of cheating might have serious results.

Midnight came and went, and my journalistic blood pressure rose steadily. When the official announcement came it was well after 1 A.M. and much too late for Monday's paper.

My irritation became rage when I got back to New York eventually and discovered what had happened. The front page of *The New York Times* on Monday had carried the story of the cheating, but it had not been my story. The paper had picked up a wire-service story sent through by a local "stringer" ahead of the official announcement — a story so inaccurate that it later became the basis for legal proceedings in England.

So not only had I passed up my first, and probably last, chance of a world scoop out of respect for the World Bridge Federation — respect that many journalists would think was misplaced — but I had been scooped on my own front page. Although they were kind enough not to say anything to me at the time, the editors of *The New York Times* no doubt shook their heads sadly. They had sent me to cover the Championships — the only American paper to have individual coverage — and then had had first news of a story of world dimension from an agency.

Even when I could write my story in Buenos Aires, I was not sure what to write. I contented myself with an account that did not go too far beyond the official statement, for I was not at all sure to what extent it was proper for me to use, in my capacity as a reporter, knowledge I had as a key witness. I still hoped, as did everyone else concerned, that the world impact of a scandal that could damage the game could in some way be contained.

On my last day in Buenos Aires I was able to catch up with my sleep and my work. The two accused players did not appear at the final banquet, but I had an unexpected encounter the next morning just as I was leaving the hotel. Reese was standing on his own in the lobby and beckoned me over. I had no idea what was coming. A blow? A bribe? A diatribe? It turned out to be a civil offer to send me some hands from the European Championship in Ostend, as he had done on occasion for my predecessor. I returned a civil acceptance, but it turned out to be unnecessary because I got to Ostend myself.

There was no direct plane to New York on Tuesday, so I had to take a "local" stopping at Santiago, Lima, Panama, and Miami. Fortunately I had company, the Solomons as far as Lima, and Kehela and Garozzo all the way. I seized the opportunity to talk to Kehela, who was anxious that the defense case should be presented as fairly as possible. At my request, he wrote out a few sentences on a scrap of paper, giving me something I could quote if an opportunity came up.

The opportunity came up immediately. When we landed at Kennedy Airport I called my office and found the paper had been trying to reach me for the previous twenty-four hours. They wanted a full story with every possible detail, so I staggered into the office, drooping with fatigue, and hammered out a piece that was later quoted by newspapers all over North America. At the finish I introduced my Kehela quotation with a few words saying that many leading players hoped that the punishment would not be too heavy. As it turned out, the quotation was cut and I came under fire in some quarters for apparently recommending a soft line toward the British pair.

We were now waiting for the British, and there was some speculation about what action would be appropriate. A few leading players expected suspension from tournament play for one or two years, but in perspective that seemed inadequate. Shortly before, the Greater New York Bridge Association had imposed a one-year suspension on a player who had been caught watching the play at other tables and making notes on his scorecard about deals he had still to play. The offenses did not seem comparable.

The first news from London was that a meeting had been adjourned because the W.B.F. report was not available. The next news was a shock. The British Bridge League had decided not to accept the World Bridge Federation verdict of "Guilty," a verdict that had been conveyed privately and not published to the world. Instead it had invited Sir John Foster, Q.C., M.P., to preside over an independent tribunal to examine the whole affair.

In June, Becker and I were invited to testify before the tribunal, on the understanding that we should find the money for our fares. The British Bridge League, as I well knew, was just as impecunious as the World Bridge Federation. The League did not realize that Mrs. Hayden had played a vital part in the whole affair, so I suggested that she should come too. This was agreed, and the money for three transatlantic plane tickets was provided by the World Bridge Federation and American sources. But for the money problem I would have suggested that Gerber also should testify. However, it seemed that our evidence together with that of Swimer and Butler should be more than sufficient to convince Sir John — a misjudgment, as it turned out.

Agreeing to go to London was one thing, but finding a date was quite another. I had a family holiday planned for July, and a heavy work schedule. The Summer National Championships were at the beginning of August, and Sir John Foster was going to be out of England for the whole of that month. We settled for late September, a three-month delay that infuriated Reese and Schapiro. They made widely reported comments about the "insufferable and iniquitous" behavior of the Americans in holding up the inquiry, but subsequent events made their complaint something of a joke. When we testified in September it was clear that we had not held up anything because we were not the last of the witnesses. Swimer was not heard until November, and it took until the following May to complete the hearing of the evidence.

While we were negotiating about dates I received a strange telephone call from the New York office of the London *Daily Mail*. I was told that the paper was following the story closely. Schapiro had been interviewed several times; and he insisted that a study of the deals played in Argentina would prove them to be innocent. In England the copies of the hand records had not been made public: the British Bridge League had them, and so did the accused players. So when the *Daily Mail* said, quite reasonably, "All right, if they prove you're innocent let's see them," Schapiro offered to sell them a set — for one thousand pounds.

I was able to tell the *Daily Mail* that they could have copies of the deals from the American Contract Bridge League for the cost of xeroxing. If they cared to wait a few days they could have the Tournament Book, containing most of the significant deals, for $2.50. However, what the newspaper would have been able to do with this technical material is difficult to imagine. This impertinence of Schapiro's was followed soon afterward by the news that Reese was working on a book about the whole affair.

The trip to England in September allowed me to meet many old friends and avoid a few new enemies. Outside the Tower of London, one of the tourist spots I showed proudly to my fellow-witnesses, a sailor gave an unusual performance. After members of the audience had bound him firmly with solid chains and padlocks, and I had by invitation stuck a bayonet down his back for luck, he gave an impressive exhibition of wriggling out of an impossible situation. It occurs to me now that he and Reese were two of a kind.

As I expected, the European bridge players were familiar only with Reese's version of the affair. He had been interviewed several times on radio and television, and his loyal friends had faithfully circulated certain myths. The prosecution side of the story had not been heard, because Butler and Swimer were maintaining a dignified silence.

We paid a lightning visit to Ostend, where the European Championships were just ending. Several leading journalists were eager to hear our side of the story, and we were prepared to tell them. As a result, one of Europe's leading bridge personalities changed his mind about giving evidence for the defense.

Back in London I spent more than a full day giving my testimony. Most of this was on cross-examination by Caplan, the defense counsel, who began by asking me whether I had had any previous experience of cheating cases. I was happy to tell him that I had served for several years on the Rules and Ethics Committee of the English Bridge Union, but he was more interested in establishing that I had been a potential witness in a European case dating from 1957. Presumably this was to be used to show that I was a hardened accuser.

Much time was spent, or perhaps wasted, while Caplan held a hand of cards in a variety of ways and asked me whether his finger position looked natural or unnatural. We had some discussion about psychic bidding, and I put forward the suggestion that the frequency with which Reese and Schapiro had made risky psychic bids over the years was evidence of "special understandings" on previous occasions. This was rather more than my questioner wanted to hear, and my answer was legally condemned as "nonresponsive" to the question.

I had earlier suggested to the British Bridge League solicitor that the past record of Reese and Schapiro should be put before the inquiry, but he did not wish to be involved in side issues that would be difficult to prove. But as I found when I began to write this book sixteen months later, the difficult may not be impossible.

HOW THE CASE WAS HANDLED IN BUENOS AIRES 9

THE MAIN issue in this case is whether or not two famous players cheated. In the period following Buenos Aires that issue tended to become submerged in a variety of side issues. A popular game on both sides of the Atlantic was to throw brickbats at the World Bridge Federation for incompetent conduct of the proceedings, or to criticize the witnesses for the parts they had played.

Undoubtedly one or two matters could have been handled in a slightly better way, which is hardly surprising considering that a situation of the gravest importance arose at the tail end of a championship. But on the whole the witnesses and officials emerge with credit from a most difficult situation. Most of the criticisms were made by people who were not present and show a total lack of understanding of the situation. But to keep the record straight, they should be answered.

WERE THE WITNESSES THE RIGHT PEOPLE?

Someone who thinks he has detected cheating in a bridge tournament has four options.

He can ignore the suspicion altogether. This timid course would be against the interests of the game and, more specifically, against the interests of those who have to play against the cheats, if cheats they are.

Alternatively, he can content himself with passing round the word that X and Y are cheats, which is of course far worse than option one. The accused players become victims of rumormongering and have little chance to defend themselves. Starting such rumors is entirely reprehensible, and official bodies have often threatened heavy penalties for such behavior — although none has ever been assessed.

He who suspects cheating can inform an official immediately, a third procedure, which is certainly "correct" although it has two disadvantages. It increases the chance that the matter will become public, and any publicity is obviously most undesirable if the charges cannot be substantiated. And it decreases the chance of a firm conclusion. Bridge history, and especially the history in Chapters 12 and 13 of this book, makes it clear that tournament officials are generally reluctant to investigate charges of cheating. Nor do they have, as a rule, the necessary ability to detect, to decode, or to judge the technical aspects of the matter.

The fourth option is to collect further evidence with the aid of other witnesses, leaving open the possibility of concealing the matter altogether or advising the authorities. This was the course actually taken in Buenos Aires. The result was that five senior officials — two nonplaying captains and three members of the Appeals Committee, which deals with such matters — were able to observe the play and satisfy themselves of the truth of the charges.

WHY NOT TELL THE TOURNAMENT DIRECTOR?

Several defense witnesses in the London inquiry insisted that the proceedings in Buenos Aires were improper, that the tournament director should have been advised and should have carried out an official investigation.

The Americans "should have told the tournament director," complained Schapiro in giving evidence. "This tournament director is well supplied with assistant tournament directors and scorers. It is up to them to make an unbiased examination and not for Swimer and Butler and these Americans to spy on us."

This course that Schapiro suggested would certainly be right in an ordinary bridge tournament, but this was not an ordinary tournament. There were five good reasons for not telling the tournament director in Buenos Aires.

In most tournaments the director is the senior official. This is not so at a world championship, at which the Appeals Committee is above the director. The cheating allegations were of such importance and delicacy that they were taken immediately to the highest level. And to object to that would be rather like complaining because a general was advised about the outbreak of war before his aide-de-camp.

Second, it simply was not true that the tournament director was well supplied with assistants and scorers, although it would have been true in Europe or America. The Argentine Bridge Federation was relatively small and impecunious, and its splendid staging of the championships was a magnificent effort that stretched its resources to the limit.

The chief tournament director, Raoul Lerena, was heavily overworked. He spent a large part of each session preparing the official records, normally a separate function, and he was doing some press work as well as supervising the whole operation. He certainly did not have time to observe the play for long periods, or to attend lengthy meetings. None of the witnesses in Buenos Aires knew him well enough to be able to judge his competence in dealing with a matter far outside the normal range of a director's duties. Certainly his overworked staff would not have been up to it, judging by the assistant who was asked to check the seating of the players on the last night and came back with the wrong answer.

Nor did those concerned know Lerena well enough to be sure that they could rely on his discretion in such a vital matter. And he did in fact commit one small indiscretion during the weekend, by sending out a press story about the affair before the Executive had released its statement. Most important of all for practical purposes, Lerena spoke little English and the others concerned little or no Spanish.

Another suggested course of action is easier to dismiss.

"What should have happened, in our view," wrote Sir John Foster in his report, "is that the players should have been watched... by neutral persons (in this case neither United States, British, Italian or Argentine nationals) appointed by the Federation for this task."

Exactly two people present in Buenos Aires fitted this nationality specification. One was Kehela, who was a Canadian but not a neutral. The other was Johannes Hammerich of Venezuela, who was ill until midday on Sunday.

NOT A COURT OF LAW

Sir John Foster declared that, judged by the standards of his profession, the proceedings in Buenos Aires were "most unsatisfactory." It is surprising that he was surprised that the two committees conducted themselves like committees, which they were, rather than like an English court of law, which they were not. But let us see why the proceedings were "most unsatisfactory."

THE OVERLAPPING FUNCTIONS

In a court case a judge cannot also be a witness. He would have to disqualify himself from acting in a judicial capacity. This is not a practical rule in a bridge tournament, in which experienced and responsible observers are usually in short supply. It would be unusual for a member of a committee to disqualify himself simply because he has knowledge of a case acquired in an official capacity. Past history indicates that English committees do not concern themselves with such legal niceties.

The Foster Report complained that Butler was wearing two hats: "Mr. Butler was Chairman of the Appeals Committee, yet his evidence was of the greatest importance."

This is a very fine legal point. But one might argue that if Butler had absented himself from the meetings he would have been failing in his duty, not only to the World Bridge Federation, but also to the British Bridge League, to which he would have to report. Perhaps Butler should have refrained from voting, but such care for legal niceties would have been academic. There would then have been six votes for "guilty" instead of seven, and two abstentions instead of one.

A *reductio ad absurdum* could have resulted if Butler had disqualified himself from the Appeals Committee because he was a witness. MacNab and Von Zedtwitz would presumably have had to follow suit, as they had each conducted observations. And if Solomon had then disqualified himself because he had personally observed the same pair on a similar occasion in the past, the Committee would have been reduced to zero until Hammerich was able to rise from his sickbed.

There is even less substance in another trivial Foster complaint. "Mr. Swimer, who was also a witness, was nevertheless present throughout the sitting of the Appeals Committee," states the Report, inaccurately. Swimer left the Appeals Committee, together with Gerber, when the stage of deliberation was reached: the meeting was still going on when the celebrated encounter between Schapiro and the British captain took place outside the hotel.

SHORTAGE OF EVIDENCE?

"The Appeals Committee did not seek all the available evidence," declares the Report. "Neither Mrs. Hayden or Mr. Kehela, the American deputy-captain, were called in to give evidence."

It is perhaps true that Mrs. Hayden should have been called as a witness, even though she was in play much of the time the meetings were being held. Whether she could have added anything material to the evidence already given by Becker, Gerber, and myself is doubtful. Most of the members of the Appeals Committee had seen my copy of the Hayden notes, which was available throughout the meetings, notwithstanding Butler's failure of memory on this point. The main reason, of course, why Mrs. Hayden was not called was that the two committees were entirely satisfied that the evidence already before them was overwhelming. The committee could not have called Kehela, because no official had the slightest idea that he had any evidence to give, and he did not come forward.

As far as seeking all the witnesses goes, one might think that the World Bridge

Federation did better in a few hours than the Foster Inquiry in fifteen months. In Buenos Aires seven of those who observed were present at the meetings, although one, MacNab, said almost nothing about his own part; an eighth, Mrs. Hayden, was heard indirectly; and the ninth, Kehela, was unknown. In London six of those who observed were heard; a seventh, Von Zedtwitz, was rejected; an eighth, Gerber, was neglected; and the ninth, MacNab, was unknown.

As for the technical evidence, which Foster says was "examined very perfunctorily," the authorities gave it as much and as little weight as the subject deserved. Almost every hand that Reese and Schapiro had played during the first seven days was examined by Swimer or by me or by the two of us in consultation, in the short period between the decoding of the signals and the start of the official hearings. I had a list of twenty hands in front of me when the meetings took place on Sunday, more than enough to satisfy the Executive of the one thing they needed to know: that the hands did not point conclusively to innocence. This was a remote possibility that needed to be, and was, excluded. Indeed, the hands pointed quite strongly to guilt, although, as shown in Chapter 16, such evidence can be argued indefinitely.

The Foster Report distorts this situation: "Unfortunately the analysis of Mr. Truscott was superficial having regard to all the hands played by Mr. Reese and Mr. Schapiro... It was wrong of the Appeals Committee to rely on the small sample of eight hands produced by Mr. Truscott without considering the overall picture."

But perhaps it was wrong of Sir John Foster to rely on the oft-repeated defense statement that Butler and the Committee heard about only eight hands. Reese heard about eight hands when he was called into the meeting, but his testimony about the number of hands produced on other occasions when he was not present was given quite surprising weight.

INSUFFICIENT CHANCE FOR THE DEFENSE?

"The two players were not, in our opinion, given sufficient opportunity of defending themselves," states the Report.

Certainly the players did not get the opportunity later offered to them in London during a fifteen-month inquiry. But they were given rather more opportunity than they would have been given on any ordinary bridge occasion. Bridge committees normally give players accused of any irregularity one opportunity to state their side of the case. Reese and Schapiro had two opportunities.

At both meetings they said very little beyond denying the charges. Reese indicated that there was no way in which he could deny the charges and admitted later in the day to Solomon that the committee could not have reached any other verdict on the evidence before it. The World Bridge Federation was prepared to hear anything the accused players had to say, but they could not, in the circumstances, wait forever. As MacNab observed pertinently long afterward: "How long does sitting silent constitute a defense?"

A SOFT VERDICT

The chief criticism in America of the proceedings of the World Bridge Federation was aimed at the action taken after the verdict.

A bridge committee dealing with an irregularity, whether it be a minor ethical lapse in a local tournament or a cheating case in a world championship, has certain responsibilities. If it finds that an irregularity has been committed, it has a duty to take some appropriate action, even if it merely warns the player or players not to repeat the offense.

The first intention of the World Bridge Federation in Buenos Aires, after the guilty verdict was reached, was to make a public announcement of the fact and perhaps suspend the players from world competition. The chief spokesman for this view was Von Zedtwitz, who had to leave during the Sunday afternoon discussions. After his departure, some members of the committee advocated a softer line. There were three factors involved.

There was some nervousness about the legal position of the Federation. The members of the committee did not know whether forthright action could lead to a libel suit — a fear that subsequently led to the appointment of an official counsel to the Federation.

There was a general feeling that the publicity would be bad for the game. So the committee attempted to minimize the public impact of the affair by concealing the verdict and trying to conceal the details of the accusation. As it turned out, this policy produced exactly the opposite effect. If the Federation had announced a verdict and a sentence, there would have been a nine days' wonder but no Foster inquiry, no book by Reese, and no book in reply by me. Instead the affair received continuing publicity and is still a matter of controversy almost forty years later.

A final factor that influenced the committee was a feeling that it was destroying the reputations of two famous players and that justice should be tempered with mercy. This accounted for the rather artificial manner in which the names of the two players were omitted from the official announcement, a gesture made at Reese's request in the interests of Schapiro.

The announcement read:

> Certain irregularities having been reported, the Appeals Committee fully investigated the matter and later convened a meeting of the Executive Committee of the World Bridge Federation. The Captain of the British team was present.
> As a result of this meeting the Captain of the British Squad decided to play only K. Konstam, M. Harrison-Gray, A. Rose and J. Flint in the remaining sessions and very sportingly conceded the matches against North America and Argentina...

The Executive Committee responsible for this announcement included: Charles Solomon, W.B.F. president; General Alfred Gruenther, W.B.F. honorary president; Carl'Alberto Perroux, W.B.F. vice president; Robin MacNab, A.C.B.L. president; Waldemar Von Zedtwitz, A.C.B.L. president emeritus; Geoffrey Butler, W.B.F. Appeals Committee chairman; Johannes Hammerich of Venezuela, W.B.F. assistant secretary; and Dr. Labougle of Argentina.

Conceding two championship matches that had already been won is something that had never before happened in the history of the game. Even if the press had not already known the details, it would not have been difficult to associate the two unnamed players with the irregularities.

THE WORLD BRIDGE FEDERATION REPORT

In my opinion the only substantial failing of the World Bridge Federation was the manner in which it reported the case to the British Bridge League.

The decision of the Executive to refer the case to the British Bridge League for disposition made it necessary for the report to be comprehensive and accurate. A lengthy report, including statements from all the witnesses, could have been compiled the day after the tournament ended. It could have been drafted, checked, and cross-checked by all those principally concerned.

If this had been done, it is likely, but not certain, that the British Bridge League would have accepted the Buenos Aires verdict. As it was, the two reports were compiled by Butler alone, while he was still suffering from shock and lack of sleep. The result, as can be seen in Appendix C, was a confused, incomplete, and inaccurate document.

The reports could and should have been edited and revised by Solomon and others concerned. In fact, they were mailed to Solomon from England a week or two later with a request for prompt return so that the British Bridge League could deal with the matter. It did not occur to Solomon that the British Bridge League would do anything but accept the report and the verdict and proceed to take some disciplinary action. In view of the urgency, he contented himself with some minor corrections instead of attempting a complete revision.

The reports shuttled back across the Atlantic to London and there contributed to a British Bridge League bombshell.

HOW THE CASE WAS HANDLED IN LONDON

A BRITISH BOMBSHELL

THROUGHOUT the history of bridge, officials and committees have almost invariably avoided public and positive action in cheating cases. The World Bridge Federation followed this pattern in Buenos Aires, and the British Bridge League followed suit in London.

The intention of the international body, admittedly not very clearly expressed, was that the British authorities should take disciplinary action against the two players who had been found guilty — action that could well have been taken in Buenos Aires.

It was far harder for the British Bridge League Council to pass a sentence of suspension on the two accused players than it would have been for the Federation.

Most of the members of the Council had known Reese and Schapiro for many years, and some of them were close friends and associates. It was rather like expecting members of a family to sit in judgment on one of their own number. Equally important was the climate of public opinion in England. The average bridge player was quite naturally horrified at the thought that England's most famous pair would cheat in a world championship. Without any knowledge of the facts, they reasoned: "It can't be true, therefore it isn't true."

The Council therefore had two strong reasons for avoiding responsibility if it possibly could: personal feelings for the accused players and the pressure of public opinion. In spite of this, the Council came close to accepting the "guilty" verdict on the basis of the inadequate information available to them. Apparently a nucleus of pro-Reese members was able to veto such an action.

There were several steps the Council could have taken if it was not prepared to accept the findings of the world body on the spot:

1. It could have listened to statements from all those concerned immediately available to them — Butler, Swimer, Reese, and Schapiro. As it happens, this would have given the Council an incomplete picture, because neither British official was in a position to give a detailed account of the American evidence.

At it turned out, Butler gave only a short formal report, and the Council did not hear Swimer at all. British captains have invariably submitted a report to the Council after returning from an international championship, and to discontinue the practice when there was a matter of highest importance to report might be considered strange, especially since Swimer was waiting patiently outside the door.

2. The Council could have asked the World Bridge Federation for a far more comprehensive report, including statements from all the principal witnesses. This would have entailed a delay of a month or two, but this would have been trifling compared with the fifteen months ultimately consumed.

3. The Council could have appointed a subcommittee to study all the evidence. This would have been difficult in practice, for most of the English members of the Council would have had to disqualify themselves because of their close personal relationship with the accused players, and the Welsh, Scottish, and Irish members lived too far from London to be able to attend frequent meetings.

In the end, the Council settled for a fourth alternative, which shifted the responsibility elsewhere — an independent inquiry. This was a bombshell for the officials of the world body and for the American witnesses, all of whom had expected disciplinary action. Instead they were faced by a rehearing of the whole case.

THE FOSTER INQUIRY

At first sight, most members of the bridge-playing public, especially in England, probably approved of the action of the British Bridge League in setting up the Foster Inquiry.

Sir John Foster was a lawyer of great distinction. Neither he nor his chosen associate, General Lord Bourne, could possibly be suspected of any bias for or against the accused players. If they had a natural bias against the very idea that British representatives would dishonor their country's name by cheating in international competition, this would have been true of any judge or jury that could have been found in London.

A major disadvantage was that the two judges were almost completely ignorant of bridge. Sir John Foster described himself as a player in the eighteenth class, while General Lord Bourne was apparently a nonplayer. Lawyers have to be able to adapt themselves and often have to acquire a superficial understanding of intricate subjects. But the two judges were to be severely tested in the months to come.

THE HEARINGS COMPARED

In one respect the British tribunal had a major advantage over the Buenos Aires hearing: time was not a factor. The committees in Buenos Aires met for six or seven hours before reaching a verdict, which is probably longer than has ever been devoted to such a case during the progress of a tournament.

The Foster Inquiry had thirty sittings spread over eleven months. (It got underway two months after the World Championship, and a month elapsed between the conclusion of the hearings and the announcements of the findings.) In this time it was possible to introduce a vast mass of evidence — much of it remote from the issues in the case and some completely irrelevant. (It may be doubted, for example, that it helped Sir John Foster materially to know that Harold Franklin had captained the British women's team on more than three occasions.) But there were three respects in which the English tribunal was at a disadvantage compared with the original hearing.

In Buenos Aires the trail was fresh. All the witnesses could remember clearly what they had seen and done during the previous forty-eight hours. In London the scent was a cold one. Butler testified three months after the original events; Becker, Mrs. Hayden, and I four months afterward; Swimer six months; Reese seven to nine months; and Schapiro nine months. Witnesses with poor memories, and this applied particularly to Butler, Swimer, and Schapiro, were fully entitled to say that they did not remember the precise sequence of events, who said what, and the reasons for particular actions.

Secondly, the eight judges in Buenos Aires were all highly experienced bridge administrators. They understood the workings of the tournament game, they could assess for themselves the importance to be attached to the different types of evidence, and most of them had had experience of similar cases in the past. The two London judges knew almost nothing about bridge.

Thirdly, and most important, the original hearing was better supplied with witnesses. The committee heard directly or indirectly from eight of the nine people who conducted observations — and they would have heard the ninth if he had come forward at the time. The London inquiry heard six of the direct observers, five speaking for the prosecution, one for the defense.

WHICH SIDE HAD THE ADVANTAGE IN LONDON?

The prosecution had one obvious advantage. The World Bridge Federation had already decided clearly against the accused players. The defense had two obvious advantages. Their case was presented last, so their witnesses could, and often did, make statements that could have been rebutted if the prosecution had been able to recall witnesses or call new ones.

Also, the onus of proof was on the prosecution, and it turned out that Sir John Foster expected a very high standard of proof. He made it clear that he would not give a Scotch verdict of "not proven", and he applied the test that would be appropriate in a criminal case: the charge must be proved beyond a reasonable doubt. It was the doctrine of "reasonable doubt" which resulted in the acquittal.

The defense had several less obvious advantages, all of them based on one factor — money. In a legal contest between an organization and one or two individuals, the organization usually has a financial advantage. In London it worked the other way round.

The British Bridge League, whose underpaid secretary I was for several years, had very limited revenues and no accumulated capital. All its income was devoted to financing British representatives in international competition. The English Bridge Union subscribed £500, later increased to £1000, toward the cost of the inquiry and so saved the League from bankruptcy. The League could have avoided the expense altogether if it had chosen to do so, because there was an outside offer to pay the whole costs of the inquiry.

The offer came from Crockford's, a London card club with a great tradition. In recent years the club has neglected bridge in the interests of such gambling activities as chemin de fer. The club was interested in the case because Reese was one of its leading members and Schapiro was employed by it at one of its gambling subsidiaries. Tim Holland, one of the owners of Crockford's, was determined to give the accused players every possible support; he went so far as to post notices in the club asking members to support Reese and Schapiro, and some visitors who ventured an opinion on the other side of the case were made to feel distinctly unwelcome. (A year or so later one properly invited visitor was actually asked to leave because Schapiro suspected that he belonged in the opposition camp.)

In these circumstances the British Bridge League felt constrained to decline the generous offer of Crockford's. The League could see that a verdict of "not guilty" might be questioned in some quarters if the whole proceedings were financed by Crockford's.

The result was that the defense had unlimited funds, while the prosecution had to count every penny. This had three direct consequences.

1. The counsel briefed for the defense, Leonard Caplan, a Queen's Counsel, was vastly more experienced than his opposite number, Simon Goldblatt. Goldblatt was careful and conscientious, but Caplan was more forceful and won most of the arguments about points of law.

2. The prosecution did not wish to pay the substantial cost of preparing a transcript. The defense was willing to pay, so a transcript was prepared that was the sole property of the defense.

3. The defense could afford to pay the expenses of numerous witnesses, most of whom had no direct connection with the case. The prosecution could afford very little for such expenditures. If more money had been available, Gerber would certainly have been brought from Texas, and perhaps other witnesses of lesser significance would have been asked to testify.

This advantage for the defense would have been substantially reduced if the inquiry had been conducted in accordance with American legal principles. Depositions from Gerber, MacNab, Von Zedtwitz, Solomon, and perhaps others would have been admitted as evidence.

PUBLIC OR PRIVATE

For several good reasons, the Foster inquiry was held in private. Neither the press nor the public was admitted, as they would have been in an ordinary legal case.

All the statements made by witnesses had "qualified privilege," which meant that they could not be made the subject of a slander action — although there would be no such protection for repetition outside the inquiry.

The secrecy was largely in the interest of the accused players: the full details of the evidence against them would not come out, and they would be spared the embarrassment of continual publicity over a long period. Because the inquiry was a secret one, some witnesses spoke freely about matters that they would not have aired in public. In particular, the defense introduced various skeletons in the closet of bridge history which bore virtually no relation to the case in hand.

From the point of view of the game as a whole, there was much to be said for the argument that repeated newspaper reference to cheating should be avoided if possible. Unfortunately, the privacy was a one-way street. All the lawyers concerned in the case had a professional duty to be discreet about matters that arose behind closed doors; but the accused players had no such obligation. Leaks that were likely to benefit the cause of Reese and Schapiro or to embarrass their opponents occurred frequently, and of course the transcript was defense property.

This point arose in connection with possible further legal proceedings, and was put strongly by the prosecution counsel:

GOLDBLATT: ". . . this Inquiry is held largely by the decision of my learned friend and his clients as a private inquiry. That being so, it is highly undesirable, to put it no higher, that the facts which are given at the present inquiry, except in so far as you feel they need to be incorporated in a report which you make, should be retailed beyond this Inquiry. I am seeking to arrive at that result."

SIR JOHN: "I do not see much of a danger at the moment."

He may have changed his mind a year later, when the "full" story of the proceedings of the inquiry was published by Reese in *Story of an Accusation*.

THE MYSTERY OF THE MISSING NOTES

One of the oddest features of the Foster inquiry was that all the primary documentary evidence disappeared. The original notes of Butler, Swimer, and Mrs. Hayden, all of which had a bearing on law suits that were likely to materialize in the British courts, could not be found when the inquiry was complete. Mrs. Hayden had left her notes with the inquiry rather reluctantly and only when assured categorically that they would eventually be returned to her.

The lawyers concerned denied any knowledge of the notes, and a letter to Sir John received this reply:

"I am afraid an exhaustive search for your notes has been without result. The notes were certainly not taken out of the room by Lord Bourne or myself, or anybody acting with our authority. They were kept in a drawer in the room."

So the notes must have been taken by someone without authority.

THE FOSTER REPORT *11*

THE COUNCIL of the British Bridge League met on August 9, 1966, and considered the Foster Report. After two and a half hours it gave out an official statement:

> The joint report by Sir John Foster and Lord Bourne into certain allegations of cheating at the world championships in 1965 made against Messrs. Reese and Schapiro was received by the Council today. After full discussion of the arguments and recommendations by Sir John Foster and Lord Bourne the finding in the report that Messrs. Reese and Schapiro were not guilty of cheating was accepted. A copy of the report will be sent to the World Bridge Federation.
>
> The Council wishes to express its sincere thanks to Sir John Foster and Lord Bourne for having conducted the Inquiry as a public duty and without fee, and to the assessors and all witnesses who voluntarily attended to give evidence at the Inquiry.

The Council refused to disclose the contents of the report, and although it was eventually given to the two defendants, it was not published in England until long afterwards. A copy was duly sent to the World Bridge Federation, without condition, and was then passed to the delegates representing various parts of the world. In January, 1967, the American Contract Bridge League published the Report in its Bulletin, perhaps because a copy had reached the bridge press.

The reluctance of the British Bridge League to publish the Report was generally attributed to legal motives: doubts about whether the Report was "privileged," and a desire to prevent its being used by the accused players as a basis for legal action. The contents of the Report suggest another motive for this reluctance: many readers might feel that the judges had strained considerably to arrive at an acquittal based on "reasonable doubt."

There is good reason to think that the Council itself was not happy with the Report and its verdict and that a substantial body of opinion favored rejection. The "full discussion" eventually brought about the realization that the League would make itself look quite ridiculous if it rejected the findings of an expensive and protracted inquiry that it itself had set up.

This is borne out by the cold tone of the official statement. If the members of the Council had been satisfied that the two players were innocent victims of an unjustified accusation, they would no doubt have expressed their sympathy for Reese and Schapiro and congratulated them on emerging triumphant from a long and trying ordeal. They might also have considered censuring Ralph Swimer for giving false testimony and considered removing Geoffrey Butler from his position as president of the League. They did none of these things and an examination of the report suggests the explanation.

THE REPORT ANALYZED

The Foster Report, with footnotes added, is given in Appendix B. The original consists of slightly more than ten typed pages, a total of 302 lines.

One would expect such a report to be a balanced document, setting out clearly the evidence on both sides, but this is not the case. A great part is devoted to criticisms of the conduct of the hearings in Buenos Aires, and Sir John apparently viewed his role as that of an appeal judge in a lower court. In the body of the report the arguments put forward by the defense are repeated at great length in an uncritical fashion. The arguments for the prosecution are mentioned briefly and in some cases ignored altogether. Perhaps Sir John and General Bourne viewed the report as a means of explaining and justifying their verdict to the British Bridge League. Certainly it reads far more like a speech for the defense than a balanced judicial appraisal.

Almost half the Report was not concerned with the issues in the case. (The origins of the inquiry and its procedures took 39 lines; there was a 4-line summary of the two types of evidence; a description of the proceedings in Buenos Aires and criticisms of them took 89 lines, which are discussed in Chapter 9; there were 7 lines outlining the doctrine of reasonable doubt; and 6 lines of verdict.) Of the part of the report devoted to the main issue — whether Reese and Schapiro cheated — 127 lines are devoted to a partisan presentation of the evidence and arguments for the defense. The direct evidence for the prosecution is condensed into 21 lines.

THE DIRECT EVIDENCE IN THE REPORT

The evidence of Becker, Mrs. Hayden, Truscott, Swimer, and Butler, which formed the basis for the original verdict of guilty, occupies only one-fifteenth of the Report. An almost equal space is devoted to the reasons for rejecting the testimony of the prosecution witnesses, almost all of which concerns Swimer. Butler's testimony is dismissed as "not clear corroboration," a judgment based on a distorted view of his recorded observations.

The Becker-Hayden notes are barely mentioned, and it is impossible to tell by reading the Report that these constitute conclusive evidence on their own. The implication of the Report is that these are rejected because of a theoretical possibility that these might have been manufactured subsequently to support the case. This would indicate reprehensible conduct by Becker, Mrs. Hayden and Truscott of a far more serious nature than cheating.

This suggestion was based on the flimsy reason that Butler did not recollect these notes, either in his evidence or in his report. No evidence was offered to suggest why three renowned bridge personalities should behave in such a way. Becker and I were on very friendly terms with the two accused players, while Mrs. Hayden barely knew them. The idea that these notes had been manufactured subsequently ("improved" was the tactful word used by the defense counsel) could have been disproved quite easily if other American evidence had been available at the inquiry.

The evidence of Gerber is not mentioned in the Report, presumably because he did not come to England. At any rate, it should have been clear that his evidence also had to be dishonest if the two accused players were innocent.

Perhaps the most astonishing feature of the Report is the complete absence of any reference to the a priori evidence: that a variation of fingers by one player is highly suspicious; that similar variations by his partner make suspicion a virtual certainty; that if this were an innocent mannerism it would show itself in the play as well as the bidding; and, strongest of all, the mannerism would not disappear, as witnesses said it did, when the two players played with other partners. Such arguments, discussed in detail in Chapter 18, were not mentioned at all by Sir John.

THE KEHELA EVIDENCE

The Report devoted twenty-six lines to the evidence of Kehela, or rather more than it did to all the other direct, recorded observations. This evidence became one of the two factors that caused Sir John to have "reasonable doubt" even though:

1. Kehela took no notes and his evidence was based on his recollections of a period when he was in a shocked state. He himself says that he does not remember clearly the events of that day. In fairness it should be said that all those immediately concerned were in varying degrees of shock, and this accounted for several subsequent discrepancies of recollection. The only person apparently quite unmoved was Reese, who when faced with the charges had the presence of mind to send a message postponing a minor appointment.

2. Kehela testified that he was entirely satisfied at the time that the two players were cheating. Subsequently he had "doubts."

3. He indicated to Gerber at the time his intention of ensuring that the defense case was fairly presented.

4. Kehela was known to have a feeling for Reese amounting to hero worship.

THE INDIRECT EVIDENCE

The indirect evidence, or the evidence from deals, takes up one-fifth of the whole report, or three times as much as the direct evidence. Practically all the testimony on this subject came from defense witnesses, both in respect of the hands themselves and the significance of such evidence. Although the two assessors apparently produced a report giving their opinion of the importance of the indirect evidence, their assessment is not quoted.

In this context, hands can be argued at great length, and are so argued in Appendix A. In spite of the contentions of various defense witnesses, the history of such cases shows that technical evidence of this kind is very rarely conclusive.

"There was no sign of cheating in the bidding or play of the cards" is the sweeping verdict of two judges who know almost nothing about the game. This contrasts strangely with another opinion: "In my view, the hands strongly confirm a knowledge of the heart suit," stated B. Jay Becker, who knew almost everything about the game.

UNCRITICAL JUDGMENTS

The authors of the Foster Report made many statements in favor of the defense to which there were obvious answers. In some cases the answers were given during the hearings but were ignored. Also included were many factual inaccuracies, while many arguments for the prosecution were omitted altogether. The following list deals with these in the order in which they appear in the report, ending with the omissions:

1. *"Mr. Butler's evidence, confined to watching 9 of the hands . . . was that there was correspondence in some 5 or 6 hands."*

This misrepresents the fact that all Butler's positive observations agreed with the code. See Chapter 5.

2. *"Mr. Swimer, who was also a witness, was nevertheless present throughout the sitting of the Appeals Committee."*

He was not.

3. *"Against [categorical evidence from several prominent players] must be set a number of considerations: the crudity of the signals. . . ."*

There is an answer to this argument. See page 162.

4. *". . . the concoction of a code to communicate information which is not as valuable as other information which could have been communicated less crudely and more economically in the number of signals."*

This statement is based on defense testimony provided largely by Reese himself. The answer is on pp. 160-162.

5. *"At some of the sessions in which they were alleged to be cheating, there was no point in their doing so since Great Britain could not win the tournament and in the last session at which observation took place, Great Britain was defeating the Argentinians anyway."*

There is no basis whatever for these statements, although they were often repeated by the defense. Great Britain had a chance of winning until the end of play on Saturday, at which point Italy had beaten the American team. In the Argentinian match the margin of victory was potentially crucial. This was brought out at the inquiry, and although it was apparently not understood by Sir John Foster, the British Team was thoroughly aware of the position at the time. See page 158.

6. *". . . Mr. Reese and Mr. Schapiro were on bad terms before the tournament . . . and . . . the two players had a row at Buenos Aires."*

This is undoubtedly true, and it is unlikely that two players would start cheating in such circumstances. But two habitual cheats would be no more likely to stop cheating merely because their relationship was deteriorating than they would be to change their system.

7. *"Mr. Reese and Mr. Schapiro played worse than their usual form in Buenos Aires. . . ."*

An established cheating partnership might be expected to play rather worse than usual if they were quarreling conspicuously. But the evidence shows that they were much the most effective of the British pairs, in spite of what the defense witnesses had to say on the subject. See pp. 156-157.

8. *". . . the players should have been watched either by the Tournament Director . . ."*

This would have been conspicuous and impractical for various reasons. See page 74.

9. *". . . or by neutral persons."*

There were none.

10. *"Allegations of cheating are made fairly frequently and . . . without real basis in International Bridge."*

Reese and Schapiro were accused of cheating five times during International Championships. In the forty-year history of the game up to 1965 there were only two or three other cases — which scarcely justifies the term "fairly frequently."

11. *"Mr. Swimer was a witness whose powers of observation and recollection were marred by difficult relations with the two players."*

No evidence was offered to suggest difficulties between Swimer and Reese. On the contrary, the evidence showed that Reese had often chosen Swimer as a teammate and had voted for his appointment as captain.

12. *"We do not believe that Mr. Schapiro would consent to cheat because he was unwilling to play the Little Major . . ."*

This curious argument is considered on page 181. Why should this be true merely because Schapiro said it to Swimer? The inclusion of an implausible statement in the confession merely indicates that there was dishonesty somewhere — a fact that was obvious for other reasons.[1]

13. *". . . or that Mr. Schapiro would have chosen the English Captain to whom to confess as their relationship was distant and to an extent antagonistic."*

The only substantial evidence to support this statement came from Schapiro himself. Clear and independent evidence to the contrary could have been made available. See pp. 182-183.

---

1. The great legal authority falls into the trap of assuming that the details of a confession will necessarily be true; the guilty often distort the facts in order to make their offense seem less serious. — A.T.

14. "We cannot understand why, if this confession took place, Mr. Swimer never reported it at Buenos Aires . . ."

Swimer treated the confession as confidential although he had not promised to keep it a secret. See page 52.

15. Kehela "had come to the conclusion that Mr. Reese and Mr. Schapiro had not been cheating."

This is rather more than Kehela recalls saying to the inquiry — and there is no transcript of his evidence.

16. "Mr. Reese and Mr. Schapiro played badly in Buenos Aires, below their form and certainly no better than the other British pair against whom there were no accusations of cheating."

See No. 7 above.

17. "Clearly the Appeals Committee attached importance to this 'indirect evidence' . . ."

As one who was present at the meetings much of the time, I can say that it was clear that the committees regarded the hands as very small beer.

18. ". . . unfortunately the 'analysis' of Mr. Truscott was superficial having regard to all the hands played by Mr. Reese and Mr. Schapiro."

On the contrary, I would say that my analysis was astonishingly prompt and thorough. Of the ten sessions played by Reese and Schapiro at the time the code was broken I had been through five within two hours, and most of the balance when I met Swimer ten hours later.

19. "Mr. Truscott had told him [Butler] that . . . 'this pair had never played a heart contract without a fit and had avoided a heart contract if the fit was unsuitable.' This is not true."

It is most decidedly true of the five sessions about which I reported to Butler and Swimer. In the whole tournament there was only one hand in which this was not true (U.S. 74), and this hand was found by Swimer and duly reported by me to the W.B.F. on Sunday.

20. "The 8 hands produced to Mr. Butler by Mr. Truscott were Italy 22, 23, 25, 26, 34, and 117 and USA 30 and 36."

This is quite untrue: I produced twenty deals to Butler and Swimer. The only testimony about eight deals came from Reese and referred to his confrontation twenty-four hours later.

21. Truscott "did not find at that time any hands which the players had failed to locate a good fit in the heart suit."

The implication is that my analysis is at fault here, but the records show that I was right. The only deal in which it can conceivably be said that Reese and Schapiro failed to locate a good heart fit is Argentina 141, which was not played until Saturday night, in the session that Swimer and Butler observed.

22. "It was wrong of the Appeals Committee to rely on the small sample of 8 hands produced by Mr. Truscott without considering the overall picture."

The Appeals Committee had twenty deals, eighteen of which had been shown to Butler the previous day. Two were added later that had been noted by others: U.S. 50 and Italy 131, the numbers of which were unknown to me at the time.

Finally there were three major omissions in the Report:

23. It did not refer to Gerber's observations, which checked the code.

24. It ignored the basic evidence of the remarkable finger variations made by two partners during the bidding only and disappearing with a change of partnership.

25. It ignored the photographic evidence, which supports the accusations. See Chapter 17.

THE CONCLUSION

Sir John ended by referring to the indirect evidence of hands and to the evidence of Kehela, then saying:

"The direct evidence as to the exchange of finger signals, strong as it is, cannot be accepted because of the reasonable doubt which we feel on these two grounds."

This hardly amounts to a triumphant vindication of two innocent men.

THE PAST HISTORY 12

PAST ACCUSATIONS of cheating were not brought into the London inquiry, because the prosecuting attorney did not consider them to be within his terms of reference. This restriction of the prosecution allowed the defense counsel to obtain, without challenge, what amounted to character references for the two accused players. As will be seen, some of the tributes from the witnesses were at best forgetful and at worst disingenuous:

Butler agreed with the defense counsel that he was not aware of "a breath of suspicion" against Reese or Schapiro.

Konstam "never found them anything but extremely ethical and extremely fair. I do not know anyone who has thought differently."

Harold Franklin of Leeds, England, one of the world's top tournament directors, said that he "had never had to consider any sort of complaint against them in sixteen years." Reese quoted the statement in this form without revealing the qualification: Franklin was referring to complaints made to him in his official capacity.

Some of the accusations that will be described in this chapter were certainly known to the leading personalities of English bridge, among whom Butler, Konstam, and Franklin must be numbered.

The defense counsel, Caplan, made great play with these one-sided character references in his summing-up of the case. He asserted that the accused players had been "almost magically free from accusations of this kind . . . If they had been cheating in the past, . . . I suggest it is quite impossible that they should have had the kind of reputation which they have had for integrity."

The inherent improbability that two experts would start to cheat when a long-standing partnership was in the process of dissolution apparently influenced Sir John Foster, and must naturally influence the bridge public. For this reason the bridge history that will be revealed in this chapter and the two following is significant in the case. And there is another reason.

If it is possible to establish a link between the affair in Buenos Aires and an earlier accusation, such evidence will be of great importance. The establishment of such a link would certainly be difficult, but as will be seen it is not impossible.

BEFORE THE WAR

Many young bridge experts, quite naturally, like to make a living from the game. Playing, writing, organizing, and teaching are likely to have more appeal than a more orthodox occupation with regular hours. This was particularly true on both sides of the Atlantic in the thirties, when jobs were scarce and wages were low.

One such in England was Iain MacLeod, who soon pushed bridge aside, served with distinction in the war, and rose to the highest ranks in the British government. Another was Terence Reese, who learned bridge at his mother's knee and established his reputation while studying at Oxford University. Soon afterward he was playing regularly at Almack's, one of the senior London card clubs and the bridge home of several of the greatest British players.

Unfortunately, the committee of the club and several of its leading members arrived at the conclusion that Reese's considerable winnings were not due simply to skill and luck. Two accusations were made against him. One followed a gin rummy game in which he won substantially against an older man who subsequently demonstrated that the cards were marked. Reese was able to point out that the accuser had taken the cards home with him after the game and showed the markings on the following day, opening up the possibility that the evidence had been manufactured.

There was a technical prelude to the second accusation. A famous player, waiting to cut in on a bridge game, was astonished to see Reese plunge into a grand slam with an aceless hand. This was long before the Blackwood convention had gained currency in England, and there seemed no technical reason to know that there was no ace missing — especially as his feminine partner was a highly erratic performer.

Some time later, the aces were found to be marked in a rubber bridge game in which Reese was taking part. The cards were locked in a safe by the club secretary; Reese was subsequently asked by the committee to resign from the club, and did so.

He was told that the matter would be kept private partly on account of his youth and partly because he was starting a professional career as de facto editor of the *British Bridge World*. But he was also told that the episode would be made public if he committed any similar offense in the future. Thirty years later, that time seems to have come.

In 1939 the small world of London bridge experts was intrigued by the news that Reese was bending his fertile brain to methods of cheating — quasilegally. He informed S. J. ("Skid") Simon, one of the great personalities in the English bridge world, that he had devised a signaling system that would convey an enormous advantage.

"Don't you believe it," responded Skid. "You'll lose more than you gain by getting your wires crossed." A unique team match was promptly agreed upon, in which the Reese team would be permitted to cheat in any way it pleased but would be subject to penalty if the signals were detected. Reese arranged to play with the late Jimmie Naughton, and invited Bob and Jim Sharples to complete the foursome. He supplied his teammates with a complete code, which they were expected to practice and master.

The match was never played, for two reasons. The Sharples withdrew from the project, partly because they found that their efforts were clumsy and partly because they did not wish to be exposed to suspicion in regular events. Also, Reese had trouble finding a suitable setting for the match. He applied without success to the great Dick Lederer, who ran a popular establishment:

"If you're thinking of going through with this after the Almack's business," roared the enraged proprietor, "you're an even bigger *?!*# than I think you are. The match won't be played in my club."

POSTWAR FAME

When tournament bridge revived in Britain after World War II a number of bright new stars made their presence felt. Prominent among them was Boris Schapiro, a player of Russian origin who had lived part of his life in Belgium. He quickly gained a reputation not only as a shrewd performer but also as a person of ready wit and coarse speech.

The Gold Cup is Britain's most important competition, equivalent to the Vanderbilt or the Spingold in the United States. Schapiro won the first three postwar Gold Cups, in each case with a different group of teammates. On the third occasion he played with Terence Reese, the start of a partnership that was to endure for seventeen years.

The first postwar European Championship was played in Copenhagen, and Reese and Schapiro contributed substantially to Britain's victory. They were again on the winning team in Paris in 1949, but on this occasion they were the target of Scandinavian suspicion. A plan to post observers was ruined by an excitable Norwegian woman who rushed up to the secretary of the European Bridge League and alleged that the two players were foot tapping. The official committee naturally decided that the evidence was inconclusive, and no action was taken.

The president of the European Bridge League at this time, Sir A. Noel Mobbs, was also the chairman of the British Bridge League. When the championships were over he summoned the British Captain, M. Harrison-Gray.

"Are you aware," he asked, "that your team was accused of cheating in Paris?" He explained what had happened, and expressed the view very strongly that no one who had been under suspicion, whether the charge was proved or not, should ever play for Great Britain.

Gray consulted his vice captain, Leslie Dodds, and together they persuaded Mobbs not to veto the selection of the accused players, on the ground that this would pander to the jealous foreigners. Instead, Mobbs announced his intention of giving the pair a stiff warning. Soon afterward the British Bridge League announced the selection of Reese, Schapiro, Gray, and Adam Meredith for the 1950 European Championship, but three factors caused Mobbs and the League to have second thoughts.

The first was a poker episode at Crockford's Club, where Reese and Schapiro often played in the same game. Two poker players working as a team can gain a considerable illegal advantage, and they were watched by experts who suspected them of doing so. One player, for instance, might make a bet or raise that would work to his colleague's advantage.

The matter was clinched, as far as the club was concerned, when Schapiro cashed a check at the desk made out by Reese for an amount which would equalize their winnings in the session that had just been played. Reference to the club accounts showed that this had happened on previous occasions. It was expected that the players would be asked to resign, but Crockford's, apparently nervous about possible legal action, was content to ban them from playing at the same table. Some time afterwards Schapiro did resign from the club. He became a member again many years later.

A second factor that influenced the British Bridge League was an international match between England and Eire in which Reese and Schapiro gave a classic display of needling. According to a magazine report, which put it politely, "The Irish allowed themselves to be harried and hounded by their opponents' braggadocio." The Irish naturally resented this performance, and it seemed likely that they would refuse to play in the Championship if they would be called on to play against their tormentors. One or two European countries had similar reservations about playing against the foremost British partnership, and this was a third factor in the mind of the British officials.

So in March, 1950, four months after the original team announcement, the British Bridge League nominated a six-man team from which Reese and Schapiro were excluded. Guy Ramsey, the editor of the *Contract Bridge Journal*, which was the official publication of the English Bridge Union, described this as a "bombshell" in an editorial.

"They were hailed at Copenhagen as the pair of the tournament; they were certainly effective in Paris; they played for Crockford's when that Club defeated the Americans.

"So — why?"

He suggested that there was a feud between some of the originally selected players, a statement that was more prophetic than factual. Then he went on:

The British Bridge League "made its decision on the merits of the circumstances with which it was faced — a decision to which various factors contributed. It had been our intention to elaborate upon these 'imponderables', dotting the i's and crossing the t's in our often-criticized fashion; but in view of all the issues involved, we refrain.

"We limit ourselves to the endorsement of the B.B.L.'s view that mere technical supremacy is not, and must never be, the sole criterion for national representation."

It is doubtful whether many readers were able to read between the lines of this delicately worded statement. But there is no doubt about the basic fact: Britain's outstanding partnership had been dropped from the team after receiving a positive invitation to play. It would be difficult to find a parallel in international bridge history.

BACK IN FAVOR

The British team, without the services of Reese and Schapiro, retained its European title in the 1950 Championships by the skin of its teeth. Mobbs retired from his official positions, and the past was buried and forgotten — at any rate, by the British Bridge League.

For the 1950-51 season the new chairman of the League was Geoffrey Butler, who was well disposed toward the two famous experts. A scheme put forward by Reese for the elaborate trials procedure described on page 63 was accepted, and he felt confident of his ability to influence the officials. He even proposed a "deal" that would have made nonsense of his own plan: he wanted Gray and Adam Meredith to play together on the team with himself and Schapiro, even though the other two players were entered with different partners. If Gray would play ball, Reese was ready to guarantee him a place on the team.

Provoked by this attempted maneuvering, and prodded by certain other experts, Gray decided to make a gesture. After playing in one session of the trials, he wrote to the British Bridge League and withdrew. At the same time, he offered to give his reasons to the League's Council. He gave two reasons. One was an objection to Reese's maneuvers behind the scenes. Another was that he wanted an inquiry to be made into the performance of Reese and Schapiro, who were the subject of many rumors at the time. Putting it as tactfully as possible, he suggested that it would be unfair to the leading British pair to send them abroad under a cloud, and that everyone would be happier if an inquiry was held.

The Council rebuked Gray for entering the trials and then withdrawing. He was suspended from international competition for a year, without any publicity, and eight years elapsed before he again represented Great Britain. The authorities also rejected his request for an inquiry, claiming that Mobbs had held an inquiry after the 1949 episode. This was an exaggeration, for all Mobbs had done was discuss the situation with another senior statesman.

In the next issue of the *Contract Bridge Journal*, Reese reported Gray's withdrawal in these terms:

"There comes an age (not necessarily measured in years) beyond which success in this competitive game is hardly won, and Gray must be congratulated on recognizing this."

Sixteen years later, teams led by Gray and Reese clashed in the semifinal of the British Gold Cup. When 48 of a scheduled 64 deals had been completed Reese trailed by the massive margin of 119 International Match Points. He conceded the match.

The London experts were not so complacent about the situation as the League. One prominent player claimed, perhaps optimistically, to have broken a code, and two others, Guy Ramsey and Jack Marx, independently made notes of suspicious hands played during the trials.

Marx, a member of the winning British team in 1950 and one of the originators of the Acol system (see footnote page 17), took the trouble to visit Mobbs and ask him to do what he could to arrange for a highly secret inquiry, in the hope of preventing an international scandal. Mobbs professed to be most disturbed but said he could only pass the suggestion to some leading members of the Council. The eventual answer was that nothing could be done until someone made a formal accusation — which was exactly what Marx wished to avert.

Much the most sensational deal was this one:

NORTH
♠ A K Q 10
♡ K 6 4 2
◇ J 9 5 3
♣ J

WEST
♠ J 9 8 7 5
♡ 9 3
◇ 10 8 6 2
♣ 8 2

```
    N
 W     E
    S
```

EAST
♠ 6 3
♡ 10 7
◇ Q 4
♣ K 10 9 7 6 4 3

SOUTH
♠ 4 2
♡ A Q J 8 5
◇ A K 7
♣ A Q 5

North-South were vulnerable, and in one room, Robert D'Unienville and I, who were partners, bid and made seven hearts, scoring 2210. In the other room Reese brought off a remarkable bidding coup which he subsequently described in the *Contract Bridge Journal* as follows:

> At the other table West passed, [Leslie] Dodds opened with one spade and, sitting East, I interposed a whimsical one notrump. [Jordanis] Pavlides doubled and, when this came round to me, I passed. I played the hand with great tenacity but was unable to record a trick: seven down, 1300 to the opponents.
>
> The pass of one notrump doubled has been the subject of much uninstructed comment. Some have held that it was a wild gamble, successful only because the opponents happened to have an easy slam. If the matter is examined more carefully it will be seen that the pass can hardly lose at the score. That the opponents have a vulnerable game is obvious from the way the bidding has gone. If one notrump is not more than three down, there is a useful gain; if it is four down, the loss is very small — probably 700 as against 650 or 660. The loss exceeds one match point only if it goes five down and the opponents cannot make a slam.
>
> This is not a likely result, for if North-South can make eleven tricks in defense against one notrump, the odds are that they can make twelve tricks playing the hand in their own best contract.

In short, a non-vulnerable player whose partner has passed should never be nervous (at international match-point scoring) of playing in a doubled contract at the range of one against vulnerable opponents. From the other side's point of view, it is a mistake to double when there is any prospect of a slam, and the hand is instructive for that reason.

There are several technical points that can be made in answer to this ingenious explanation. One is that five down seems a much more likely result than three down. A second is that the diamond queen is far more likely to be worth a trick in defense than in one notrump doubled. A third is that even if the opponents can make a slam there is no certainty that they will bid it.

In any event, this particular bidding triumph has never been repeated, as far as I know, by Reese or anyone else. A possible nontechnical explanation of his action is suggested on page 178.

Reese and Schapiro carried an inexperienced pair of students to victory in the final stages of these trials. But Britain failed to retain the European Championship in Venice, where the Italians won the first of their many titles.

The following year, in 1952, the Championships were held in Ireland. The pattern of suspicion reappeared, and an accusation was made, ironically enough, by a player who became a violent defender of the partnership after Buenos Aires. The following account of this episode was written by Ewart Kempson:

"In 1952 in Dublin Mrs. Markus openly stated that R & S were cheats.[1] All hell broke loose . . . G. Fell, the captain of the Men's Team[2], wanted to have Mrs. Markus boiled in oil there and then, but I persuaded him to leave things alone until after the championships because the women (I was their captain) were out in front and, in fact, won without losing or drawing a single match. Fell agreed and the matter was shelved until the championship ended. . . ."

And stayed shelved.

---

1. The accusation related to psychic penalty doubles that Reese and Schapiro were employing. The suggestion was that the partnership was better informed than the opposition about what was happening on such occasions. A.T.
2. It was the European Championships and Mrs. M. was playing for the British women's team, while R & S were on the men's. A.T.

WORLD CHAMPIONS

The newspapers gave front-page coverage to one remarkable episode at the 1955 match in New York, where Reese and Schapiro were making their first world championship appearance.

Two deals occurred several days apart which were identical down to the last spot card. Alvin Roth, a member of the American team, not only recognized the hand when the dummy came down, but reconstructed the unseen hands, spot for spot, for the benefit of an incredulous tournament director. Nobody wished to believe that the laws of probability had been temporarily suspended, so this freak was attributed to perfunctory shuffling by Adam Meredith, coupled with the unwise use of new decks throughout the match.

But an even bigger news story was in the making behind the scenes, although it was never made public. At a meeting of the United States team immediately after the first session of the match, Lew Mathe, one of America's greatest players, announced that in his opinion Reese and Schapiro were cheating. He had observed what he believed to be a signal during the play of the hand. When Reese and Schapiro were defending, one of them would sometimes make a clear-cut movement when his partner was thinking about a second-hand play. Mathe worked out the meaning of the signal and checked it on subsequent occasions. If the defender lowered his cards, he wanted his partner to play low, and if he raised them he suggested a second-hand high play. Later in the match, Mathe was able to have a little sport by reading the signals and basing his play upon them.

Mathe's teammates were prepared to believe that he was right, but he made no impression on the authorities. Al Sobel, long the chief tournament director of the A.C.B.L., clearly believed that Mathe was imagining things and wished to be completely fair to the visitors. Anxious to prevent any international disharmony, he took a strong stand.

"I suggest you forget about this and get on with the play," he told Mathe. "If you insist on making an official protest and your accusation cannot be substantiated, it could lead to your being barred from playing in the American team."

Despairing of any official action, Mathe took an unofficial step. He arranged for a leading expert to sit and watch the play, noting suspicious mannerisms and attempting to interpret them. At the end of the Championship the expert submitted an inconclusive report: there were plenty of grounds for suspicion, and plenty of technical evidence that Reese and Schapiro had played "too well," but no clear-cut identification of signals.

One psychic maneuver by Schapiro in this match would make anyone's hair stand on end.

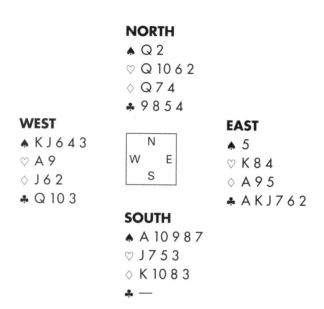

NORTH
♠ Q 2
♡ Q 10 6 2
◇ Q 7 4
♣ 9 8 5 4

WEST
♠ K J 6 4 3
♡ A 9
◇ J 6 2
♣ Q 10 3

EAST
♠ 5
♡ K 8 4
◇ A 9 5
♣ A K J 7 6 2

SOUTH
♠ A 10 9 8 7
♡ J 7 5 3
◇ K 10 8 3
♣ —

North was the dealer, and neither side was vulnerable. The bidding was:

WEST	NORTH	EAST	SOUTH
Roth	Schapiro	Ellenby	Reese
	1♣(!)	pass	1♠
pass	2♣(!)	pass	2◇
pass	pass	3♣	pass
3NT	all pass		

To open one club with no lead-directing advantage is remarkable enough. But the rebid of two clubs is unique: a player who has made an opening psychic bid invariably passes his partner's response. To rebid in such circumstances courts disaster, for the responder's next action may be a leap to game or even beyond.

Schapiro came close to talking his opponents out of a laydown game, but they managed to back into the auction successfully.

I included this deal in the first edition because it was weird. I did not understand it. A year after the book appeared, a Californian reader sent me an explanation. He had noticed something that I, and others, had overlooked: 96 deals earlier, which is obviously 3 x 32, the identical deal appears in the World Championship book. The players had forgotten, perhaps accidentally or perhaps not, to redeal it. On the first occasion, Schapiro passed with the North hand and the opponents reached the obvious three notrump. Two days later, against different opponents, he remembered. Since East was known to have long, strong clubs, he presumably thought that bidding and rebidding clubs would discourage the opposition. His effort failed, but it was certainly creative in unusual circumstances.

Contrast this with Al Roth's actions on another hand in the same match, when he recognized the dummy. As described previously, he called the director, Al Sobel, and explained that he had played the deal before. Sobel said it was impossible, but Roth went off into a corner and laboriously reconstructed the complete deal — correctly. There were thus two different approaches to a similar situation.

The match itself was a slight disappointment as a spectacle, for the British team built up an invincible lead at an early stage and was never in danger of defeat.

Two sour notes slightly marred the final victory banquet that honored the British team. Lew Mathe congratulated only Meredith, Konstam, Leslie Dodds, and Jordanis Pavlides. And Terence Reese made a short speech criticizing the organization of the match and the arrangements made for the press.

For five years after they won the world title Reese and Schapiro were free of all suspicion. Oddly enough, however, they were involved in two cheating cases in 1957 — but not quite on the same side of the fence.

One of them arose in the European Championship, where allegations of cheating were made against a leading pair. A libel case eventually resulted in England, and a number of leading figures in the bridge world would have given evidence if the case had not been settled out of court at the last moment. Five of them — all later concerned in the Foster Inquiry — were Jimmy Ortiz-Patino, the original accuser; Terence Reese, a potential witness for the accused players; Boris Schapiro, Geoffrey Butler, and the author of this book, potential witnesses on the other side.

More significant to the present story was a case in London. Two little-known players rocketed into the public eye when they won the London knockout team championship and later won a large cash prize in a French tournament. Some of their victims in the team event found some of their bids and plays so extraordinary that a dossier was submitted to the English Bridge Union Rules and Ethics Committee.

The committee found them guilty, but its verdict was later reversed by an *ad hoc* Appeals Committee headed by Kenneth Konstam. In the final of the championship the exonerated duo beat a team that included Reese, Schapiro, and Gray. Another series of unusual deals was collected, but no further official action resulted. This was one:

WEST	EAST
♠ A Q J 6	♠ 10 5 4 2
♡ A K Q 5	♡ 6
◊ Q 10 5 4 3	◊ A K 9 8 2
♣ —	♣ Q 10 8

East was the dealer and both sides were vulnerable. The bidding, using methods described by the players as "normal approach-forcing", was:

WEST	EAST
	pass
1◊	1♡
2♠	3◊
4◊	4♠
4NT	5◊
6◊	pass

East's psychic response of one heart as a passed hand and West's failure to support his partner's suit at any stage are both striking. The prosecution contended that this deal, together with a series of others with the same theme, indicated illicit knowledge of the heart suit.

Two important points arise from this episode. In 1957 Reese and Schapiro became aware of the possibility of signaling the length of the heart suit. And they also became aware of the dangers of taking extravagant advantage of such knowledge.

In Oslo the following year the British team failed narrowly to win the European title. One sensational deal that could have changed bridge history was widely reported:

NORTH
♠ Q 4
♡ Q J 10 4 2
♢ 10 9 4
♣ 7 4 2

WEST
♠ A J 9 5 2
♡ 9 7
♢ K Q J 3
♣ A J

```
      N
   W     E
      S
```

EAST
♠ K 10 8
♡ K
♢ A 7 2
♣ K Q 8 6 5 3

SOUTH
♠ 7 6 3
♡ A 8 6 5 3
♢ 8 6 5
♣ 10 9

East-West were vulnerable.

It is easy to see that East-West could readily have made six clubs. Six spades depends on the guess for the spade queen, and the British declarer who reached this contract misguessed and went down — losing the European title and a possible world title in the process.

The bidding in the other room was:

WEST	NORTH	EAST	SOUTH
	Schapiro		Reese
	pass	1♣	1♠
dbl	pass	pass	2♡
3♡	pass	3♠	pass
4♠	all pass		

There is, of course, no way of knowing whether East-West, who were scientific and accurate bidders, would have reached a slam if their bidding had not been interrupted by Reese's remarkable psychic overcall.

Many years later South's situation on the first round of bidding was given to a large panel of international experts by a French bridge magazine. One Swedish expert suggested an overcall of one heart to indicate a lead. Every other juror without exception not only voted for a pass by South but also expressed astonishment that they had been asked such a simple question. Some of their comments were:

Dormer[2]: "Pass — unless I am forced to bid by having a gun stuck in my back."

Trezel[3]: "Pass. I don't think my hand will produce a game opposite a partner who has passed!"

Reese himself: "Pass. It would be ridiculous to bid without even raising the level of the auction."

But if one happens to know that partner has exactly five hearts, the psychic overcall would become less ridiculous.

Before returning from European championships to the world scene, it should perhaps be mentioned that Reese and Schapiro had practically no occasion to use their traditional Acol bidding methods in international play between 1960 and 1965.

The only exception was the second half of a crucial match against Italy at Baden-Baden in 1963. In the course of a successful recovery, Schapiro had to respond to an opening bid of one club. He held:

♠ K J 5 ♡ K Q J 10 8 ◇ J 6 2 ♣ J 6

One heart is an automatic response with this hand, and no expert on either side of the Atlantic would consider anything else. The only makable game will often be four hearts if the opener has three or four cards in the suit. However, Schapiro chose to respond two notrump. Concealing the heart suit did not hurt the partnership, because Reese held a singleton in the suit.

The second of the four world championships in which Reese and Schapiro represented Great Britain was the Team Olympiad at Turin in 1960. The twenty-nine competing teams were divided into three qualifying sections, in each of which a round robin was played. The top two teams in each section qualified for a round robin final.

One deal in the qualifying stages caused considerable gnashing of teeth in the Canadian camp.

---

2. Albert Dormer, British player and writer.
3. Roger Trezel, one of the French players concerned and a former world champion.

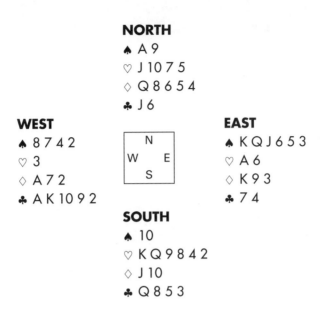

NORTH
♠ A 9
♡ J 10 7 5
♢ Q 8 6 5 4
♣ J 6

WEST
♠ 8 7 4 2
♡ 3
♢ A 7 2
♣ A K 10 9 2

EAST
♠ K Q J 6 5 3
♡ A 6
♢ K 9 3
♣ 7 4

SOUTH
♠ 10
♡ K Q 9 8 4 2
♢ J 10
♣ Q 8 5 3

Both sides were vulnerable. The bidding was:

WEST	NORTH	EAST	SOUTH
Elliott	Reese	Sheardown	Schapiro
		1♠	1NT
4♠	dbl	pass	5♡
pass	pass	dbl	all pass

The lead was the club king. The result was down three, 800 to Canada. When the hand was replayed the British East-West pair bid the laydown spade slam and scored 1430. Britain gained 630, or 6 (old) international match points, sufficient to give them a small half-time lead in a tight match.

If North-South had been playing the Gardener notrump overcall (see pp. 206-207), South's first-round action would be comprehensible, although certainly risky when vulnerable. And using this convention, North would not have doubled four spades.

But the notrump overcall purported to be natural showing 16-18 points. In an honest partnership such an action might lead to all kinds of disasters, but it is completely safe if both players have knowledge of each other's heart holding and approximate point-count. North can double, and confuse the issue further for the opponents, in the knowledge that his partner will bid five hearts.

Without illicit knowledge, South's dummy in five hearts doubled might include a singleton heart and more in spades. The resulting penalty of 1100 or

1400, preventing East from making, or perhaps failing to make, four spades, would surely prove a lack of liaison in hearts.

The Canadian team, built around Eric Murray and Sam Kehela, who subsequently became known as one of the world's great partnerships, just failed to qualify for the finals. Murray offered his help in recording the final matches and found himself on duty in the closed room for the clash between Britain and France which decided the world title.

Two of the deals he recorded struck him as so remarkable that he was able to recall them accurately six years later. On one of them Schapiro held this hand:

♠ A 10 9   ♡ J 9 2   ◇ A Q 5 4   ♣ Q 10 5

After two passes he opened with one notrump, which would have been entirely orthodox using a weak notrump. But he was vulnerable against non-vulnerable opponents, and the notrump bid in the methods of his partnership showed 16-18 points.

It is most unusual for an expert to explain his bidding as he puts down the dummy, but Reese did on this occasion after he had passed. He announced that he had decided to underbid his hand, and he had. The dummy was:

♠ J 4 3   ♡ K 8 7   ◇ J 7 2   ♣ K 8 3 2

It is easy to see that a sound game contract would have been missed if Schapiro had held 18 points, which was possible, instead of 13 points, which was impossible. This odd performance has obviously nothing to do with the heart suit, but it follows a pattern that is discussed and explained in Chapter 20.

The other deal that astonished Murray was a quiet partscore deal on which Reese held as North:

♠ 9 8 7 5   ♡ 7 4   ◇ 9 8 2   ♣ A Q J 8

His side was vulnerable, and the bidding began:

WEST	NORTH	EAST	SOUTH
	Reese		Schapiro
		pass	1 ♡
dbl	pass	2 ◇	pass
pass	?		

A pass seems automatic at this point, but Reese emerged with a bid of two spades. This could have led to serious trouble, with West likely to have four spades, but Schapiro's hand contained Q-J-4-3 of spades and all was well.

Although these deals had no great effect on the score, it was apparent that the French players were distinctly unhappy about the extent to which fortune, or whatever it was, was smiling on the English pair.

Murray is never reluctant to say what he thinks, and when the play was over he spoke to Reese.

"I think it's only fair to tell you," he announced, "that your opponents are quite convinced that they were being cheated."

The only reply from Reese was a snicker.

This chapter has described some remarkable deals and a number of accusations made against Reese and Schapiro before Buenos Aires. One more accusation is so important that it needs two chapters to itself.

THE OAKIE STORY 13

DON OAKIE, of San Jose, California, was one of America's leading players. He was a member of the American team that defeated France for the World Championship in 1954, a win that preceded a long string of European successes. At home he won four national titles and innumerable regionals and was an active bridge writer, teacher, and administrator. He was a member of the National Laws Commission, a highly select body, and represented Northern California on the National Board of Directors.

Apparently an American kibitzer (spectator) professed to have observed that when we held up our cards to show them to the spectators before the bidding began we held them in the right hand when we were strong, in the left hand when we were weak. A more obvious or naive way of signaling could scarcely be imagined. The American officials reported the allegation to the British tournament director, Harold Franklin. He promised to keep his eyes open when we got back to Britain and later wrote to the Americans to say there was nothing in it. (Reese: *Story of an Accusation*)

In 1954 I played against Reese and Schapiro in an exhibition match in a department store in London. Although we lost the match and Lew Mathe made some complaint about the English team in general, the only item that I noticed was Schapiro's tendency to overexplain the cleverness of his actions or to deride the shortcomings of his opponents. Although I thought this unsporting, it never occurred to me then that perhaps something was being covered up.

When our team lost to the English in New York the next year, Lew Mathe again made some allegation of irregularities, specifically against Reese and Schapiro. Since I was not there I tended to discount the report as due to bridge ego.

In Turin in 1960 my team lost some ridiculous matches and failed to qualify for the finals. We were penalized for slow play in the preliminary rounds but did succeed in beating the other American team in our division (some English paper had printed the suggestion that we might throw the match).

My wife and I did some sightseeing — she does not play bridge — but for one session prior to the final day I went to the playing area to kibitz and get the news.

Reese and Schapiro were on Bridge-O-Rama, and I watched from the audience. As the bidding and play unfolded on the screen I recalled what Sonny Moyse often pointed out in *The Bridge World*: Reese and Schapiro seemed to be able to enter the bidding with light and semi-psychic bids with impunity. Their defensive play, likewise, appeared to go beyond the capabilities of players engaged in an actual contest.

I had entered that evening without undue suspicions. By the end of it I was certain that Reese and Schapiro were up to something.

On the final day the British team, racing the French for the world title, played against an American team. In the afternoon session I took a seat in the Open Room above and slightly behind Schapiro. The match had drawn a good attendance, and the choice of seats was limited. I had a good view of the cards in Schapiro's hand and an unobstructed view of the table top and Reese.

During one of the opening boards I was struck by the peculiar manner in which Schapiro was holding his cards. He held in his right hand *both his playing cards and his pipe*! Contrasted with Reese's long-fingered, flexible, and artistic hands, Schapiro's hands are small and pudgy and appear anything but dextrous. In any event, the appearance of both cards and pipe in the right hand was a jarring note. Many of the spectators were taking notes, so I begged a piece of paper from one of them and began a record.[1] I first noted that Reese had his cards in his left hand with all four fingers together behind the cards. As the hand progressed I also noted that he held four high-card points.

I continued to record the hand used to hold the cards, the number of fingers showing, and the point-count. From Board 25 onward I recorded the board numbers also, and there were two consecutive "right hands."

On Board 27 Reese had shifted back to his left hand with three fingers showing and it appeared there was some variation in the height at which he held his cards. Accordingly I noted, by means of a small-sized L, that the hand was held lower than usual. Since it developed that he held only 6 high-card points, it dawned on me that there was a relationship between the high-card strength of the held hand and the hand in which it was held.

Up to this point my notes showed:

---

1. These notes are reproduced on pp. 116-117. — A.T.

	Hand	Fingers	Points
	L	4	4
	L	3	6
25	R	2	18
26	R	3	13
27	L	3	6

A pattern began to emerge. I was now sure that Reese was signaling and realized I must check Schapiro also. For the rest of the session, as my notes show, every time a player held less than 10 points he used his left hand, and every time he held more than 10 points he used his right hand.

There was no longer the slightest doubt that the two were signaling at least the information that their hands were of either less than average or better than average strength. Even though the English team was letting its lead slip, I was convinced that additional signals were being used. Odd auctions were occurring accompanied by odd defensive plays. I continued the record of the number of fingers displayed behind his cards by Reese — I could not see Schapiro's from my position — but was unable to decode these signals if that is what they were.[2]

In the interval between sessions I took my notes and sought out Harry Fishbein, the erstwhile captain of the team on which I had played. Needless to say he was as sickened by the apparent evidence as I was and queried me closely on my notes and observations. When play was about to restart he said: "Go on back, Don, and continue to keep your record. I'll take care of this."

As I returned to my kibitzer's seat I could see Fishbein in close consultation with Charles Solomon and Alvin Landy[3]. During the second or third deal the three of them came over and stood on the outside of the group of spectators — no seats were available. They watched about six boards, and at an opportune moment when the participants were intent on the play I caught their eye and gave them a questioning look. Each in turn gave me a confirming nod, and they left shortly afterwards. To my surprise they made no reappearance until the match was over. Equally surprising was the American team's managing to avoid defeat, the French becoming world champions as a result.

It was no surprise that the pattern of hands continued, with only one small discrepancy. On Board 48 Reese apparently deviated by holding the cards in his

2. Such a decoding would have been virtually impossible on the scene of action, and Oakie never had at his disposal the records of the deals. — A.T.
3. Respectively vice president and secretary of the World Bridge Federation — A.T.

left hand despite some 11 high-card points. It should be noted that it was necessary to follow the play of the hand with care in order to count Reese's points. I could look in Schapiro's hand to count his. Since my record was not checked back against the actual hand records it is possible that a variation of a point or possibly two on one or two hands might show up.

Within minutes of the end of the match I met the three officials and asked them if they were completely convinced by what they had seen. All three said that the evidence was incontrovertible and that they were satisfied beyond the shadow of a doubt. There can be no question that this was the case, since it is unthinkable that any of the three could have brought himself to leave the table — while the game was in progress — if not totally convinced by what he had already seen.

Some time later we met again and were joined by Julius Rosenblum, the captain of one of the other American teams. (I do not know whether he had watched any of the play as the other three had.) I asked them what they intended to do about it.

Solomon and Landy dwelt at some length upon the impossibility of replaying the Olympiad, the fact that the English had not won — they had finished second — and the terrible damage that could be done to international bridge by the publicizing of such a scandal. Finally they requested me most urgently not to tell anyone what I had seen and most particularly not to let word of it get to Albert Morehead of *The New York Times* or Sonny Moyse of *The Bridge World*.

When I asked why I should keep my knowledge to myself they asked me what I wanted. I said: "I want your assurance that no American pair will ever have to play those two again."

Landy said: "I don't know how we'll do it, but we'll do it." On this we shook hands and I agreed to keep silent.[4]

I heard no more of the matter until a year later, when a story about accusations against some French players was printed in the A.C.B.L. Bulletin. Having kept silent, I wrote to Landy and asked what he had done to keep his end of the bargain. His answer was far from satisfactory. He told me that he had talked the matter over with British tournament director Harold Franklin, who had then consulted a solicitor. The solicitor had told Franklin that the evidence was inconclusive, and the whole matter had been dropped.

---

4. When I spoke to Landy in 1987, shortly before his death, he had no recollection of saying this and doubted that he would have made such a promise. Perhaps the worried officials, looking at the matter from their administrative angle, were not giving all their attention to Oakie, who was expressing a player's point of view. Not unnaturally he was thinking in American terms, and it did not occur to him that future opponents of Reese and Schapiro in England and Europe were in need of protection. — A.T.

Feeling that this reply liberated me from the terms of the agreement, I sent the facts in the case along with my correspondence with Landy to Jim Ferguson, then president of the American Contract Bridge League. I sent copies to all the members of the board of directors, and I understand that Landy, Solomon, and Fishbein testified to the board at its meeting in Houston in 1961.

And there it rested for more than five years.

The notes taken by Don Oakie during the 1960 world championship in Turin. They are described and interpreted in various chapters of this book.

Totals from second half.

		Runs			Shapiro
41	R_L	3	14	R_L	11
42	R_L	2	14	L	3
43	L	2	6	R_L	15
44	L	4	1	L	9
45	R_L	2	15	R	13
46	L	4	0	R	23
47	R	2	12	R	16
48	L	2	11	L	9
49	L	4	6	R	15
50	R	3	19	R	2	14
51	L	4	4	R	18
52	L	2	8	R	13

53	L	4	6?	L	8
54	L	3	8	L	8
55	R		14	R	11
56	L	4	7	R	3	15
57	L	8	7 equal.	R	7	13
58	L		?	R	10
59	R		18	L	2	7
60	L		8	R	1	18

SEVEN YEARS LATER 14

THE EPISODE at Turin was the first thing mentioned by Reese when he was informed of the charges against him in Buenos Aires. He indicated this as an example of the American proneness to make unsubstantiated accusations.

Butler was puzzled by this reference, and Solomon was puzzled that Butler was puzzled. The matter was explained, but Butler did not absorb the details. As in other matters relating to a weekend that shocked him severely, his memory was faulty. In his draft report he wrote:

"Mr. Solomon said that at the end of the Olympiad in 1964 in New York certain allegations had been made against them and the Director H. Franklin of England had undertaken to report these allegations to Mr. Butler, Chairman of the British Bridge League. Mr. Butler said that Franklin had not done so and this was news to him."

Solomon and Landy corrected the chronological error, and the final report read:

"Mr. Solomon said that at the end of the Olympiad in 1960 in Turin alleged irregularities had been reported to the Director H. Franklin of England who had undertaken to report them to Mr. Butler, Chairman of the British Bridge League. Mr. Butler said that Franklin had not done so and this was news to him."

This implied a failure in duty by Franklin, and he later asked to have the record set straight. It was true that he had not reported the matter to Butler and the League, although he had eventually told Reese and Schapiro. It was not true that he had been asked to make an official report.

Eighteen months after Buenos Aires, Solomon wrote the following letter to Butler:

November 15, 1966

DEAR GEOFFREY,

As to the 1960 affair, let me try to give you a picture of what occurred — after this description, perhaps you will understand why there is a twilight zone concerning the facts as they unfolded.

First, I hope you will remember that I did not introduce this matter into the record. It was only after Reese, defending himself, stated that Americans had always been making wild accusations against him, that I spoke up. I then said: "Several Americans did make allegations against the partnership in 1960 but in fact, instead of pressing the matter, nothing was done about it."

I then asked, "Didn't you know about this, Geoffrey?" It was actually a rhetorical question — I was sure you had heard all about the case.

Undoubtedly, this short sentence, which really had nothing to do with the 1965 case, should have been deleted; but somehow in reading our joint report it slipped by even Alvin Landy and others who read it very carefully. It is true that I approved what was said, signed it, and sent it back to England. At the time we had no thought that the matter would go beyond your League. Also, time was against us. You were compelled to hurriedly prepare the statement and I did not have too much time to examine it in detail.

Now let me tell you what happened in Turin. Several American players who had failed to qualify watched the final match that involved Reese-Schapiro against Schenken-Harold Ogust. Incidentally, the Americans won the match,[1] which naturally materially weakened the American view that something abnormal was being perpetrated.

I personally saw about eight hands, and in truth, the hand movements did correspond to the code which Don Oakie, a famous player and a thoroughly trustworthy citizen, told us about. Harry Fishbein, the captain of this squad, saw about fourteen boards. He, too, felt that the hands of the contestants were "going up and down" in accordance with the code.

Still, the evidence was far from conclusive.[2] After discussing the matter with the Secretary (Landy) and the Vice-President (Solomon) it was decided that it would be unwise to raise the issue at that time. There could not be a hearing because many of the members of the committee had already left Italy, and also it would be a question of testimony from one or two non-playing Americans as against a denial by Reese-Schapiro. Since we had just cleaned up the ugly Como mess, it was decided to give our WBF a chance to get on its feet, and so we dis-

1. Solomon's recollection was slightly faulty here. Britain gained a winning draw, and collected three victory points out of a possible four. But the one victory point the British did not get was vital, because it gave the French the world title. — A.T.
2. This is an example of the general reluctance of official bodies to press charges in such cases. Oakie's notes provided enough data for further decoding which could have been done at the time. — A.T.

missed the matter officially. Perhaps, in the light of what has happened, this was injudicious, but that was what we determined "on the spot."

Nevertheless, we did not wish to ignore these serious charges, so we talked to Harold Franklin, the English Director, in an informal way. We did not want the issue to come before the B.B.L. at that time with this limited evidence.

With no directions at all, we asked Mr. Franklin to carry on as he thought proper. He was not commanded to do anything. Indeed, we didn't want to blow the case up unless there was further evidence against the alleged offenders. Franklin, after consulting with his attorney, apparently thought it was unwise for him to do any further investigating, and he wrote Landy to that effect. The case, therefore, was dropped.

Scores of players on this side of the Atlantic knew about the charge and I feel many players in Great Britain knew about it.[3] I am still astounded that you had not heard anything concerning this incident.

As you know, I had nothing to do with the case in South America. I was actually surprised when you called me to attend the early morning session of the Appeal(s) Committee. I remained out of the picture, as much as a member can, until Reese raised the question as to the past. Obviously "this past" did not play a prominent part in the final decision of the arbiter. It is not even mentioned in the final report; also there was much character support for Reese and Schapiro and lots of evidence against them if the prosecuting attorney had wanted to obtain it.

Under the circumstances, however, I do feel that Franklin's integrity is unnecessarily in the balance. Although he could have done more than he did, we cannot condemn him for failing to act when, in fact, we followed the same indecisiveness ourselves.

Please keep in touch.

As always,
CHARLES SOLOMON

---

3. Probably not, apart from Franklin, Reese, and Schapiro. I did not hear about it until I moved to America. But in 1963, Rixi Markus, who often visited New York, informed Harrison-Gray that Reese and Schapiro had been watched in Turin and that it was a national disgrace. — A.T.

A BELATED DECODING

A month after this letter was written, Reese's book was published in England. I borrowed a copy that reached New York and decided that some reply was called for.

In January, 1967, I wrote to Oakie and asked him what had happened in Turin. To my astonishment, I received within a few days not only the full account that constitutes Chapter 13 but also a photocopy of his original notes. In a letter he wrote:

"I do not have a copy of the hands played at Turin and have only original notes and memory to refer to. I suppose you will be able to get the hand records for a cross-check.

"You will be curious about the finger notations and the small Ls and Ms next to the large Ls and Rs that recorded in which hand Reese was holding his cards. At the time I was positive that the two had some system for showing the number of cards held in particular suits as well as a means whereby they could ask for the lead of any specific suit (some defensive plays were inexplicable otherwise). Reese varied the number of fingers on the back of his cards and I recorded them — when you get the hand records you will be interested to see if you can decode these signs from seven years ago. The height at which the hand was held might have had a significance so I noted it as low or medium through the first half but discarded the listing after Board 45.

"The finger notations on Schapiro were only on boards 50, 56, 57, 59 and 60, since through most of the match I sat towards his side of the table and couldn't see the back of his hand."

I certainly was interested in attempting some decoding, and I immediately met with some success and some frustration. The obvious move was to compare Oakie's notes with the hands recorded in the Turin World Championship book published by the American Contract Bridge League, and I had a copy in my bridge library. I found to my disgust that the last twenty deals watched by Oakie, Numbers 41-60, were missing altogether from the book. As this was a crucial session which included a famous deal, the only likely explanation was that the editors did not have the records of this session at their disposal.

There were thirteen deals on which a clear comparison was possible: 25-28, and 31-39. Whether this was a sufficient sample for decoding purposes was doubtful, especially as in this session Oakie was interested primarily in the alternation between left hand and right hand, so there was no guarantee that his finger observations were completely accurate.

The task proved unexpectedly simple. A routine first move was to test the Buenos Aires heart code, and it fitted — not completely, but well enough. In eight of the thirteen deals the code fitted. On three occasions on which Reese held four hearts Oakie noted three fingers — a confusion paralleled when Becker watched Reese from a similar angle five years later. On two occasions in which Reese held five hearts, Oakie's notes did not fit. Once he recorded one finger, which would be likely enough if Reese was in fact showing two splayed fingers, and once he noted three fingers, which would be a clear discrepancy.

There was one small puzzle: the first two deals noted by Oakie are unnumbered. It seems likely that he wrote them down from memory *after* he had borrowed a piece of paper. The first numbered deal is 25, and one might suppose that the unnumbered deals are 23 and 24. If that is so, his point-count observation was wrong by three points and by two points and the heart code does not fit.

But if one assumes that Oakie missed one deal while borrowing paper and organizing his note taking, things fall into place. His point-count observation is then wrong by one point in each case, and the heart code does fit both deals.

THE LAST LINK IN THE CHAIN

To possess recorded finger observations of twenty-two extra deals but no official records with which to compare them was quite infuriating. A small step forward was made by researching the bridge magazines that reported the tournament. Harold Franklin had written a long article in the October, 1960, issue of *British Bridge World*, and this included three deals that were not otherwise available. In all three cases Oakie's notes fitted the signals, and that made the score 11-5 in favor of the heart code.

I was not very optimistic about making any further progress, for it seemed likely that the original records were no longer in existence. Nevertheless I asked Richard Frey, editor of all the publications of the American Contract Bridge League, to arrange for a search. He was not hopeful, because all such material was deposited in the League's basement, which was crowded with the obsolete business and membership records of an organization with a membership of nearly two hundred thousand.

Frequent harassment of Frey's overworked staff eventually produced a discouraging answer: an employee in the packing department had spent several unproductive hours searching in the basement, and the assumption was that the records were not there. I would be welcome to come and look for myself, an invitation I put aside because I was about to leave on a Caribbean cruise.

When I got back to New York I found that serendipity, that art of making fortunate discoveries by accident, had taken a hand. The League was clearing out its records in preparation for the removal of its offices to Greenwich, Connecticut, and was throwing out much obsolete material. The office manager came upon a dusty package that seemed to belong to the editorial department. He called down Tannah Hirsch, Frey's chief assistant, who found himself with a bundle of material from Turin which included the records of the final match, which Oakie had observed.

As it happened, Hirsch and I were taking the same plane to Seattle for the Spring National Championships. He lived in an apartment near Kennedy Airport, so I drove over to see him en route. I produced my copy of Oakie's notes, and he produced the Turin records. I called out the notation I had for each deal, and he announced the number of hearts held.

There were now twenty more deals on which it was possible to compare Reese's fingers with the record, and every one fitted the code. There were six deals on which Schapiro's fingers could be compared, and every one fitted the code.

It was the end of the road.

A comparison of the fingers noted by Oakie and the hearts actually held by Reese:

Board	Hearts	Fingers	Board	Hearts	Fingers
?	?	4	42	2	2
?	?	3	43	2	2
25	2	2	44	4	4
26	5	3	45	2	2
27	6	3	46	4	4
28	4	4	47	2	2
29	3	3	48	5	2
30	3	3	49	4	4
31	1	1	50	3	3
32	2	2	51	4	4
33	3	3	52	2	2
34	4	4	53	4	4
35	5	1	54	3	3
36	4	3	55		
37	4	3	56	4	4
38	4	3	57	1	1
39	2	2	58		
40	4	3	59		
41	3	3	60		

A comparison of the fingers noted by Oakie and the hearts actually held by Schapiro:

Board	Hearts	Fingers
50	2	2
56	3	3
57	3	3
58	1	1
59	2	2
60	1	1

DIRECT EVIDENCE *15*

WHAT IS THE DIRECT EVIDENCE?

In the preceding chapters the observations of thirteen witnesses are described:

1. B. Jay Becker
2. Dorothy Hayden
3. Alan Truscott
4. John Gerber
5. Waldemar von Zedtwitz
6. Ralph Swimer
7. Geoffrey Butler
8. Sam Kehela
9. Robin MacNab
10. Don Oakie
11. Alvin Landy
12. Charles Solomon
13. Harry Fishbein

All these thirteen witnesses in Buenos Aires and Turin were completely satisfied that cheating had taken place at the time they concluded their observations. One, Kehela, subsequently had "doubts."

Leaving aside Kehela, who regarded his own evidence as inconclusive, there were twelve persons of high standing in the bridge world who said from personal knowledge that the two accused players were cheats. If the two accused players were innocent, it follows that the evidence of these twelve experts must be inconclusive, mistaken, or dishonest. Whether any of these alternatives is possible will be considered in this chapter.

THE RECORDED OBSERVATIONS

Five separate sets of observations belong in the record relating to the heart suit:

1. The Becker-Hayden notes, used for breaking the code (15 positive observations, all fitting the code; 4 queried observations, 3 of which fitted the code).

2. The Gerber notes, made before the code was broken (9 positive observations, 8 fitting the code).

3. The Swimer notes, made with knowledge of the code (38 positive observations, all fitting the code; 2 observations relating to undecoded voids).

4. The Butler notes, made with knowledge of the code (12 positive observations, all fitting the code; 3 queried observations, 2 of which fitted the code; 2 observations relating to undecoded voids).

5. The Oakie notes, made five years before the code was broken (37 positive observations, 31 of which fit the code).

In addition, there was the observation made in Turin of the hand used to hold the cards:

6. The Oakie notes, made largely after his decoding (76 observations, 75 of which fit the code; one fails to fit by one point).

All the details of the Buenos Aires observations were assembled by the prosecution counsel, Simon Goldblatt, and presented to the Foster Inquiry.

THE MATHEMATICS OF COINCIDENCE

Any calculation of the possibilities of coincidence depends on what initial assumptions are made. Precisely what the assumptions are is not of the greatest importance, because the results are overwhelming in any event.

A convenient assumption is that four different mannerisms exist and are noted and that they are equally likely to occur. The chance that anyone could guess which mannerism would come next at any point would be one in four. The chance of ten consecutive correct guesses would be one in 4^{10}, or one in slightly more than a million. No doubt mathematicians would be able to suggest superior procedures, but this will serve for the purposes of the heart-and-finger observations.

For the point-count-and-hand observations, if we assume that players use one hand or the other at random, the chance of coincidence is obviously exactly even for each observation.

The defense in London was not based on any possibility of coincidence. Instead it was suggested that the notes were not a genuine record, and that at least some of the evidence was dishonest. Sir John Foster's verdict implied that he believed the defense suggestion that some evidence was dishonest and that coincidence was out of the question. "The direct evidence is bound to raise suspicion," he stated in his report. "If accepted, the odds against the observed fingers corresponding in so many cases to the number of hearts held were so astronomical (running into millions to one) that the only conclusion would have been that the two players were cheating."

Because the Report arrived at a "not guilty" verdict, it is clear that the direct evidence was not accepted. So we shall now consider the witnesses and consider whether there were reasonable grounds for rejecting their evidence.

BECKER, MRS. HAYDEN, AND TRUSCOTT

The evidence of the Becker-Hayden notes is conclusive on its own, for the odds against "coincidence" are about a billion to one. Nor can it be said that the three players were "mistaken."

The case for the defense was that this evidence was given dishonestly, although the wording was less blunt. Caplan, the defense counsel, suggested that the notes could have been "improved" after the conclusion of the Championship. He also hinted at coincidence but was clearly without any hopes that such an argument would hold water.

The only support the defense was able to offer for the suggestion that these notes were not an accurate contemporary record was a lapse by Butler. He did not understand at the time that these notes had been taken and therefore did not refer to them in his official report from the World Bridge Federation. The other members of the Appeals Committee were better informed. MacNab and Von Zedtwitz had been present at the Saturday morning meeting and were fully aware that notes had been taken.

GERBER

Gerber's observations were known to the London inquiry but were ignored by the defense and by the Foster Report — apparently because he did not travel from Texas to give evidence. His observations, made before the decoding, would convince most people. The odds against coincidence are better than 16,000 to one.

Apart from his own evidence, Gerber confirms the authenticity of the Becker-Hayden notes and must be a party to a "conspiracy" if one existed. Such a theory must assume some talented acting, for it was obvious to MacNab and Von Zedtwitz that there was some strain between Gerber and Becker about permission to inform officials about the signals.

The motives attributed to Gerber for his "dishonesty" were not very substantial. He had spoken sharply to Schapiro on the subject of cigars, and of course he was an American.

VON ZEDTWITZ

Von Zedtwitz watched a full session before the code was broken, and he was satisfied that the finger movements were deliberate and meaningful. He remembered one two-finger-spread signal that corresponded to a five-card heart holding, which the defense would no doubt have described as a coincidence if this affidavit had been accepted in evidence.

SWIMER

Swimer's observations on their own represented ample proof of the charges, for the coincidence chance would be more than 4,000,000,000,000,000,000,000 to one. His account of Schapiro's confession, if accepted, would also be conclusive.

Sir John Foster accepted the defense contention that all Swimer's evidence was dishonest. The fact that Swimer had been somewhat annoyed with Schapiro two years earlier was suggested as the motive for dishonesty, and his last-minute revelation about the confession is used to indicate his unreliability. How much credence should be placed in this assessment can be judged by reading Chapters 4 and 21.

BUTLER

Butler's observations on their own represented sufficient proof, for the coincidence chance of his unqueried observations would be 16,000,000 to one.

The defense did not question his honesty or competence[1] or suggest that he had reasons for conspiring against the two accused players. Instead they suggested that he had been influenced by what he expected to see — that he was told that a player with three hearts would show three fingers and so he based his notes on the number of hearts he could see rather than the number of fingers. One might think this a remarkable piece of delusion or self-persuasion for a responsible official.

KEHELA

Kehela watched without taking notes and was satisfied at the time that the players were cheating. Later he had "doubts" and testified that he had seen a forty to fifty per cent correspondence with the code. This represents much more than a random correspondence but much less than three other observers noted during the same session.

MACNAB

MacNab's evidence is equivalent to Kehela's, but is quite positive. He watched a series of deals during the same session, and noted a succession of cases in which the code fitted and none in which it did not.

OAKIE

Oakie's recorded observations fall into three categories. First, his finger notations made five years before Buenos Aires are sufficient proof of the heart code. Thirty-one out of his thirty-seven observations checked out against the hearts actually held, and four of the remaining six were examples of the confusion between three

---

1. Some curious and irrelevant testimony was introduced to show that Butler was not a teetotaler. The same could be said about almost everyone in the case with the possible exception of Reese. He was ready to admit that his head swam after one small glass of sherry. – A.T.

and four fingers which other observers found when watching Reese from an angle. The coincidence figure for this would be astronomical.

The left-hand/right-hand signal was also proved beyond a shadow of doubt. The coincidence figure in this case would be one in 2^{75} or one in 64 thousand billion billion.

The significance of his medium/low observations, analyzed on pp. 165-166, is also strong evidence.

LANDY, SOLOMON, AND FISHBEIN

These three witnesses watched some eight deals in Turin and verified Oakie's left-hand/right-hand allegation. In this case they gave convincing proof that they were not motivated by any American bias against Reese and Schapiro, because they decided not to take any action although convinced of the truth of the charges. The coincidence chance in their case would be one in 2^{16}, or one in 85,536.

Whatever may be said about the witnesses in Buenos Aires, it is abundantly clear that the three Turin officials could not have been part of a gigantic conspiracy. To frame two players for cheating and then go to great pains to protect them by concealing the evidence would make no kind of sense.

THE CONSPIRACY THEORY

A conspiracy theory, or a theory of multiple independent dishonesty, would have to go considerably further than attacking the reputations of the twelve witnesses under discussion. If Oakie's notes are fraudulent — and there is expert testimony to the contrary — the defense would have to explain how they came to correspond with documentary evidence which was not available until two months after copies of the notes and the story of their decoding had been circulated to several other people.

CONCLUSION

The direct evidence leaves only two possibilities. Either Reese and Schapiro were cheating as alleged, or they had become the victims of a gigantic conspiracy in which many of the conspirators went to great trouble to defeat the object of the conspiracy.

THE INDIRECT EVIDENCE 16

"It is the duty of an 'independent' commission to be very critical of 'expert' evidence, especially if the expert body is under any suspicion of being interested in a particular conclusion." — Professor Hugh Trevor-Roper, Oxford University historian, in the introduction to Rush to Judgment *by Mark Lane.*

Expert evidence is a familiar feature of legal cases. Doctors testify about diseases, injuries, and the contents of the stomach. Firearms experts testify about guns, shells, distances, angles, and marksmanship. And so on. Some of this evidence is clear-cut: if two fingerprints match, it is little use pleading coincidence. But much is open to debate and can be interpreted in different ways. It is not uncommon for medical experts to contradict one another.

Technical evidence based on bridge hands is vastly more unreliable and subjective, because an enormous variety of factors can influence a bidding decision. System, style, psychology, and a wide range of technical elements play their part. If two pairs using the same bidding system are given a series of hands to bid, the results will rarely be identical. The multiplicity of choices can be seen clearly by examining "The Master Solvers Club" in *The Bridge World*, in which experts have been known to pick as many as ten different bids in a particular situation. A given pair, even a given player, will not be consistent. If a regular partnership is given a hand to bid twice, with a gap of perhaps a year, the odds are against their duplicating the bidding sequence.

Because players are not consistent in their habits, it may be very difficult indeed for one expert to say whether another is likely or unlikely to make a particular bid — assuming the bid has any kind of plausibility.

JUDGING BY RESULTS

In a team match the profitability of a cheating system is unlikely to be as great as ten per cent. Much of the time the information gained will not help. The result may depend on the actions of the opponents, or of the four players in the other room. Much of the time a cheating partnership will achieve without trouble something that an honest partnership would manage with much mental exertion.

In his book Reese points proudly to the fact that the British team lost 23 points on 29 deals which were quoted in London as evidence of illicit signaling. This statistic has even less meaning when it is appreciated that he carefully excluded from consideration the British match against Argentina, in which the six deals put forward by the prosecution gave the British team a net gain of 40 points.

THE TOLERANCE FACTOR

If two bridge players decide to cheat by using illegal signals, the presumption is that they plan to evade detection. If they make a large number of improbable bids and unusual leads and are consistently successful, suspicion is likely to be aroused. But if the players are content to take small advantages, with an occasional lapse into "brilliancy," they are likely to get away with it. There are many borderline situations in bidding and play in which special knowledge of a partner's hand can be used quite imperceptibly.

The cheat must therefore be careful not to stray outside the limits of normality. But unless he has remarkable self-control, he will once in a while make a revealing bid that could have been avoided with little disadvantage. It was generally recognized that Reese had far greater self-control than his partner, both at the table and away from it.

Schapiro neglected the tolerance factor on the following Turin deal:

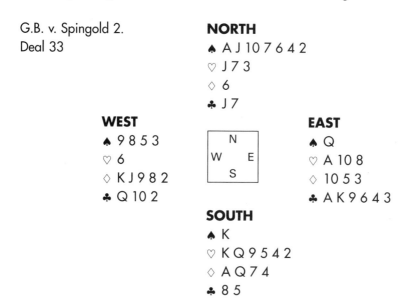

G.B. v. Spingold 2.
Deal 33

NORTH
- ♠ A J 10 7 6 4 2
- ♡ J 7 3
- ◇ 6
- ♣ J 7

WEST
- ♠ 9 8 5 3
- ♡ 6
- ◇ K J 9 8 2
- ♣ Q 10 2

EAST
- ♠ Q
- ♡ A 10 8
- ◇ 10 5 3
- ♣ A K 9 6 4 3

SOUTH
- ♠ K
- ♡ K Q 9 5 4 2
- ◇ A Q 7 4
- ♣ 8 5

1. Reese at the World Team Olympiad, Turin, 1960. His opponents are Rapee, right, and Silodor, left. (Credit Moisio, Turin)

The Photographic Evidence

2. Schapiro in play in Turin against Rubin and Grieve. He is showing two fingers, and has two hearts. (Credit Moisio, Turin)

The Great Bridge Scandal

3. Reese holding his cards up for the spectators to see at the start of Deal #4, Great Britain v. Italy, Buenos Aires, 1965.

The Photographic Evidence

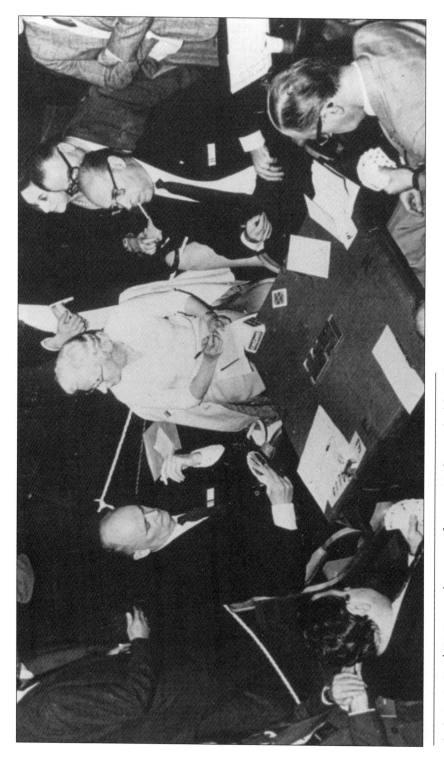

4. Later in Deal #4 Reese shows two fingers. He has a doubleton heart.

5. Great Britain v. North America. The third day of play. Schapiro has one finger showing, and has one heart.

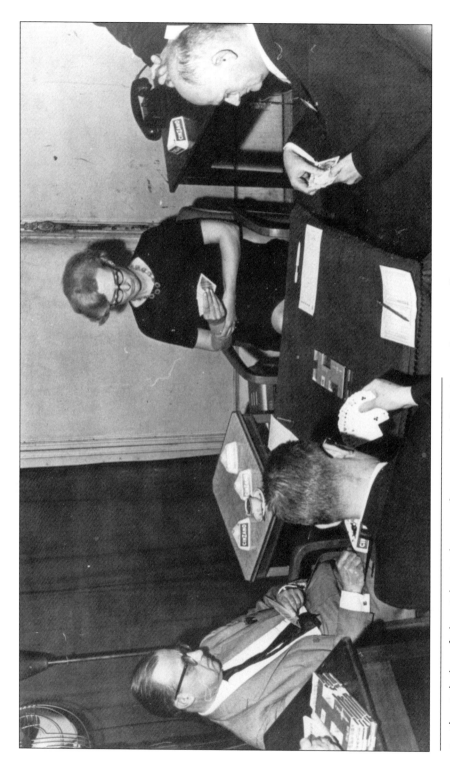

6. The sixth day of play. Schapiro has one finger extended. He has no hearts at all.

The Great Bridge Scandal

7. Reese in play with Flint on the sixth day. Observers were satisfied that no signals were exchanged.

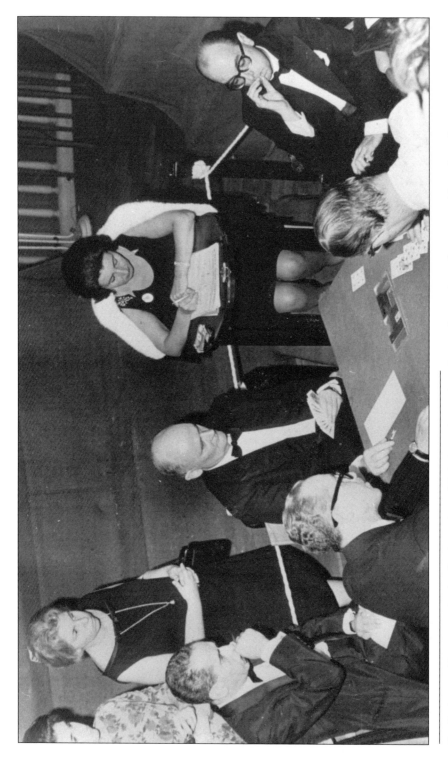

8. Swimer taking notes in the final session of Britain v. Argentina. Reese shows three fingers and has three hearts.

The Great Bridge Scandal

Neither side was vulnerable. The bidding:

WEST	NORTH	EAST	SOUTH
Ogust	Reese	Schenken	Schapiro
	1♠	2♣	2♡
pass	2♠	pass	4♡
all pass			

Almost any expert, English or American, would open three spades on the North hand, practically without thought. But such a preemptive bid becomes less automatic if one happens to know that partner holds at least 10 points with a six-card heart suit. One spade then becomes a more flexible choice, especially if there is no danger that partner will assume the normal values for an opening bid.

Whether a player who has opened the bidding with a 7-point hand, as North has, can afford to bid again when his partner bids two hearts is debatable. But what is clear is that South's second-round jump to four hearts is extraordinary. Any good player would bid three diamonds automatically on the second round with the South hand. The right final denomination could be spades, notrump, hearts, or even diamonds. (North might have five spades and five diamonds.)

The bid of four hearts showed an unnecessary lack of regard for the tolerance factor. South would have excited no suspicion if he had bid three diamonds, received a heart preference from North, and continued to game. But it was the last day of a long and tiring tournament — and incidentally one of the deals which Oakie was observing — and Schapiro took the short route to the contract he wanted to reach. This indiscreet bid was followed by tired play.

East won the first two tricks with his high clubs and shifted to the spade queen. The contract then failed in some way that the records do not explain, but it should have been made. Whether or not South overtakes his own spade king with dummy's ace, he makes the contract by leading high spades from dummy at every opportunity. South's play converted the potential profit from the bidding into a loss. The American North opened three spades and made ten tricks when the defense failed, quite understandably, to find the heart ruffs to beat the contract. One wonders whether Reese and Schapiro would have found them.

That Schapiro paid less attention than his partner to the question of "tolerance" can be seen by examining the hands in Appendix A and elsewhere in this book. He was responsible for the great majority of the partnership's "brilliancies" and the eccentricities.

CAN HANDS PROVE GUILT OR INNOCENCE?

The brief answer is that it is possible but unlikely. There has been only one case — a French one — in which players were adjudged guilty simply on the basis of technical evidence. In a number of other cases the technical evidence has been inconclusive. There were two important cases in England that hinged on technical evidence. In one, two expert committees arrived at diametrically opposite conclusions (see page 105). In another, the members of the investigating committee disagreed on the significance of the hands put forward.

If a pair is alleged to have illegal knowledge of the heart suit, it is certainly conceivable that the records of a long match may disprove the charge. That is why, in Buenos Aires, I immediately took a look at the hand records at my disposal. My conclusion was that the records, without being decisive, supported the idea that the players had knowledge of the heart suit.

If the accusation had been made against Reese and Schapiro ten years earlier, when they won the world title in New York, there would have been no difficulty at all in demonstrating their innocence from technical evidence relating to the heart suit. (But, as shown elsewhere, there are indications that other kinds of signals were being exchanged.)

A few hands from the 1955 Championship are worth giving to point the contrast:

Deal 46

Reese	**Schapiro**
♠ A 8 6	♠ K 7 5 2
♡ A Q 10 9 5	♡ —
◇ J 2	◇ 10 5 4
♣ Q 10 5	♣ A 9 7 6 4 2

The bidding was:

Reese	**Schapiro**
1♡	2♣
2♡	pass

Although Reese struggled home with eight tricks, it is obvious that he was in a silly contract. A partscore in clubs or spades would have been very much easier to manage. With knowledge of the heart layout, Reese would have rebid three clubs, and so, perhaps, would Schapiro.

The very next deal was this:

Deal 47

Reese	Schapiro
♠ 4 2	♠ A 8 7 6
♡ K 9 4 2	♡ A Q 8 7
◇ K Q 8	◇ A 10 7 4
♣ A Q 7 3	♣ K

The bidding was:

Reese	Schapiro
1♣	2◇
3◇	3♡
4♡	4♠
5◇	6◇

There was an unavoidable trump loser in six diamonds, and the contract was down one. Six hearts, which was bid and made by the United States pair holding the same cards, would have been better. If Reese and Schapiro had been sure that they had a four-four fit in hearts they would no doubt have been more successful and avoided a disaster.

A final example:

Deal 146

Reese	Schapiro
♠ 10	♠ K 8 5 3
♡ A 6 4 3	♡ K Q 10 7
◇ —	◇ 9 8
♣ A K Q 8 7 5 4 3	♣ 9 6 2

Reese preempted with five clubs over an opening bid of one spade, and Schapiro pushed to six clubs over five diamonds. The opener bid six diamonds, and after two passes Schapiro tried six hearts. When this was doubled on his right, he at once retreated into seven clubs, doubled and down one. If he had known that Reese held four hearts he would have stuck to his guns and made a doubled slam.

The stark clarity of these deals should be contrasted with the Buenos Aires hands offered by the defense, which are certainly arguable — and are argued in Appendix A.

A DECISIVE FACTOR?

The evidence from the hands was the chief reason offered by Sir John Foster for his "not guilty" verdict. He stated that this indirect evidence was examined only "very perfunctorily" in Buenos Aires.

He accepts uncritically a myth propounded by the defense: "The eight hands produced to Mr. Butler by Mr. Truscott were Italy 22, 23, 25, 26, 34 and 117, and U.S.A. 30 and 36." These were eight hands I had quoted to Reese out of a list of twenty when the chairman of the World Bridge Federation Executive Committee meeting indicated that enough was enough. The members of the Appeals Committee had heard the full list at an earlier stage in the proceedings.

Several months later, Reese's counsel told Butler that I had showed him (Butler) eight deals, and that six of them were from the match against Italy. As Butler had no particular reason to remember in detail what I had showed him, he answered, quite naturally, "I would accept that, of course, if you have evidence."

The evidence was never forthcoming, for an obvious reason. The defense was claiming that the abbreviated version given to Reese was the same as the list given to Butler, Swimer, and members of the Appeals Committee earlier. I testified to the contrary, and I have since found my original typed copy which includes twenty deals.

Swimer examined most of the Reese-Schapiro deals that were not at my disposal, so nearly all the ground was covered. Between us we found only one deal (U.S. 74) that seemed in favor of the defense.

"It was wrong of the Appeals Committee to rely on the small sample of eight hands produced by Mr. Truscott without considering the overall picture," states the Foster Report. "We had a very full analysis, lasting over twenty-two days, of all the hands that might have a bearing on these allegations . . . ."

With a few hours in which to make a decision, the World Bridge Federation clearly could not devote twenty-two days, or even one day, to considering a relatively minor part of the evidence. The members of the Appeals Committee, either at its formal meeting or during the private meetings on the previous day, spent perhaps two or three hours on this topic.

The six people present at the Appeals Committee meeting included four high-ranking experts and two experienced players. They were completely satisfied that the hands did not point strongly to innocence — the only interpretation that would have had any significance in the face of the direct evidence.

Two persons with very slight knowledge of the game[1] were satisfied at the end of twenty-two days of testimony that the hands did point to innocence. But it may not be a complete coincidence that 21-1/2 days of that period were devoted to the technical evidence of the defense witnesses.

THE TECHNICAL WITNESSES

The prosecution called no technical witnesses, no doubt in the belief that the hands would speak for themselves. And although four of the five prosecution witnesses were experts, they were given very little opportunity to discuss this side of the case: Becker and Mrs. Hayden were not invited to give any technical opinions, and for much of the twenty-two days that the inquiry devoted to the subject, the counsel for the B.B.L., a fair amateur player, was arguing with experts of world renown testifying for the defense.

For Sir John Foster and General Lord Bourne to listen to twenty-two days of highly technical argument was not only a complete waste of their time, and that of others concerned in the Inquiry, it was a procedure likely to produce a distorted judgment. There was an obvious, convenient, and effective alternative that would have saved both time and money.

Both sides should have been asked to produce written submissions on the technical evidence, with the opportunity to present written answers and rebuttals. This material should then have been submitted to an expert panel, largely or entirely non-English and non-American. This jury would then have given individual and secret opinions on the worth of the technical evidence. Each juror would have been asked to say whether the hands were inconclusive or whether they pointed slightly, strongly, or overwhelmingly in any particular direction. The consensus of the experts — who would have been selected by agreement of both sides — would have been available to Sir John Foster without placing any strain on his limited knowledge of the game.

---

1. Sir John was quite conscious of his own limitations as a bridge player. In discussing a deal on which Reese picked a heart lead rather than a spade from this hand:

    ♠ 8 6 5 4 3 2   ♡ K 9 5 3   ◇ 9   ♣ 8 7

    he observed: "Speaking as a player in the Eighteenth Class here . . . the only chance is perhaps there is only one stop in hearts, and so you play either your three of hearts or your king in the Eighteenth Class." If he ever reached the seventeenth class, Sir John no doubt gave up the idea of leading the king.

WHAT ACTUALLY HAPPENED?

The inquiry listened at great length to a small panel of experts that not only was selected by the defense but was predictably biased in favor of the defense.

These witnesses were:

1. Jeremy Flint. He was Reese's regular partner during the previous three years and together they had devised the Little Major system. They were the closest of friends — far closer than Reese and Schapiro were during the same period — and had twice won the British Masters Pairs title.

2. Kenneth Konstam. He was a regular teammate of the two accused players from 1948 on. He was teamed with them when he won five of his seven international titles and three of his five major British titles. A verdict of "guilty" in the inquiry would have removed some of the glory from his own reputation.

3. Harold Franklin. He was Britain's chief tournament director and an occasional teammate of the two accused players. For more than a decade he had a very close professional association with Reese. They were collaborators in a successful bridge program on radio and in various journalistic capacities.

4. Jimmy Ortiz-Patino. He is a Swiss international expert and was a bridge comrade of the two accused players — a friendship that with Reese extended to the golf course. In giving evidence, he was in a sense repaying a debt: eight years earlier he and his partner had been accused of an ethical lapse in a European championship and Reese was the only leading authority who gave them public support.

Ortiz-Patino was presented to the inquiry as a player with a special interest in cheating allegations. "On several occasions I was mixed up directly in allegations," he testified. That he was the original accuser in one of the most famous European cases was apparently not brought out (although my being a supporting witness on that occasion was cited as evidence that I was a witch-hunter).

These four technical witnesses should certainly have been barred from membership in an expert jury on account of their close association with the two accused players — who themselves gave evidence on the hands at very great length.

This consideration would not have applied to two other witnesses, although their sympathies can be judged from their volunteering to give evidence for the defense. But whether they would have been selected as members of an impartial jury of international authorities is distinctly doubtful. They were:

5. Irénée Bajos de Hérédia. He was the chief French tournament director, and he volunteered to give technical evidence for the defense. Some of his statements were of an extravagant nature and suggest a highly egotistical personality.

6. Eric Figgis. He was a statistician and an experienced tournament player who at the request of the defense compiled tables intended to indicate the relative performance of the various players.

An impressive list might be made, if full information were available, of the technical non-witnesses for the defense. Reese circulated the hands, and his comments, to a number of European experts who did not choose to give testimony for him. Some of them refused because in their opinion the hands pointed to guilt rather than innocence.

THE ASSESSORS

Sir John Foster and General Lord Bourne were not left without guidance in technical matters. Two expert players were appointed to advise them as "assessors."

But there are two reasons for believing that this was not an entirely satisfactory procedure.

First, the assessors were not sufficiently independent and free from all suspicion of bias. Neither would have been eligible for an expert jury of the type suggested on p. 137; the two assessors were:

A. Tony Priday, a timber merchant and bridge writer, was European Champion in 1961 when he played with this author. This link with the prosecution is more than balanced by his longstanding partnership and friendship with Jeremy Flint and by his association with Reese. All three were members of a team that won the Gold Cup, the most prized British event, in 1964, and they continued to be teammates while the inquiry was in progress, although Reese was not an active player.

B. Alan Hiron, a mathematician and bridge writer, was professionally associated with Reese in a journalistic capacity. His wife was Reese's secretary and "injected a certain amount of 'acid'" into Story of an Accusation. Hiron was nominated by the defense for the position of assessor and was clearly committed to that side of the argument.

Second, one would have expected two such assessors to prepare a report on the overall significance of the technical evidence. Presumably no such report was made, for there is no reference to it in the Foster Report, where one would expect it to be quoted. Instead Sir John offered his own summing-up: "The evidence about the bidding and play did not support the allegations of cheating."

It is not surprising that he should have gained that impression after listening to defense testimony on the subject for 21½ days. He cites three deals[2] in his report as conclusive but does not mention any of the deals that point in the opposite direction.

THE INFALLIBILITY OF INDIRECT EVIDENCE

"Mr. de Hérédia, Mr. Ortiz-Patino, Mr. Flint and Mr. Konstam," states the Foster Report, "were quite categorical that if a pair cheated, then this could be detected in the record of their bidding and playing the cards."

Bridge authorities are not noted for modesty, and such statements amount to a doctrine of personal infallibility. This is reminiscent of the police chief who announces dogmatically: "There are no undetected murders in my precinct." All these defense experts had very good reason to know that certain partnerships have been under frequent suspicion but that no action has been taken against them simply because evidence from hands is generally inconclusive.

Konstam and Flint had every reason to recall a famous London case in which two players who had achieved sudden success were accused of cheating on the basis of hands alone. They were found guilty by the Rules and Ethics Committee of the English Bridge Union and then appealed to the Union's council. There was no machinery for appeals, and an ad hoc committee was set up headed by Konstam. The original verdict was reversed. In this case one of the committees must have been wrong. The evidence may be "written in the hands," but those who read the evidence are certainly fallible. In a later English case the members of the committee could not agree on the significance of the technical evidence. There are many similar examples.

To distinguish between a pair that cheats within the "tolerance" and a pair that has merely a tendency to unorthodoxy is almost impossible by reference to hands alone. In such cases experts are about as likely to agree as they would be if asked to vote on bidding systems or a ranking of top players.

Hérédia's self-esteem went a good deal further than stating that examination of the deals would always prove or disprove cheating. He insisted that he would prefer the evidence of hand analysis to the evidence of observations — at any rate, to observations made by others. This sweeping generalization is quite astonishing, because it is made quite irrespective of the weight of the two varieties of evidence.

---

2. Two of them are U.S. 74 and Argentina 141, shown in Appendix A. In the third, Italy 58, Reese made a defensive error that knowledge of the heart suit would have helped him to avoid.

It would seem common sense to prefer overwhelming evidence of one kind to limited or inconclusive evidence of another.

Hérédia could be compared to an amateur Sherlock Holmes who examines some footprints and announces that the maker of the prints is bearded and six feet tall and has red hair. If it is demonstrated that the man is five feet six and clean-shaven with black hair he refuses to believe it.

CONCLUSION

Those who wish can form their own "expert" opinions on the technical evidence by studying Appendix A and the arguments offered on both sides. For the overall picture, it is perhaps worth pointing out that the Reese-Schapiro eccentricities at Buenos Aires were all related to the heart suit.

On both occasions that a psychic bid was made, it was in the heart suit. When an ace was underled successfully, it was the heart ace. When a dangerous semi-psychic overcall of one notrump was made, hearts offered a safe landing spot. And when a one notrump opening bid was made with a singleton, the singleton was in hearts. The defense was unable to offer any comparable examples of unorthodoxy related to any other suit.

But whatever may be thought of the merits of the hands, it is at any rate obvious that it is not difficult to make out a plausible case on both sides of the argument. Considering the wide variety of factors that may influence a player in making his bids and plays, which even at world championship level can be affected by human error, it is not surprising that many authorities, unlike the witnesses in the London Inquiry, believe that hands, like statistics, can prove anything.

THE PHOTOGRAPHIC EVIDENCE *17*

PERROUX told Gerber in Buenos Aires that he would like to see photographic evidence of the alleged cheating. The American captain replied that it would hardly be possible to arrange for such proof at the tail end of a championship in a foreign country. Nevertheless, a news agency story that was dispatched around the world before the World Bridge Federation issued its release suggested, quite wrongly, that photographs had been taken to prove that cheating had taken place. Even if arrangements could have been made, the wisdom of such an action would be doubtful. The sudden appearance of a photographer on a long-term basis could hardly fail to alert the accused players.

Many hundreds of photographs are taken at world championships for general press purposes. A few of these may accidentally have a bearing on cheating charges, and this is true of the Buenos Aires affair. Unfortunately, the photographer who did most of the work died soon afterward and his records were destroyed. There are six Buenos Aires photographs shown in this book, and four of them have a direct bearing on the accusation. They are shown in chronological order. A reproduction of an original hand record appears opposite as a sample.

Just before the first edition of this book went to press, two significant photographs taken in Turin in 1960 came to light in the files of the A.C.B.L. These are given first. All the photographs appear after page 132.

1. WORLD TEAM OLYMPIAD, TURIN, ITALY, MAY 1, 1960

In the second round of the final matches, Great Britain played a United States team — there were four American teams in all — known as "Vanderbilt I." In this photograph Reese is facing the camera and looking down at his cards. Schapiro's head is visible in the foreground. The American players are the late Sidney Silodor, on the left, and George Rapee, on the right. The British nonplaying captain, Louis Tarlo, is sitting in his privileged seat behind Silodor.

There are two faint clues to the hand in progress, and these are perceptible only if someone with good eyesight examines the original photograph closely under a strong light. The writing on the scorecards being used by Reese and Silodor can be faintly perceived, and suggests that about half the session, i.e. ten deals, has been completed. In addition, the face of Silodor's cards can be seen, and

The hand record of Deal 4, Great Britain v. Italy. Such records were the basis for the decoding and technical analysis in the case.

the card on the extreme left appears to be the heart jack. It can therefore be conjectured that this was Deal 11, on which Silodor's heart suit was J-10-5-4-2, and on which Reese held:

$$\spadesuit \ Q J 7 5 \quad \heartsuit \ Q 6 \quad \diamond \ A K 5 3 \quad \clubsuit \ J 8 3$$

It is easy to see that Reese is showing two fingers, that he is using his right hand, and that his cards are being held close to the table.

If the identification with Board 11 is correct, all three codes fit. He has two hearts, corresponding to two fingers. His cards are being held in the right hand, with more than 10 points. And, the low-level position of the cards, in the right hand, shows 10-14 points (see pp. 165-167).

2. WORLD TEAM OLYMPIAD, TURIN, ITALY, MAY 2,1960

A day later Great Britain played the United States "Spingold I" team. This time Schapiro is facing the camera, and Reese's head is in view. Bill Grieve, on the left, is putting down his dummy, and Ira Rubin, on the right, watches alertly. Jeremy Flint's face is visible in the top left-hand corner, below the flag.

In this case the deal can be identified without trouble. The opening lead is the diamond three. Grieve has already produced a six-card club suit headed by ace-king-jack, and is fingering the spade ace. Rubin's scorecard clearly shows that the session is about two-thirds completed. It is Deal 14, which was:

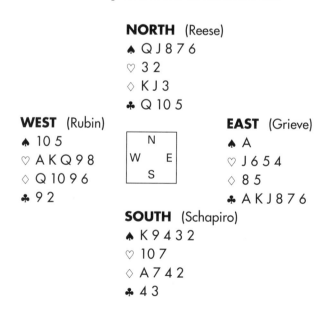

NORTH (Reese)
- ♠ Q J 8 7 6
- ♡ 3 2
- ◇ K J 3
- ♣ Q 10 5

WEST (Rubin)
- ♠ 10 5
- ♡ A K Q 9 8
- ◇ Q 10 9 6
- ♣ 9 2

EAST (Grieve)
- ♠ A
- ♡ J 6 5 4
- ◇ 8 5
- ♣ A K J 8 7 6

SOUTH (Schapiro)
- ♠ K 9 4 3 2
- ♡ 10 7
- ◇ A 7 4 2
- ♣ 4 3

Schapiro's position fits all three codes. He is showing two fingers for two hearts, and the left-hand medium position indicates 6-9 points.

3. BUENOS AIRES: THE FIRST DAY

The first session of play in the World Championship. Around the table from left to right are Boris Schapiro, wearing glasses and looking toward the camera; an Argentinian scorer; Sergio Osella, the Italian nonplaying co-captain (jointly with Perroux); Giorgio Belladonna, one of the stars of the Italian Blue Team; Ralph Swimer, sitting in the captain's seat within the ropes; Terence Reese, holding up his cards so that the spectators sitting in the grandstand behind him can see; and (West) Walter Avarelli, who was the other member of the Italian pair.

A section of the grandstand is visible behind Belladonna, and it seems that a lady has removed her shoes for greater kibitzing comfort. Swimer is looking very relaxed. It is clear that the bidding has not yet started. After taking this shot the photographer must have moved to the far side of the table to take the more significant shot which follows.

This is deal Number 4, which can be seen by looking at the board from Schapiro's angle.

THE HAND RECORD

In the top left-hand corner of photograph #3, an Argentinian scorer is shown entering the cards on the official record of deal Number 3. The back of his head is visible in the foreground of the photograph that follows.

The bidding and play of each deal was entered by another scorer sitting diagonally opposite Swimer. The scoring was of high quality, although "Belladona" was a spelling slip. There are two errors on the printed form itself: "triks" and "commulative."

The final step in the preparation of the records was the entering of the bidding and play from the Closed Room, together with the international match-point score and running total. This was done by the chief tournament director, Raoul Lerena, using a scoring record made by another scorer in the Closed Room. Lerena's complete record of deal Number 4 is reproduced on page 143. It will be seen from this record that Reese holds two hearts, the ten and the three.

4. THE TWO-FINGER SIGNAL

Deal Number 4 at a slightly later stage. The players, from left to right, are Belladonna, Reese, Avarelli, and Schapiro. Also in view are Swimer, sitting far left; Chief Tournament Director Lerena, standing left; Mrs. "Dimmie" Fleming, British journalist, sitting between Reese and Avarelli; and Geoffrey Butler, with glasses, behind Avarelli.

Reese has two fingers together behind the cards, and two fingers tucked between the cards. According to the heart code this would show a doubleton heart, and the record shows that he held two hearts. Reese suggests that this photograph is "meaningless" because he is about to make the opening lead. Even if this statement is true, it is difficult to see that it has any relevance.

There are two other points worth noting in this photograph. If Reese is about to lead, he is leading with his left hand — an unlikely procedure for a right-handed player. In all the other photographs he is holding his cards in his left hand, which is the natural way to proceed after the bidding is over. Another curiosity is that the cards are not fanned evenly. There is a sizable break five cards from the right and a smaller one two cards from the right. (Oddly enough, Reese gives this photograph in his book without indicating that it was part of the evidence or revealing that he had a doubleton heart.)

5. BEFORE THE DAWN

Deal Number 32, Great Britain v. North America. This was the third session on the third day of play, Monday, May 17. The deal was:

East-West vulnerable

NORTH
♠ 10 2
♡ Q J 9 8 7 3
♢ K J 6
♣ K 5

WEST
♠ 5 3
♡ 10 6 5 2
♢ 7 5 4 2
♣ Q 3 2

EAST
♠ Q J 9 8 6 4
♡ K
♢ Q 8
♣ A 8 6 4

SOUTH
♠ A K 7
♡ A 4
♢ A 10 9 3
♣ J 10 9 7

The bidding was:

WEST	NORTH	EAST	SOUTH
Reese	Becker	Schapiro	Hayden
pass	2♡	2♠	4♡
all pass			

Schapiro has led the spade jack, a Rusinow lead of the lower of touching honors, and Mrs. Hayden has laid down the dummy. Becker is planning the play, and Mrs. Hayden is looking very relaxed. Schapiro has his left forefinger extended and the other three fingers curled back below the cards. He has a singleton heart, so this corresponds with the code. This was three deals before Becker noticed the coincidence of V-shaped finger positions which aroused his suspicions.

This deal was played on Bridge-O-Rama, and the players are in a bleak backstage area. The author is shown on the right, holding a microphone and relaying the bids and the plays to the Bridge-O-Rama audience. (This was the only time during the week that I performed this duty, and I enjoyed myself by duplicating the English and American accents. Unfortunately "Paass—pass—no bid" was rather wasted on the Argentinian spectators.)

6. THE MYSTERIOUS VOID

Deal Number 68, Great Britain v. North America. The same four players in the same Bridge-O-Rama room, but three days have elapsed. This is the second session on the sixth day of play, Thursday, May 20, and there is a different announcer. This deal is shown on page 220 in Appendix A. Reese and Schapiro reached a contract of five spades and just made it.

By this stage both Becker and his partner believe that they are being cheated but do not know how. Mrs. Hayden is looking grim and determined, perhaps resolved not to allow her awareness of the finger variations to affect her game, as it had in the disastrous session that preceded this one. Schapiro again has his left forefinger extended. This deal was offered by the defense at the London Inquiry, because Schapiro holds a heart void. Because the prosecution never suggested what signal was used when a void was held, this photograph can be regarded as neutral.

The other observations regarding a heart void were made by Butler and Swimer. Reese held a heart void on boards 127 and 131 against Argentina. Butler, sitting behind the players, noted four fingers for Reese on both occasions. Swimer, sitting opposite Reese, did not note the number of fingers — perhaps because the arrangement of the fingers on the back of the cards was not clear-cut and countable.

But both observers indicated — Swimer on 127 and Butler on 131 — that Reese had his cards in his right hand and held his left hand down. This is suggestive; but it does not fit the photographic evidence such as it is.

The signal for a void will probably remain a mystery.

7. THE NEGATIVE EVIDENCE

Deal Number 99, Great Britain v. Argentina. The players around the table from left to right are Reese, Egisto Rocchi, Flint (lighting a cigarette) and Luis Attaguile. Konstam is sitting between Flint and Attaguile. This was the first session of play on Saturday, May 22, and during it both Gerber and I observed some of the play. We were both satisfied that the cards were being held in an entirely natural manner. This photograph demonstrates three points that can be tested quite easily by personal observation at any tournament.

First, in normal circumstances all four fingers show behind the cards. (See also Belladonna in the first photograph in this chapter.) Becker testified in London that he had subsequently observed a large number of players other than Reese and Schapiro and had not found one who did not hold his cards with four fingers touching some portion of the backs.

Second, it is quite easy to see that both Reese and Attaguile must be displaying four fingers to their partners. In London, the defense denied that Swimer and Butler would be able to judge the fingers shown by a player they were sitting beside.

Third, all the cards are fanned evenly. (Any exception is rare.)

8. THE END OF THE INVESTIGATION

Deal Number 138, Great Britain v. Argentina. The last session of the match, on the eighth day of play. Alberto Berisso of Argentina, holding a cigarette to his mouth, has just led the diamond six. Schapiro has started to expose the dummy, and the clubs — A-K-8-7-5-2 — can be seen. Marcelo Lerner, the other defender, is, like Reese, waiting expectantly for the rest of the dummy.

Reese has three fingers showing, and has his little finger tucked below his cards. His heart holding is K-9-2, so the fingers correspond to the code. This is approximately the angle from which Becker and Oakie had some difficulty in determining whether three or four fingers were being shown by Reese.

During this session Swimer observed and took notes. He is sitting on the left, looking white and strained, and his hand is firmly covering the notes that are on his lap.

SUMMING UP THE PHOTOGRAPHS

Of these eight photographs, six have a direct bearing on the affair. Three of the six — numbers 6, 7 and 8 — were available to the London inquiry.

On all six deals Reese shows two fingers twice and three fingers once and Schapiro shows one finger twice and two fingers once. On five occasions (subject to some doubt in one case) the fingers correspond to the heart holding in accordance with the code. On the sixth occasion the player has a void, for which the code offers no interpretation.

It should be emphasized that the photographs are in no sense a selection. The author has included every significant photograph that he has been able to find.

FINGER VARIATIONS 18

It Appears that neither side appreciated the significance of one admission made by Reese in the London Inquiry. "I have for thirty years held the cards in different ways at different times," he stated, "and there is evidence of that."

Bridge experts are extremely conscious of the importance of avoiding mannerisms that might be misunderstood or give rise to suspicion. So if it were true that Reese had for thirty years varied the number of fingers showing behind his cards — as he attempted to prove by producing two or three photographs at the London Inquiry — someone surely would have noticed the fact. And if any partner, opponent, or kibitzer had observed this fact and pointed it out to him, he would have had a clear duty to correct his habits and make a conscious effort to hold his cards in a consistent fashion.

In his career up to 1965, Reese probably played at least 100,000 deals of bridge. Perhaps 5,000 of those were played on occasions of high importance in the decade prior to 1965. On this basis, a lifelong innocent mannerism would be twenty times as likely to be noticed as a deliberate signal used on selected occasions in recent years.

Few players have the slightest idea how they hold their own cards or how the cards are held by their partners or opponents. This is as it should be. But if you take the trouble to look, you will see that practically all players hold their cards with all four fingers clearly in view behind the cards. This can be tested quite easily by wandering from table to table at any tournament or bridge club. You would have to search very hard to find a player displaying one, two, or even three fingers in a natural and innocent way, and a player who holds two spread-out fingers behind his cards must be as rare as a twelve-card suit. The use of any one such position regularly and innocently is possible, although surprising. The use of a series of such positions innocently within a single session is so wildly improbable that credulity must be strained to an extreme limit.

If it were possible to find such a player, the mannerism might be attributed to nervousness (although this is the last quality anyone would associate with Reese). But the odds against finding such a player's partner with the same peculiarity would then be astronomical. Yet this is what the defense asked the London Inquiry, not to mention the bridge public, to believe: that two of the world's most famous players both quite innocently varied their grip on their cards from one deal to the next and in so doing produced finger positions that could hardly be called natural.

Photographs showing that Reese had held his cards in different ways on previous occasions in his career could be open to more than one interpretation. It would have been impressive, of course, if the defense had produced photographs of other experts with similar finger mannerisms. They did not do so. The defense could hardly deny — and did not deny — that the two players were varying the fashion in which they held their cards. This was attested to by the defense witness Kehela, as well as by all the prosecution witnesses and several photographs. The defense case was that the two players were indulging in an innocent mannerism.

Some persons might think that such evidence on its own would be sufficient indication of guilt, without detailed observations or decoding. It was sufficient for a leading Australian authority who studied all the published material about the case from a neutral position far removed from Buenos Aires, New York, and London:

"Having now read the W.B.F. and the British evidence and verdicts, I remain (sadly) convinced that the conclusion reached by the W.B.F. has not really been shaken except by legal technicalities. Unless and until somebody can explain why not one but two of the world's most experienced players should develop mannerisms of almost identical type, then I shall remain convinced that the W.B.F. finding has not really been challenged."

But the evidence of the finger variations goes very much further than the sheer improbability that such a mannerism would be adopted innocently by both players. An innocent mannerism would evidently be a consistent one, irrespective of time and place. But there was ample evidence in Buenos Aires that the fingers variations were "switched off." The observers testified that the cards were held normally, with four fingers showing, when the play was in progress. There is no clear evidence relating to the point at which the finger variations disappeared, but it seems likely that it was after the first trick had been played. Two of the photographs show finger positions corresponding to the code after the opening lead has been made but before a card has been played from dummy.

Even more significant is the evidence that the finger variations disappeared when the two accused players were in action with other partners. Swimer watched fourteen deals in which Schapiro played with Konstam. I watched two or three deals in which Reese played with Flint. And Gerber watched a number of deals in both these sessions. In every case the cards were held normally with all four fingers in clear view. These observations were made partly in order to establish, beyond any possible doubt, the innocence of the other British players. But they also constitute an argument for the prosecution which can hardly be answered other than by disputing the honesty of the witnesses.

GENERAL ARGUMENTS FOR THE DEFENSE 19

THE BRITISH bridge public has had very limited information about the Reese-Schapiro case. The only public statements came from Reese, with the exception of formal announcements by the British Bridge League. His book *Story of an Accusation* has been widely read, but there has been no statement of the prosecution case.

The very fact that the World Bridge Federation had found the two players guilty in Buenos Aires was hidden from the British public when the American Contract Bridge League decided to publish this information in August, 1965. This was published by newspapers all over the world except in Britain, where the laws of libel are particularly favorable to plaintiffs. Readers of the *Scottish Daily Mirror* were able to read about the international finding of guilty, but only if they purchased the first edition of that paper. Before the second edition appeared, the paper's legal department had taken a hand.

Reese and his supporters offered a number of general arguments for defense, and these carried weight at all levels, from the player in the street to Sir John Foster. The answers to these were seldom made available. In this chapter these general arguments are put forward forcefully and vividly by Victor Mollo, an outstanding player-writer who represents the orthodox British view of the case. The answers are by the author.

WAITING FOR BECKER

Argument

If two players cheat — and have, as their accusers now say, cheated for years — who is likely to find them out? Would it be an opponent in action during a world championship, his attention riveted on the game, fighting for every match point, card by card and pip by pip? Or would the discovery be made by one of the tournament directors, scorers, journalists or perhaps by some members of another team, all of whom can watch at their leisure with nothing to distract them? Surely the culprits are much more likely to be exposed by the latter than by the former.

How is it, then, that so many expert observers saw and suspected nothing until B. Jay Becker suddenly showed them the light? And is it a pure coincidence that Becker had more than once before suspected his opponents of cheating?

Which, in short, is the more probable explanation of what happened — that a suspicious player imagined seeing something that was not there, or that the whole regiment of onlookers and officials was out of step — except Becker?

Answer

Of course it is unlikely that any particular person will be the first to detect illicit signals, just as it is highly unlikely that any particular person will win the Irish Sweep. But as the World Championship is set up, a player is more likely than a nonplayer to spot signaling. This is not simply because a player at the table has a better view of his opponents than anyone has, and has some leisure to observe while he is dummy or while the opponents are conducting a bidding duet.

In Buenos Aires only one of the four rooms was open to spectators — the roped enclosure surrounded by wooden staging which Mrs. Hayden in her story referred to as the "pit." The other three rooms each contained four players and one scorer. In one of these rooms there was also an announcer with a microphone. The next year, in the 1966 World Championship, all four rooms were closed, and the chance of signal interception by a spectator became zero. The theoretical possibility that something might be noticed by a scorer, official, or tournament director can be ignored, for they have their own duties to see to and rarely have sufficient expertise in the esoteric area of cheating. In no major case have charges of cheating ever been brought by an official.

Becker had not "more than once before suspected his opponents of cheating." On one occasion in a thirty-five-year career he supported allegations brought by someone else, which is hardly the same thing.

It would be more accurate to say that a whole regiment of onlookers and officials was in step with Becker. Eight other people confirmed that both players were varying their fingers in an apparently systematic manner and saw, to a greater or lesser extent, a correspondence with the heart code.

As was shown in Chapter 12, it is far from true to say that expert observers suspected nothing until Becker showed them the light. He was not even the first to observe and note the finger variations, a distinction that belongs to Don Oakie.

A SUSPICIOUS RECORD

Argument

Many bridge players are by nature suspicious of one another, and the Americans seem to be more so than most. That, at least, has long been the view in Paris and in Rome, no less than in London. The Europeans point to the record.

The Americans accused an Italian pair of cheating in the World Championship of 1958 at Como, and an American player was later suspended by the A.C.B.L. At Turin, no one was accused openly, but there were rumors in plenty during the Olympiad, and they spread far and wide, for one or two of the Americans did not trouble to hide their suspicions.

Not only, say the Europeans, is this a record of suspicion, it is a suspicious record.

Answer

Mollo is wrong about Turin, where he was not present. The American suspicions developed at the very end of the tournament, and far from spreading them far and wide, the Americans went to great trouble, as described in Chapter 13, to prevent any rumors from circulating. The only non-American informed was the English tournament director.

That leaves one other case prior to 1965 in which Americans made accusations[1] against Europeans. Against that, there were a number of cases — five come to mind immediately — in which prominent European players were formally accused by Europeans. In his book Reese carefully leaves the reader with the impression that some of these accusations were made by the wicked Americans.

THE RELUCTANT CHEATS

Argument

Since players intent on cheating can do so only in partnership with each other, one would expect them to play together whenever possible. Yet for months before Buenos Aires, Reese was anxious to end his long partnership with Schapiro and to play, instead, the Little Major — which Schapiro spurned – with Jeremy Flint. Why? Did he expect to do better playing the Little Major honestly than Acol dishonestly? If so, he clearly had little confidence in his system of cheating, and the question arises: Why

---

1. Reese describes a completely trivial episode in which an American player muttered something about "telepathy" when an English opponent made a good lead, but there was neither suspicion nor evidence nor accusation.

should a man risk so much for so little? Why should Reese jeopardize his reputation and his livelihood, derived entirely from bridge, for signals of such dubious value?

Conversely, if the heart code was, after all, a worthwhile weapon, how is it that Reese and Schapiro put up such a poor performance against the Italians? It was much their worst match up to that time against the Squadra Azzurra.

The accusers must somehow escape from the horns of this dilemma: If Reese and Schapiro's cheating was ineffective, why did they cheat? If it was not ineffective, why did they not fare better?

Answer

Mollo covers three separate issues here.

WHY TURN HONEST?

Men have been known to abandon an old mistress for a new wife, and gangsters who turn to legitimate enterprises sometimes find them more profitable and satisfying than crime. But in neither case can a lapse from new and virtuous paths be regarded as unlikely.

There is no doubt that Reese fell in love with his creation, the Little Major, and wanted to play it whenever possible. Equally, it is certain that Reese and Schapiro were not on speaking terms for several months before Buenos Aires. When Swimer insisted that the two players play together, the tension and discord between them were reduced but not dissipated. One would expect some loss of efficiency in such circumstances: two players who like and trust each other will do better, other things being equal, than two who do not.

But one would not expect the players to abandon old habits, either in bidding or in cheating.

WHY TAKE THE RISK?

It would certainly be improbable that two bridge players would begin to cheat at the end of long and distinguished careers. But no one has suggested that this was a beginning except those on the defense side setting up a man of straw to knock down. On the contrary, players who have cheated over a period of many years are likely to find it as difficult to abandon their illicit methods as a smoker finds giving up tobacco. Successful flouting of any code of laws breeds a feeling of immunity.

A world bridge championship was at stake, and both Reese and Schapiro were passionately anxious to win. To play honestly would certainly have reduced their chances, and what must have seemed a remote chance of detection was no deterrent.

WHY DID THEY PLAY BADLY?

The brief answer is that their overall results were good even though they made errors. Reese and his supporters have repeatedly said that the partnership played badly, but the evidence offered to support this statement is quite feeble.

The results in Buenos Aires show clearly that Reese and Schapiro were by far the most effective British pair. The British team did much better when Reese and Schapiro were playing together than when they were not; the two did much better as a partnership than they did when separated; and they were well ahead of the average team performance in each of the three matches. This is shown by the table on page 157.

In one way it is slightly surprising that Reese and Schapiro had such good results, for Schapiro made a number of clear-cut errors and was not in good form. The combination of effective results with some technical incompetence is difficult to explain — especially if they were playing honestly. But pairs that cheat will always produce better results than their technical performance would seem to justify: their illicit knowledge gives them an edge over their rivals in many bidding and defense situations.

In a long match between expert teams, the score of any pair that plays a substantial part is likely to be close to the average score of the team. The table opposite shows that Reese and Schapiro were almost half a point per board better than the team as a whole. So it may be true that they played "badly," but they certainly did not play ineffectively. Losses on the individual swings were more than balanced by gains on the partnership roundabouts.

	Boards Played	IMPs Won or Lost	IMPs per Board
GREAT BRITAIN V. NORTH AMERICA			
Reese-Schapiro	48	+ 89	+ 1.9
Reese-Flint	34	- 53	- 1.6
Schapiro-Konstam	34	- 41	- 1.2
Total when R-S did not play as pair	76	- 43	- 0.6
Total for team	**124**	**+ 46**	**+ 0.4**
GREAT BRITAIN V. ITALY			
Reese-Schapiro	96	- 52	- 0.5
Reese-Flint	34	- 57	-1.7
Schapiro-Konstam	20	- 21	-1.0
Totals when R-S did not play as pair	48	- 69	-1.4
Total for team	**144**	**-121**	**- 0.8**
GREAT BRITAIN V. ARGENTINA			
Reese-Schapiro	54	+ 96	+1.8
Reese-Flint	56	+ 88	+1.6
Schapiro-Konstam	62	+ 73	+ 1.2
Totals when R-S did not play as pair	90	+132	+1.5
Total for team	**144**	**+ 196**	**+ 1.4**
COMBINED SCORES ON THREE MATCHES			
Reese-Schapiro	198	+133	+ 0.7
Reese-Flint	124	- 22	- 0.2
Schapiro-Konstam	116	+ 11	+ 0.1
Totals when R-S did not play as pair	214	+ 20	+ 0.1
Total for team	**412**	**+121**	**+ 0.3**

TOO LATE TO CHEAT

Argument

At no time was the crazy pattern of the Buenos Aires affair so sharply defined as during the closing session of Britain's match against Argentina. It was then that the accusers gathered the most damaging links in the chain of visual evidence on which they based their case. Yet at no stage in the Championship did the accused have so little incentive to cheat. They had, in fact, no incentive at all. The result of the match was in no doubt. Britain's victory by a huge margin was assured, and so, too, for all practical purposes, were the final placings in the World Championship. To exchange illicit signals at that point was rather like doping a horse after the race.

Even had Reese and Schapiro cheated before, they surely would not have done so in that last session. It was too late, for the die had been cast.

ANSWER

The unimportance of the final session against Argentina is a myth that has been widely circulated. There was no doubt that Britain would win the match, but the players were well aware that the margin of victory was of great potential importance.

When the session started — the session in which Butler and Swimer observed and made notes — the match between Italy and North America was still in the balance. The Italians led by 16 points and were perhaps 3-1 favorites to retain their world title. But if the Italians lost to the Americans, the British still had a chance. The three teams would each have won two matches, and the rules provided for a play-off between the two teams with the best "quotient." The quotient is the figure obtained by dividing IMPs won by IMPs lost for each team.

Before Saturday evening's play the British quotient was inferior to their rivals' as a result of their heavy loss to Italy. So the British players knew that it was of great importance to pile on points against the Argentinians and improve their score against the Americans the following day.

"We've got one chance in eighteen," Schapiro told me on Saturday afternoon. He was allowing for the chance that America would beat Italy, the chance of improving the British quotient, and the chance of winning the play-off match. I thought his estimate was distinctly optimistic, but I was aware of a factor which he had not taken into account.

Certainly the British team did not play the last session against Argentina as though it were "going through the motions." The British won 68 IMPs and lost only 3, an overwhelming victory that would not be achieved by a team that had lost interest in the proceedings. When the plays were over, the American loss to

Italy had killed the last British hopes. A remarkable statement by Reese that attempts to show that he knew about the Italy-America result before it happened is discussed on page 184.

THE DEATH WISH

ARGUMENT

Suppose, for the sake of argument, that Reese and Schapiro had resolved to cheat in that last session just for the sake of increasing further Britain's formidable lead against Argentina. Would not the alarming activities all around them have stopped them in their tracks? On the previous day they had been watched by Dorothy Hayden, Alan Truscott, and John Gerber. Others, too, had flitted before them, and all, apparently, had taken notes. Now, suddenly, during a session that presented so little interest in itself, they found seated beside them Ralph Swimer, the British captain, and Geoffrey Butler, the chairman of the British Bridge League. Both were taking notes busily after every board. To complete the scene, the American vice-captain, Sammy Kehela, was moving around in the foreground.

Short of calling the police, what more could anyone have done to alert Reese and Schapiro? Yet we are asked to believe that hand after hand, oblivious of watchful eyes and sharpened pencils, they kept up their finger exercises, signaling hearts relentlessly, just to deal a few more blows to the prostrate Argentinians. Didn't it occur to them that they might be spotted? Or did they have the death wish?

ANSWER

Lawbreakers never think they are going to be caught, whether the laws they are breaking be those of God, man, or the World Bridge Federation. First offenders look nervously at shadows, but the old hand who has never been caught is supremely confident, whether he is cheating at cards, cracking a safe, or selling the Brooklyn Bridge.

Bridge experts on occasions of high importance are completely absorbed in the game and pay little attention to what is going on around them. Schapiro claims that he once proved this in an unusual way by arranging for a beautiful prostitute to stand facing Reese for part of an important contest. That he was completely unaware of her presence was a testimony to his asceticism as well as his concentration, for the lady was nude.[2]

---

2. The episode was stage-managed by Schapiro, who collected on a substantial bet as a result of Reese's lack of perception. An unkind person might suspect a confidence trick.

Reese and Schapiro would no doubt have been alerted if the officials had wheeled in movie cameras, as some critics have since suggested they should have done. But as it was, nothing in the least unusual occurred. On Friday afternoon the Bridge-O-Rama match between North America and Argentina was of little interest except to local fans loyally rooting for the gallant but outgunned representatives of their own country. The cognoscenti flocked to watch the clash between Reese-Schapiro and Forquet-Garozzo, two partnerships with strong claims to being regarded as the best in the world.

Some seventy or eighty people were watching, and it was natural that I should be there, together with other journalists. It was natural also that the Americans not engaged elsewhere should watch the performance of their chief rivals. Whether Reese and Schapiro were aware that Mrs. Hayden and Becker were standing in the background, or that Gerber had made a brief appearance, is highly doubtful, however.

Geoffrey Butler, in his capacity as a British selector, had conscientiously watched Reese and Schapiro, notebook in hand, for almost twenty years, both in national trials and in international matches. His presence in Buenos Aires would have been no surprise to the two players. The presence of Swimer was even less remarkable. British captains at that time customarily watched their players in the Open Room as a matter of duty and kept a record of the contracts and results. Swimer had done so throughout the week, and if he had been absent on this occasion Reese and Schapiro would have been the first to ask: "Where's Ralph?"

THE HEARTS MYSTIQUE

ARGUMENT

If two players make up their minds to use signals for one purpose only — and only one has been alleged in this case — which would it be? Would they really give top priority to the length of their hearts? Is it not more likely by far that they would choose to convey illicit information about the relative strength or weakness of their bids, and especially of their passes, to tell each other when to balance and when to desist, when to look for close slams and when to seek cheap sacrifices? Alternatively, sooner than enumerate hearts, would they not prefer to warn each other that a psychic or semi-psychic bid or some flagrant falsecard, perhaps, is on the way? Why should cheats — or anyone else for that matter — be obsessed with one particular suit?

There is room in bridge for many strange theories, and some experts — though surely not many — may subscribe to the view that hearts have properties denied to other suits. There is not a tittle of evidence that Reese and Schapiro have ever been of that cult or that they have shown the least interest in it. The accusers must prove otherwise. Until they do so, the hearts mystique can hardly be taken seriously as an adequate motive for cheating.

ANSWER

Only one type of signal was detected and decoded at Buenos Aires, but there are very good reasons for thinking, as shown in Chapter 20, that Reese and Schapiro did use other signals at Buenos Aires and on earlier occasions elsewhere.

The effectiveness of a heart-length signal compared with other cheating devices is a question to which I have given considerable thought since Buenos Aires. I now believe that a pair would gain more from heart signals than they would from any comparable maneuver.

Clearly, any signal must have a wide application: to devise a signal to cover such rare eventualities as a psychic bid or a falsecard would be stupid. (Note that a heart signal will sometimes tip off such shenanigans.) There are three types of signal, apart from a suit-length device, that could be considered candidates for a cheater's first choice.

One is the maximum-minimum signal, which will make it possible for a player to make an accurate judgment in the bidding. A second is a stop-go signal, by which a player can advise his partner whether a passive policy or an active one seems preferable. A third is a suit signal, which will suggest a lead in spades, hearts, diamonds, or clubs. The heart-length signal is more valuable than any of these, largely because it is profitable to the user in both the bidding period and in the defense. The other signals are significant during the bidding or the defense, but not both.

The bidding advantage of knowing about the heart suit is fairly obvious. The defense advantage is equally important, but less obvious: opening leads become much more accurate, and counting the hand becomes simple. If you know one of partner's suits, your chances of working out his complete distribution are greatly increased.

The increased defensive efficiency resulting from knowing partner's heart holding is virtually undetectable. And it is worth noting that Reese and Schapiro had the reputation for being incomparable defenders, while Schapiro was thought by many authorities to be relatively weak in dummy play — the department in which signals are of no help at all.[3]

---

3. At any rate, no help in an international tournament. At lower levels it has been known for a woman player as dummy to get up and powder her nose in a position in which she could signal to declarer the location of defensive honor cards.

If a pair decides to signal the length of one suit, the reason for picking the heart suit is easy to see. Four hearts is the game contract that eludes an expert pair most frequently, because opposing spade bids block the free exchange of information. The spade suit cannot be shut out easily because it outranks the others, and clubs and diamonds are of lesser importance – minor-suit games are rare.

For many American experts the negative double decreased the danger of "losing" the heart suit. This device was not commonly used in England at the time, but it seems that Reese and Schapiro did not need it.

FIVE-FINGER EXERCISE
ARGUMENT

From the improbable we pass to the incredible, to the "five-finger exercises," which were said to constitute the signals.

Many players on both sides of the Atlantic have been accused at different times of cheating. No players, on either side, have ever been accused of cheating so badly. The question: Why should two of the world's best players be the worst and the clumsiest cheats in history?

Signaling at bridge is absurdly easy. The cards may be fanned or folded, held in the left hand or in the right or transferred periodically from one hand to the other, or rocked on the wrist or lowered or raised or pointed this way and that. Each movement may be combined with some seemingly natural mannerism. The possibilities of signaling unobtrusively, without arousing anyone's suspicion, must be innumerable. Yet here are Reese and Schapiro, playing before the world's leading experts and most experienced tournament directors, resorting to the crudest and most blatant gestures — and so very unsuccessfully! Is it credible?

ANSWER

Several of these points have been discussed elsewhere, principally in the chapter entitled "Finger Variations," so brief answers are in order.

"Many players on both sides of the Atlantic" is an exaggeration. No leading tournament player in America up to then had ever been formally accused of cheating[4], and the number of cases in Europe do not reach double figures.

Unobtrusive signals based on movement cannot be spotted unobtrusively by

---

4. There have been cases of unsubstantiated suspicion without formal accusation. One expert, Willard Karn, was barred from a New York club in the thirties. But that was rubber bridge, not tournament play.

the partner. Players in a world championship are forbidden to stare at their partners. The finger positions in Buenos Aires were only crude and blatant when you knew about them. It is not disputed by the defense that finger movements took place, yet only two people ever noticed them independently, five years apart. And as we have seen already in this chapter, Reese and Schapiro were the most effective British pair in Buenos Aires.

And if Mollo wishes to experiment with a deck of cards, he will find it advisable to stick to four-finger exercises. If he throws in his thumb for good measure, he will drop his cards.

A SUSPICIOUS VERDICT

ARGUMENT

Had the World Bridge Federation been called upon to deal only with accusations from the American camp, they would doubtless have acted in a staid and sober manner. That they should have found Reese and Schapiro guilty without giving them a chance to defend themselves was due to an unprecedented situation. For it was not only the Americans, but the captain of the British team and the highest official in British bridge who accused Reese and Schapiro. It seemed incredible that they should take sides against their own team without good reason, and the judges, bewildered, if not bewitched, gave in without a fight.

The W.B.F.'s precipitate decision has been severely criticized, for it is contrary to every principle of justice that a verdict of guilty should be pronounced when only one side has been heard. That this should have happened was surely by far the gravest of the "irregularities" reported from Buenos Aires.

Meanwhile, Reese and Schapiro have been acquitted by another court. The reader can judge which verdict should carry the greater weight, that reached so unceremoniously during the last feverish hours of the World Championship or that of the long, painstaking inquiry conducted by one of Britain's leading lawyers, who heard both parties, listened to all the witnesses, and, with expert assistance, studied all the hands.

ANSWER

It is quite true that the evidence of the two British officials carried great weight with the World Bridge Federation: it would be astonishing if it had not. But it is certainly not true that the Executive was precipitate in its disposition of the case. In an ordinary bridge tournament such a matter would be disposed of in a single hearing; for obvious reasons it is not normally practical to conduct a one-year inquiry with full legal forms at a cost of thirty thousand dollars to decide upon an accusation of cheating. In Buenos Aires there were two separate meetings. Reese and Schapiro were called into both and were invited to defend themselves. The fact that the two players had little to say — Schapiro said virtually nothing — was hardly the fault of the Federation.

In London two judges with much legal experience and little bridge knowledge decided long after the Championship that there was "reasonable doubt" about the guilt of the two players. In Buenos Aires seven judges with some legal experience and vast bridge knowledge decided that the players were guilty. Two years later, having had ample opportunity to reconsider after reading the Foster Report and Reese's book, a slightly different Executive unanimously reaffirmed its original verdict.

Which verdict was the right one the readers of this book can decide for themselves.

"WHAT ELSE ARE WE DOING?" 20

WHEN REESE was summoned to appear before the World Bridge Federation Appeals Committee on Sunday morning his first step was to deny the charges. His second step was to ask a very curious question.

According to Robin MacNab, President of the American Contract Bridge League, Reese "shortly began inquiring whether he and Schapiro were suspected of any other lapses in deportment. As I recall his exact words they were: 'What else are we doing?', almost as if to ascertain just how deeply a code might have been plumbed."

This strange query is hardly one that would occur to an innocent man faced with unfounded charges. It did not receive any answer from the Appeals Committee. It can now be answered by showing that there is evidence from other times and places of illegal signaling by the same players.

LEFT, RIGHT, UP, AND DOWN

In Turin, Don Oakie detected and noted three variations of behavior that he thought were significant. Two of these — fingers for hearts and left-hand/right-hand for under and over average — are fully discussed in Chapters 13 and 14.

The third mannerism is also important in that it helps to explain the second.

Oakie noticed that the two players held their cards at varying levels, and he did his best to record this by writing a small "L" for low and "M" for medium beside his left-hand/right-hand notations. For one hand, Schapiro's on Deal 28, he wrote "hi" for high. Oakie discontinued this listing toward the end, but there are still thirty-two notations of hand-level capable of analysis.

The knowledge that partner has more or less than 10 high-card points is not on its own particularly valuable. This puzzled the handful of American observers at the time and enabled Reese to describe such a signal as "naive" six years later.

But such a signal becomes valuable when combined with another signal to break down the point-count further. Like this:

Points	Hand	Level
0-6	left	low
6-10	left	medium
10-16	right	low
16-20	right	medium (or high)

THE LOW AND MEDIUM NOTES

	Reese			Schapiro		
Deal	Hand	Level	Points	Hand	Level	Points
27	Left	low	6			
28	Left	low	6	Right	high	18
29	Left	med.	6	Right	low	13
30	Left	low	8	Right	low	10
31	Left	low	10			
32	Right	low	13	Right	low	11
33	Left	med.	7	Right	med.	14
34	Right	low	11	Left	med.	6
35	Left	low	4	Right	med.	14
36	Right	low	13	Right	low	12
37	Right	low	10	Left	med.	7
38	Right	low	14	Left	low	5
39	Left	low	0	Right	low	21
40	Right	low	10	Right	low	16
41	Right	low	11	Right	low	11
42	Right	low	11			
43				Right	low	15
45	Right	low	15			
50				Right	low	11

This table fits twenty-seven out of Oakie's thirty-two notations, which is as accurate as one could expect. Observations of the level at which the cards are held are likely to be less precise than observations of the hand used, the fingers showing, or the point-count.

There are only four positive discrepancies, deals 30, 31, 33, and 35. Deals 30 and 31 are discussed later in this chapter. On Deal 39 Oakie recorded Schapiro in a right-low position when he held this magnificent hand as dealer:

♠ A K 9 6 4 2   ♡ —   ◊ A K J 9 2   ♣ A Q

This is a healthy 21 points, and he opened the bidding with two clubs. This effectively removed any impression that his partner might have of a 10-14 point hand, and one can guess that the low position showed a minimum in high cards for the two-club opening.

The point range for left-medium should perhaps be listed as 6-9. The only occasion on which the left hand was used for a 10-point hand was on Deal 31, on which Reese held a worthless singleton jack.

THE TECHNICAL PROOF

Players who have illicit knowledge of partner's point-count are likely to make some unusual bids from time to time. In particular they can open the bidding with impunity when they do not have an opening bid, and they can depart from their announced opening notrump range. Reese and Schapiro did both of these repeatedly in Turin. In Buenos Aires they were strictly orthodox in both areas. After Turin they knew, from Franklin, that the left-hand/right-hand maneuver had been spotted, so it is reasonable to suppose that they gave up signaling point-count.

On four occasions in Turin they opened the bidding with one of a suit holding a hand falling far short of the normal high-card requirements. None of these bids would be likely to occur to a bidder using normal methods.

As dealer at favorable vulnerability, Reese bid one club with:

♠ K 6 5 4   ♡ Q   ◊ 7 6 5   ♣ J 8 7 6 5

In the second seat at favorable vulnerability Schapiro opened one heart with:

♠ Q 7 3 2   ♡ Q J 10 4 2   ◊ Q   ♣ J 4 2

Opposite this, Reese held a hand on which he would have opened two clubs with 20 high-card points. The example of Deal 39 suggests that Reese would have signaled right-low, in which case Schapiro would not have known the power of his partner's hand until after he had opened the bidding. The result was a grand slam depending on a finesse — which lost.

In the second seat at favorable vulnerability Reese opened one heart with:

♠ J 10 6 4   ♡ A 8 6   ◇ K 10   ♣ J 8 4 2

And in the deal discussed on page 132, Reese, as dealer, with neither side vulnerable, opened one spade holding:

♠ A J 10 7 6 4 2   ♡ J 7 3   ◇ 6   ♣ J 7

There were no comparable opening bids by Reese and Schapiro in Buenos Aires. Their bidding had suddenly become more orthodox.

THE EXTRAORDINARY NOTRUMP

In expert games the opening notrump bid is a precision tool. The players stick to the announced range, and one can predict whether a given expert will open one notrump on a given hand with about 90 per cent accuracy.

In the printed records of the World Championship for the Bermuda Bowl up to and including the 1965 event, covering twelve separate years and more than thirty-three hundred separate deals, departures from the announced range are very rare. Opening bids with one point short, such as 15-point hands bidding a 16-18 notrump, happen from time to time. Usually the player has some compensation in the form of a five-card suit or good intermediates.

There are three cases of a player's opening a notrump with one point more than his announced range. There are two cases of a player's opening with 2 points less than the advertised range. Helen Sobel, a player who had little faith in points and tended to rely on intuition, opened a 14-point hand in 1957. Kenneth Konstam opened a weak notrump with a "good" 10 points at favorable vulnerability in third seat in 1965.

There is only one case of a player's bidding a notrump with three points less than his announced range, and on that occasion he had full distributional compensation. In 1961 Gerber opened a 16-18 point notrump holding:

♠ 7 5   ♡ A K Q 7 5 3   ◇ A 5   ♣ 9 4 2

With seven playing tricks this bid was an understandable tactical move.

Yet Reese and Schapiro in Turin wandered from their notrump range in a quite astonishing way, moving Harold Franklin to comment in *The British Bridge World:*

"In all the matches against the American teams Reese and Schapiro bid one notrump on a variety of hands with good results."

The advertised range was 13-15 points not vulnerable and 16-18 vulnerable. The following examples are all taken from the records of Reese and Schapiro's play in Turin.

♠ 9 6   ♡ K 6 4   ◇ A J 6 5   ♣ 10 6 5 3

In third seat at favorable vulnerability Reese opened with one notrump. He played in three clubs doubled, one down against misdefense, and kept the opponents out of a vulnerable three notrump which would certainly have been made.

Reese	Schapiro
♠ A K J 10 2	♠ Q 7
♡ Q J 7	♡ A 9 8 5 2
◇ K 9	◇ A 8 5
♣ K 10 2	♣ 8 5 4

Not vulnerable against vulnerable opponents. Most players would regard Reese's 17-point hand as too strong for a strong notrump, let alone a weak notrump. The bidding was:

Reese	Schapiro
1NT	2NT
3NT	pass

Normally a player opening a weak notrump with Reese's hand would run a serious risk of missing a game or a slam. The danger does not exist when using the point-count hand signals as described above: the opener would know that his partner had 10-14 points, and as he has himself indicated 14-17 he knows that the responder will not pass.

♠ A 10 9   ♡ J 9 2   ◇ A Q 5 4   ♣ Q 10 5

In third seat Schapiro opened this hand with one notrump, vulnerable. This episode is described in detail on page 110.

♠ A K 10 8 7 6   ♡ 2   ◇ 9 7 4   ♣ J 10 2

Reese opened one notrump as dealer with neither side vulnerable.

On these four deals, the British pair gained on three and had one stand-off. Their profit was equivalent to 12 IMPs with the present method of scoring.

Notice that these four notrump deviations by one pair in one world championship were far more extreme than the six deviations recorded by all other players combined in the whole recorded history of world championships up to 1965. It is also noteworthy that Reese and Schapiro did not deviate from the notrump range in any other world championship. Such eccentricities are only a commercial proposition when some kind of point-count signal is in use.

Less conspicuous but also interesting are the deals on which one would expect a notrump bid which is not forthcoming. Two clear-cut examples from Turin were:

♠ K J 5   ♡ 10 8 6   ◊ A 6 2   ♣ A K J 2

This would seem an absolutely automatic vulnerable opening bid of one notrump using a 16-18 point range. But Reese opened with one club and rebid one notrump when his partner bid one heart.

If partner is known to have less than 10 high-card points, such a procedure gives added safety, because the partnership can stop in one notrump when normal bidding might reach two notrump. At the worst, a borderline game may be missed. The worst did happen in this case, for Schapiro held exactly 9 points, and the thin game was bid and made by the Americans thanks to a favorable lie of the opposing cards.

Reese	**Schapiro**
♠ A 10 7 3	♠ J 6
♡ K 10 8	♡ Q J 9 5
◊ K Q 7 6	◊ A J 4 2
♣ K Q	♣ 7 6 3

Both sides were vulnerable, so one would expect Reese to open one notrump. But the bidding was:

Reese	**Schapiro**
1◊	1NT
2NT	3NT

Schapiro did not feel any need to bid his heart suit, so the partnership achieved a bidding sequence that strongly indicated a major suit lead. A heart was duly led, when a club would have defeated the contract.

THE SINGLETON NOTRUMP

Significant deviations from the strength of a notrump opening bid are very rare indeed, but deviations from the pattern of a notrump bid are even harder to find. In the history of the World Championship up to 1965, there are only four cases of a player's opening one notrump with a hand containing a singleton, and in each case the singleton was in hearts.

Belladonna once permitted himself to open one notrump with a singleton ace of hearts. He held a powerful hand, so he had no reason to prevent his opponents from bidding hearts. The other three cases were all by Reese and Schapiro. Two of these are shown elsewhere in this book, on pages 169 and 218. The third example was this:

♠ J 10 8   ♡ K   ◇ K Q 10 7 3 2   ♣ A 9 5

In Turin, Schapiro opened this hand with a non-vulnerable weak notrump.

The normal objection to an opening notrump bid with a singleton is that partner may insist on that suit as trumps. This danger disappears if both players know each other's length in the suit. Such a bid stands to gain if the opponents have a heart fit, because they may find it difficult to enter the auction. In each of the cases on which Reese and Schapiro opened one notrump with a singleton heart, the opponents had a good fit in that suit: in one case eight cards, in another nine cards, and in the third ten cards.

If one accepts the possibility of a player's bidding one notrump while holding a singleton — and remember that no other British or American player is recorded as ever having tried such a gambit in world championship play up to that time — the heart coincidence is remarkable. The odds would be 64-1 against a player's venturing a notrump with a singleton heart on three occasions out of three if operating at random.

OPENING LEADS

Falsecard leads by expert players are exceedingly rare, for the danger of misleading partner in normal situations is vastly greater than the possible advantage from deceiving the declarer.

Most expert partnerships stick rigidly to their opening-lead methods. A few permit themselves an occasional eccentricity. But in this area, as in others, Reese and Schapiro are the exception. In their four World Championships they made twenty non-standard spot-card leads. If one checked the whole of recorded world championship history, it is doubtful whether all other players combined would exceed this total.

In Buenos Aires the British pair produced seven eccentricities:

1. The heart eight was led from A-10-8-2 against three notrump.
2. The heart five was led from J-10-7-6-5 against three notrump.
3. The diamond four was led from A-J-9-6-4-3 against three notrump.
4. The diamond six was led from 10-9-6-5 against four spades.
5. The club three was led from 9-3 against four hearts.
6. The club two was led from A-J-8-4-2 against three notrump.
7. The heart seven was led from J-10-7-6 against three notrump.

Three of the seven are in the heart suit, a point that recalls some of the evidence given at the London inquiry. Ortiz-Patino testified that Reese and Schapiro had only once departed from the fourth-best convention when leading the heart suit. As he found only one of these three cases, his investigation of the records must have been a little careless.

The other British players in Buenos Aires made no comparable off-beat leads. Reese and Schapiro between them made just one when playing with other partners. (Playing with Flint, Reese led the diamond two from A-9-5-4-2 against a notrump contract.) The Italian players use nonstandard leads but stick rigidly to their announced methods. They believe that partnership discipline and morale are most important, and altogether avoid individual experiments such as falsecard leads and psychic bids.

Reese and Schapiro seem to have been able to make these eccentric leads without any loss of efficiency. (For some comment on their leads in New York in 1964 see page 178.) Whether these opening-lead eccentricities had any direct connection with signals of some undecoded type it is impossible to say. But there is no gainsaying the basic fact: Reese and Schapiro regularly made unorthodox spot-card leads that other players of world championship class would not make.

Illegal information possessed by the opening leader permits him not only to experiment in this way but also to increase his accuracy. There is some reason to think that in earlier years the Reese-Schapiro partnership had a method by which a player could indicate possession of a long, strong suit that he would like led.

THE LENGTH AND STRENGTH SIGNAL

One of the most remarkable leads in the history of the game was made on the following deal from the 1964 Olympiad.

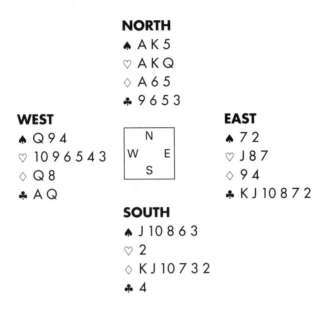

NORTH
♠ A K 5
♡ A K Q
◇ A 6 5
♣ 9 6 5 3

WEST
♠ Q 9 4
♡ 10 9 6 5 4 3
◇ Q 8
♣ A Q

EAST
♠ 7 2
♡ J 8 7
◇ 9 4
♣ K J 10 8 7 2

SOUTH
♠ J 10 8 6 3
♡ 2
◇ K J 10 7 3 2
♣ 4

Reese, sitting West, had to lead against four spades after North had shown a strong balanced hand and no other suit had been bid naturally. Reese led the club queen.

This is not a lead that would be likely to occur to anyone. But if one assumes that East had in some way indicated length and strength in clubs, the lead becomes entirely understandable. Partner will be able to overtake the club queen or not with more information at his disposal, and the declarer will be deceived about the position of the club ace.

The Italian declarer against Reese-Schapiro made his contract with an overtrick, and Italy had a chance to gain heavily on the deal. The British North reached the inferior contract of three notrump, against which the defenders could have taken the first six club tricks. But East would have had to lead a low club, and his actual lead of the jack blocked the suit.

Another example occurred in the 1955 championship. Reese held:

♠ 6 5 4   ♡ 6 4 2   ◇ A 7 4   ♣ A K 4 3

Lew Mathe on his left opened in fourth seat with one spade. The response was two hearts, which ended the auction. Reese's choice of opening lead was the diamond four. This certainly suited Schapiro, who held:

♠ Q J 10   ♡ 9 8 7   ◇ K Q J 8 3   ♣ 7 2

A signal to show a long, strong suit would explain this lead, and also the following remarkable episode. It was reported by Reese in the *Contract Bridge Journal* in the January 1952 issue.

"I must mention one comical incident in the match between my team and that of Norman Squire. I made an overcall of one heart on ♡ A-9-7, was doubled and stood it. The first thing that partner put down was ♡ Q-J-x-x-x! Contract just made. Can it ever be right to double a bid at the one-level on a trump holding no better than K-10-x-x? I must say that I do not believe in it."

Can it ever be right to overcall with a three-card suit and then stand for a double? I must say that I do not believe that. Such wild bidding would lead to frequent disasters when the dummy produces a singleton or doubleton in the suit — but Reese and Schapiro never recorded such disasters.

DYNAMITE DOUBLERS

Reese and Schapiro were celebrated in English bridge circles for their happy knack of producing effective penalty doubles out of thin air. Konstam once wrote an article on the subject, entitled "Dynamite Doubles," for a British magazine.

Such doubles of course are easier to find if the doubler has some illicit information about his partner's hand. A striking example occurred just before the Buenos Aires Championship in a high-level London event:

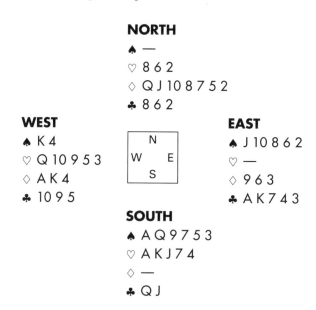

NORTH
♠ —
♡ 8 6 2
◇ Q J 10 8 7 5 2
♣ 8 6 2

WEST
♠ K 4
♡ Q 10 9 5 3
◇ A K 4
♣ 10 9 5

EAST
♠ J 10 8 6 2
♡ —
◇ 9 6 3
♣ A K 7 4 3

SOUTH
♠ A Q 9 7 5 3
♡ A K J 7 4
◇ —
♣ Q J

The bidding was:

WEST	NORTH	EAST	SOUTH
Reese		Schapiro	
			2♠
pass	2NT	pass	3♡
pass	4♡	dbl	all pass

The opening bid was an Acol two-bid, forcing for one round and showing a strong hand with at least eight playing tricks. Florence Osborn offered this description in the *New York Herald Tribune* shortly afterward:

"When North said four hearts, Reese waited happily for the chance to double, but it didn't come. Schapiro, sensing the opponents were in trouble, beat him to it. 'Boris, who fancies this kind of double, didn't wait for me,' said Reese afterward.

"South went down two tricks at four hearts doubled, losing two clubs and three trump tricks."

A player sitting East normally would not consider doubling. For one thing, South may bid further if left to his own devices. For another, North may hold four good trumps. If the red queens are traded in the diagram, for example, four hearts is made without trouble.

But if East knows that his partner has five hearts, and perhaps has some indication of strength in addition, the game becomes delightfully easy. Notice that Reese indicates that Schapiro goes in for imaginative doubles. The records show that he almost invariably chooses the right moment to make them.

WHO NEEDS BLACKWOOD?

All over the world, ninety-nine players out of one hundred use Blackwood or one of its variants to check aces in slam bidding. Reese and Schapiro, together with a tiny group of English experts, belonged in the 1 per cent of dissidents who do not use Blackwood.

Their Acol methods included the Culbertson four-five notrump, a more complicated convention, but a study of the records reveals a peculiar thing: they virtually never used the convention. Even when one would expect the four notrump bid to be used, a direct slam bid or some other move toward slam was produced.

Even players who do use Blackwood occasionally reach a slam lacking two aces. But, to the best of my recollection, Reese and Schapiro never suffered this fate even though they disdain to check the ace situation. One is forced to consider the possibility that in some way they may have known the number of aces held by partner. This would serve to explain the following "dynamite double" played in Turin against an American team.

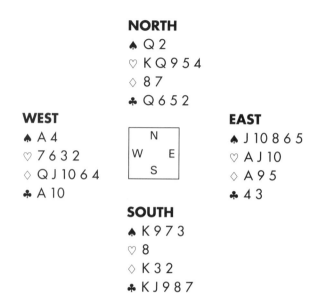

NORTH
♠ Q 2
♡ K Q 9 5 4
◇ 8 7
♣ Q 6 5 2

WEST
♠ A 4
♡ 7 6 3 2
◇ Q J 10 6 4
♣ A 10

EAST
♠ J 10 8 6 5
♡ A J 10
◇ A 9 5
♣ 4 3

SOUTH
♠ K 9 7 3
♡ 8
◇ K 3 2
♣ K J 9 8 7

East and West were vulnerable, a circumstance that caused South to try a third-hand experiment. The bidding was:

WEST	NORTH	EAST	SOUTH
Reese		Schapiro	
	pass	pass	3♣
pass	4♣	pass	pass
dbl	all pass		

The double of four clubs appears a most risky action, especially at IMP scoring. But the risk is negligible, and the prospect of a 300-point penalty is greatly increased, if West knows in some way that his partner has two aces.

WHAT HAPPENED IN NEW YORK?

If Reese and Schapiro were signaling their heart lengths in 1960 and 1965, one would suppose they had also done so in the World Team Olympiad in New York in 1964. There is no reason to think that they did — but there is some reason to think they had illicit knowledge of the spade suit.

There was a good technical cause for switching from hearts to spades and back again. In 1964, for the only time, they were playing the Little Major. In this system a one diamond opening bid shows either a spade suit or a strong notrump type of hand. An illegal knowledge of the spade suit would resolve this ambiguity and help the responder to judge the situation if one diamond was overcalled pre-emptively.

On one celebrated hand of the 1964 event Schapiro led a spade from K-9-8-6-5-4-2 against seven diamonds. Reese was void, and the ruff was the only way in which the slam could be beaten. This is suggestive, but there was a more spectacular example of spade inspiration.

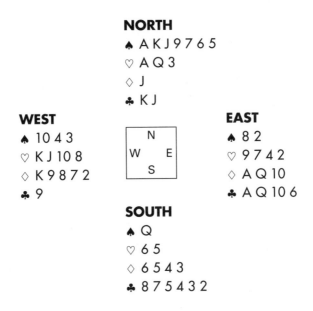

NORTH
♠ A K J 9 7 6 5
♡ A Q 3
♢ J
♣ K J

WEST
♠ 10 4 3
♡ K J 10 8
♢ K 9 8 7 2
♣ 9

EAST
♠ 8 2
♡ 9 7 4 2
♢ A Q 10
♣ A Q 10 6

SOUTH
♠ Q
♡ 6 5
♢ 6 5 4 3
♣ 8 7 5 4 3 2

Without some understanding of the Little Major, the bidding is unbelievable:

WEST	NORTH	EAST	SOUTH
	Reese		Schapiro
	1♡	pass	1♠
pass	pass	dbl	pass
2♢	2♠	3♢	pass
pass	3♠	all pass	

One heart was a two-way bid in the system. It could be a psychic opening, with very little high-card strength, in which case the opener would pass any response. Or it could be a powerful hand, needing little or no support to make a game, in which case the opener would continue bidding. The pass of one spade was therefore anti-system, for it indicated a psychic opening. It is also most odd in bridge terms, for if South had held a few spades, North would have had a good play for game.

The one spade bid was negative, but it did not deny holding spades. The pass becomes explicable only if North knew that his partner held a singleton spade as well as a weak hand.

Analysis of the opening leads points to the same conclusion. Reese and Schapiro made five eccentric spot-card leads in New York, and three of them were in spades. None was in hearts.

CONCLUSION

Apart from the Turin strength signals, this chapter does not attempt to prove cheating by the British pair. But it does suggest a number of areas in which their unusual habits were difficult to explain in terms of normal bridge — psychic bids, opening leads, imaginative doubles, and the omission of Blackwood or its equivalent.[1]

---

1. In 1951 several British experts believed that Reese and Schapiro were using a "weakness signal" which indicated a hand that was virtually worthless. This would explain Reese's psychic maneuver shown on page 101, and also another episode. Schapiro opened one club with a balanced 21 points — a standard two notrump bid in England. Opposite a yarborough, one club was just made and two notrump failed.

TRUTH AND FICTION 21

IN SOME areas of this case, witnesses on opposite sides told completely contradictory stories. In others the evidence was of such a nature that the opposing counsel had to reject it as dishonest. Three of these conflicts deserve special consideration.

THE CONFESSION

Swimer told the London inquiry, at the eleventh hour, that Schapiro had confessed to him in Buenos Aires.

Schapiro agreed that they had had a conversation opposite the hotel but denied that there was any confession. According to his version he attacked Swimer by saying: "How could you associate yourself with these American gangsters?" and continued by calling him some unprintable names. Swimer then burst into tears, and Schapiro "felt a wave of nausea come over me." There were at least four independent witnesses of this scene: Mrs. Swimer, Rose, Gerber, and Hammerich. All four formed the impression that both players were in a highly emotional state — a joint despair rather than a one-sided verbal onslaught.

The most striking phrase used by Schapiro in Swimer's version was "that evil man" in reference to Reese. Harrison-Gray recalled that he went for a walk with Schapiro just after learning of the accusation. Schapiro used the same phrase, "that evil man," and was perhaps about to confess when they were interrupted by the arrival of two other players and the moment passed.

Six months elapsed between the events in Buenos Aires and Swimer's testimony in London. By the end of that time many people either knew or guessed about the confession. Gerber was not the only official who inferred the confession from Swimer's attitude at the W.B.F. Executive meeting on Sunday afternoon. MacNab was very much alive to the situation at the time.

"I am a little confused," he writes, "about whether Swimer actually said that the pair was '110 per cent guilty.' The phrase, as such, gained much currency but this may well not have been what Swimer said.

"As I recall it, Swimer said: 'Gentlemen, I can assure you that you will not be making a mistake in finding them guilty.' It is quite possible that someone else interpreted this as the '110' statement.

"The reason I remember this so vividly is because Charlie Solomon was pressing Swimer to clarify his remark. The inference was plain that someone had confessed, but Swimer did not put it quite that bluntly. He knew only, I feel, that that was the inference we got.

"Charlie kept at Swimer to clarify himself, and I felt that Swimer was then close to tears and breaking, and I personally urged Charlie to cease pressuring Swimer, on the grounds that I thought he had already made the totality of the statement he was willing to make."

Other members of the Executive gained the same impression, but Swimer did not tell them the full story. He did, however, tell several people in confidence.

He naturally told his wife, and at her suggestion set out the full story in the famous letter to himself from Rio de Janeiro. On his return to England he told his lawyer, and shortly afterward he told Richard Preston, his regular partner.

In September, Mrs. Hayden asked Swimer in London about the confession, and his reply — "Please don't ask me anything about that" — led, as she describes (page 28), to a curious passage in Caplan's cross-examination of her.

None of this history was presented to the inquiry in London, with the exception of the letter — and that was disallowed as evidence after lengthy legal debate. If Schapiro's version of his talks with Swimer is accurate, and if he and his partner are innocent, Swimer's character and self-control must have been remarkable. He must have:

1. seized the opportunity offered by an American accusation to fabricate evidence against his old friends and teammates, acting the part of a heartbroken man most convincingly;

2. seized the opportunity offered by an embarrassing encounter with Schapiro to fabricate a confession story. This must have been an instantaneous decision, since he so well acted the part of a man overcome by emotion that several people standing some distance away were impressed (it seems hardly likely that a plotter of such consummate ability would break down involuntarily when confronted by one of his victims);

3. allowed the members of the World Bridge Federation Executive to infer that a confession had taken place, while continuing to act the part of a broken man;

4. lied to three people in confidence about the confession and written himself a letter on the subject;

all in order to prepare a delayed bombshell — almost too delayed — to present to an inquiry that was completely unforeseeable during the proceedings in Buenos Aires.

180 | *The Great Bridge Scandal*

The comments of Sir John Foster in his Report deserve examination:

"Mr. Schapiro had, according to Mr. Swimer, said that 'that evil man Reese' had forced him to cheat because Mr. Schapiro would not play the Little Major. We do not believe that Mr. Schapiro would consent to cheat because he was unwilling to play the Little Major . . . ."

I would not believe this either. To start cheating with one's regular partner after nearly twenty years to soften the blow of rejecting his new system would be strange conduct indeed.

Sir John appears to have fallen into an obvious trap. As a lawyer of great experience, he was surely aware that when criminals confess they frequently tell only a limited version of the truth. The natural reaction of a petty thief, when caught fairly and squarely, is to claim that he is a first offender and therefore entitled to leniency. According to Swimer, almost the first thing Schapiro said was: "This is the first time that it has ever happened." This would seem a likely statement for a man who wishes to hide a long record of misconduct, especially when followed by an implausible excuse.

The Foster Report gave two other reasons for doubting Swimer's testimony. One was this:

"We cannot understand why, if this confession took place, Mr. Swimer never reported it at Buenos Aires or told solicitor or Counsel for the British Bridge League, who called him as a witness."

Others might find this not too difficult to understand. Swimer felt that he had some moral obligation to Schapiro, although he had made no promises. The weight of evidence was clearly so great that the story of the confession was not going to affect the Buenos Aires verdict, and revealing it would have seemed rather like kicking a man when he is down — a course particularly distasteful in British eyes. Schapiro had mentioned suicide, and Swimer was afraid of driving him to such lengths. (Perroux had had the same consideration in mind when he abstained from voting.)

Nothing occurred to make Swimer change his mind about treating the confession as confidential until he was cross-examined by Caplan in London. It then became clear to him that his own integrity and honesty were being attacked. If his own reputation was in danger, as he believed, it is hardly surprising that he should decide to withdraw the limited protection he had given to a man whom he regarded as a cheat.

The third reason offered by Sir John for doubting Swimer deserves a section to itself.

THE CHOICE OF CAPTAIN

"We do not believe," says the Foster Report, "that Mr. Schapiro would have chosen the English Captain to whom to confess as their relationship was distant and to an extent antagonistic."

Swimer and Schapiro had frequently been teammates and were members of the same club. One would expect that they would be friendly unless there was clear evidence to the contrary. The objective evidence to support the idea that there was discord between them was distinctly limited. Two years earlier they had had an unhappy partnership in a trial, and on that occasion as well as before Buenos Aires, Swimer was omitted by the selectors and Schapiro was included.

The selection of the captain for Buenos Aires raised a vital issue, and on this point Swimer and Schapiro directly contradicted each other in their testimony. Swimer testified that Schapiro telephoned him several times, urging him to accept the captaincy. Schapiro denied this angrily:

"I heard Swimer say in evidence that I telephoned him and persuaded him to accept the captaincy. I did not even know the man's telephone number, and I was absolutely against him from the start."

The first part of this statement is an odd defense, for telephone directories are not unknown in London. Fortunately, there is independent evidence about Schapiro's views at that time. Reese, Schapiro, Flint, Konstam, and Harrison-Gray met at Crockford's to discuss whether the team should have a sixth player and who should be chosen as captain. According to Reese, Schapiro favored Dr. Sidney Lee as captain for the rather frivolous reason that he dispensed free whisky. Presumably Flint and Konstam were not asked about this meeting when they appeared as witnesses for the defense, for Reese does not mention such evidence.

The recollections of Harrison-Gray, who was not called as a witness, are quite different:

"Having made his wisecrack about Lee, Boris said it was essential to have Rose in the team and raised no objection whatever to Swimer. The only objection came from Konstam ... In the end he agreed that our choice of captain should be unanimous and undertook to write accordingly to the British Bridge League."

In the London Inquiry the prosecution presented its witnesses before the defense and so had no opportunity to rebut Schapiro's version of his relations with Swimer. If there had been such an opportunity, Richard Preston, a fellow member with Schapiro of the Hamilton Club, could have given important evidence. Says Preston:

"On at least three occasions Boris Schapiro engaged me in conversation either in the bar or in the card-room, and he told me how much he liked and admired

Ralph Swimer. He said that he was very much in favor of the suggestion that Swimer be appointed non-playing captain of the team for Buenos Aires, and furthermore that he intended to telephone Swimer and urge him to accept the captaincy."

If the evidence of Preston and Harrison-Gray is accepted, three important conclusions follow from it.

Schapiro's evidence in an important matter was dishonest.

The alleged antagonism between Swimer and Schapiro disappears.

And the flimsy motive advanced by the defense to support the suggestion that Swimer's evidence was dishonest completely vanishes.

THE HAYDEN-KEHELA CONVERSATION

The defense in London alleged that Mrs. Hayden had made "one demonstrable error" in her evidence. She testified that she had a conversation with Kehela of considerable importance on Saturday evening. They left the Bridge-O-Rama hall after an American disaster on the third deal had made an Italian victory a virtual certainty, and went for a walk. They discussed Reese and Schapiro, and Kehela explained that he had been told by Gerber about the allegations. Kehela went on to say that he had watched them play and knew it to be true, although he would not say so publicly — in fact, he would deny it if asked.

Reese points out that "there is something wrong with the timing." Kehela, on the face of it, could not have made this statement after three deals of the America-Italy match when his observations of the Britain-Argentina match, according to his own testimony, were confined to the second half of the session. The two matches were scheduled to start at the same time, but the normal delay in launching the Bridge-O-Rama session, which requires a speech to the audience and the introduction of the players, would have given the British match a start of from fifteen to thirty minutes. The nominal starting time was 10:30 P.M., and the crucial America-Italy match was played quite slowly. The third deal was probably not completed until nearly 11:30 P.M., by which time the other match would have completed 7 or 8 deals.

The conflict in evidence was circumstantial rather than direct, for Kehela gave his evidence before Mrs. Hayden and the question of conversations between them did not come up. Since then he has said that his recollections of the whole weekend are hazy because he was emotionally disturbed. He could not recall subsequently what conversations he had had with whom at what times.

There are three, and probably only three, explanations of the apparent discrepancy. The reader can decide for himself which is plausible.

1. Mrs. Hayden invented the conversation to discredit Kehela. (This is implied by Reese in his book.)

2. Kehela watched the first few deals of the Britain-Argentina match, wandered unhappily out to watch Bridge-O-Rama and talk to Mrs. Hayden, but subsequently forgot this first inspection of the British players. (This is Mrs. Hayden's own reconstruction of the episode.)

3. Mrs. Hayden has confused two conversations. The discussion after the third deal of the Bridge-O-Rama match was perhaps confined to Kehela's having been told about the code. His other statements might have been made in the course of a conversation she recalls having with Kehela much later the same night, after the play was over.

Another problem relating to the starting time of this session deserves mention.

"On our way to the Open Room," records Reese in his book, "we learned that America had fallen well behind Italy and had no chance of winning."

If he had made this statement to the Foster Inquiry it would have been easy to refute: the unspecified informant was looking a full hour into the future. This was of course a most significant point. If Reese and Schapiro had known that Italy was winning easily, they would have known that their only hope of final victory had vanished and the need to pile on points against Argentina would have disappeared. There are only two possible explanations of this discrepancy. Either Reese invented this to bolster his defense, or he suffered from a chronological confusion of a most peculiar kind.

Complete accuracy about the chronology of such complex events is certainly difficult to achieve, as Reese's book shows. At one point he refers to the Becker-Hayden notes being taken on Thursday afternoon instead of Friday. And he describes a conversation between himself and Kehela in Buenos Aires a full day after the Canadian star had returned to the United States.

AFTERTHOUGHTS 22

THE LEGAL ISSUE

Two prominent bridge players who are also lawyers were asked to comment on the case for the second edition of this book, and especially to focus on the issue of the standard of proof, which is essentially what led to two opposite verdicts in this case.

ALLAN FALK, of Okemos, Mich., is an attorney who has served as commissioner of the Michigan Court of Appeals. He is the author of five bridge books and as a player has won three A.C.B.L. national titles. He writes:

As a lawyer of some accomplishment and a bridge player of more or less accomplishment, depending more than I'd care to admit on which of my partners you ask for an evaluation, I have been asked to offer an opinion on the issue of whether the Foster Inquiry was correct in demanding that the proof of alleged cheating meet the standard in criminal cases, namely, 'beyond a reasonable doubt.'

To be asked this question concerning a matter now four decades past, in which the accused have gone the way of all flesh and have had to answer for their misdeeds, if any, to a Higher Power, proves the remarkable staying power of bridge scandals to excite the imagination, rather similar to why weekend warriors and military cadets still study the ancient exploits of Napoleon Bonaparte, Robert E. Lee and Julius Caesar, among others. In the same way, by studying major cheating scandals, we can profit from the errors of our predecessors as they investigated, prosecuted, defended, or adjudicated such issues in the past and equally benefit by emulating the good moves they made.

In countries that derive their legal system from Great Britain, criminal charges require proof 'beyond a reasonable doubt.' Centuries of legal precedent have tried to reformulate those words, but always we return to the plain meaning of the language: proof that leaves no doubt that prudent people might accept as reasonable under the circumstances. This is the highest standard of proof known to the common law. It is part and parcel of placing the burden of proof on the prosecution or, at the Foster Inquiry, on the accusers, and simultaneously cloaking the accused with a presumption of innocence. By contrast, in places like Europe and former colonies (like South America) where the Napoleonic Code (a modernization of the old Roman Law) prevails, by the time of trial the burden of proof may be on the accused. Such a concept would have been anathema to the adjudicators at the Foster Inquiry, who were quintessentially English.

However, proof beyond a reasonable doubt applies in no other context than a criminal prosecution. When William Jefferson Clinton was impeached by the House of Representatives and tried by the Senate, proof beyond a reasonable doubt was not required, even though the Bill of Impeachment charged him with 'high crimes and misdemeanors.' No criminal penalty was at issue before the Senate, which was determining Mr. Clinton's right to continue to hold the office of President of the United States.

Similarly, when O.J. Simpson was sued for wrongful death by relatives of his ex-wife Nicole Simpson and her friend Mr. Goldman, he was held liable using a mere 'preponderance of the evidence', the usual standard of proof in civil cases. In a most controversial denouement to his highly publicized criminal trial just months earlier, Simpson had been acquitted because the jury was not satisfied 'beyond a reasonable doubt' that he murdered Ms. Simpson and Mr. Goldman.

The Foster Inquiry was certainly not a criminal prosecution; had Reese and Schapiro been found guilty of using forbidden secret signals, they would have been socially ostracized by their peers, and probably barred from tournament competition and even their local rubber bridge clubs, but they would not have been at risk of incarceration or even of being assessed a fine. The fact that an adjudication of cheating would have sullied their reputations irretrievably is of no import; in a defamation lawsuit under common law, truth as an affirmative defense can be proved by a simple preponderance of the evidence.

Other sports seem to enforce their rules regularly in proceedings requiring only a preponderance of the evidence. Olympic athletes can be banned for using prohibited pharmaceuticals on proof by a preponderance of the evidence, although that means that a lifetime of hard work may be forever wasted, a penalty surely no more Draconian than what might have happened to Reese and Schapiro.

However, the presiding adjudicators at the Foster Inquiry were both experienced lawyers, and legal training teaches that when a point is conceded by the party expected to contest it, further consideration of it wastes time, money, and energy. Thus, when Simon Goldblatt, counsel to the BBL, in his opening statement denominated his role as that of 'prosecutor', and admitted that at the very least the evidence had to 'clearly prove' the charges, he effectively diverted all further proceedings down a path where the case was viewed as quasi-criminal and more proof than a preponderance of evidence would be demanded of him.

In the common law tradition, this higher than usual standard of proof is described as 'clear and convincing evidence.' In most American jurisdictions, civil charges of fraud have to meet this test, which is regarded as somewhat lower than proof 'beyond a reasonable doubt'. In practical terms, however, the distinction may be one hard to measure, even for lawyers.

Once an elevated standard of proof is acknowledged as being required by the side that has the burden of proof, it is to be expected that the adjudicators will take a fairly rigorous view as to when that standard is reached. The Foster Inquiry predictably did exactly that when, from the outset, Mr. Goldblatt condoned the use of such disadvantageous parameters. Mr. Goldblatt also seems to have acknowledged throughout that the evidence supporting the charge of cheating had weaknesses to a greater or lesser degree: there were, he said, too few direct observations and too little compelling indirect circumstantial evidence of actions that could be attributed to unauthorized knowledge of heart length and nothing else. Thus the outcome of the Foster Inquiry may well have been preordained once these guidelines were adopted.

It is still worthwhile to study the Foster Inquiry, as well as the handling of the matter by the World Bridge Federation. Mistakes were made, particularly in the initial stages, of a type being repeated currently. There was a recent case where an American expert was barred after allegations that he had repeatedly dealt the spade ace to his partner. A videotape of very poor quality supposedly showed that the spade ace was consistently on the bottom of the pack immediately before the dealing began, but no effort was made to obtain hand records to see which player actually held the spade ace on hands dealt by the accused player, or whether there was anything in the bidding or play to suggest that the accused had such information (as by using it to advantage, or at least attempting to do so). It seems like bad policy to ruin a person's livelihood on the basis of such sloppy information.

Bridge organizations in general seem atrociously slow to learn from these mistakes of the past. By studying *The Great Bridge Scandal*, modern competitors and administrators may hope to acquaint themselves with the types of evidence that should be gathered to establish a case of cheating, the flaws that might undercut the value of such evidence, and how to avoid those flaws. Perhaps they might also be inspired to imagine how technology might be used to improve the process of detection, apprehension, and expulsion, and how existing procedures may be focused or sharpened to assure essential fairness.

DENIS HOWARD of Sydney, Australia, is a solicitor. He was President of the World Bridge Federation from 1986 to 1991. He regularly represented Australia in world championships, earning a bronze medal in the Bermuda Bowl in 1971. He writes:

The credibility of the Foster Report could not hope to survive the publication of Alan Truscott's compelling and courageous book, *The Great Bridge Scandal* and the Report's 'not guilty' verdict in favour of Reese and Schapiro carries little weight, if any. However, its predictable approach to the basis on which cheating allegations should be adjudicated (Sir John Foster was an English lawyer) is worth quoting:

"The effect of a finding of cheating is just as serious for those accused as a finding of guilt of a crime. The standard of proof required in a criminal court to return a verdict is that the jury or court should be satisfied beyond a reasonable doubt. We think that the same standard should be applied here..." (see page 242)

'Beyond a reasonable doubt' is a standard of proof in criminal cases established by Anglo-American common law. In most cases, juries are left to decide whether the prosecution has sufficiently discharged that standard to permit a 'guilty' verdict to be returned. But the claim that this standard should necessarily be applied to allegations of cheating in bridge strikes me as unsound, given the nature of bridge as a game and the coalition of politics and incompetence that usually accompanies its administration. In 'The Anatomy of a Scandal', an article I wrote for *Australian Bridge* in 1975 about the Facchini-Zucchelli foot-tapping affair at the 1975 Bermuda Bowl, I made this comment:

"Legalism is an attitude of mind, frequently of assistance to the guilty. In everyday life, the combination of eyewitness reports and the suspect background of the pair involved would enable a fairly prompt conclusion to be reached on the question of their guilt. Put into the setting of formal accusation, with the yoke of 'beyond reasonable doubt' on the accuser's neck, the matter assumes a different shape. The proponents of screens were perceptive enough to realise that prevention is the easier game to win."

Circa 1977, under the presidency of Jaime Ortiz-Patino, the screening mechanism of the WBF Credentials Committee was introduced as a further protection against cheating. This Committee decides, with no reasons needing to be given, whether or not invitations to compete in WBF championships should be issued to those wishing to take part. In this context, it is amusing to reflect on the fact that although Ortiz-Patino gave evidence on behalf of Reese and Schapiro at the Foster Inquiry, he was firmly opposed on ethical grounds to Reese's participation in the 1981 World Championships as the n.p.c. of the British team (which was to have been Reese's first appearance in a world teams championship since Buenos Aires in 1965) and used the Credentials Committee to secure his exclusion.

Cheating is undoubtedly a grave threat to the integrity of bridge competition and administrators must be prepared to deal with allegations of cheating, however troublesome or distasteful. For example, a very unhealthy climate in world competition had developed in the 1970s as a result of the growing conviction in U.S. circles that some Italian pairs were cheating and the perceived failure of the WBF to do anything about it. Ortiz-Patino set out to tackle this issue after his election as WBF president in 1976 and he did so vigorously and successfully. His insistence on high ethical standards in world championships and the non-legalistic mechanisms he adopted to promote this outcome did the game a great service, although it took me some time after 1976 to recognise this.

Reverting to the Foster Report, I quarrel not only with its assertion that satisfactory indirect or technical evidence had not been adduced (Truscott and others did in fact provide persuasive indirect evidence), but also with the need to provide such evidence in the first place. It seems to me that a less onerous criterion to be adopted in cheating cases should be one of 'significant' proof. Two examples of what constitutes significant proof would be the peculiar finger signals given by Reese and Schapiro (surprisingly enough in view of its finding, the Foster Report acknowledged that there was strong direct evidence of the exchange of finger signals) and the repeated foot contact witnessed in the Fucchini-Zucchelli case. Where no credible explanation can be offered for such inherently suspicious behaviour, proof of guilt may be said to exist, without the prosecution also being required to link these physical activities to the bridge hands themselves.

That said, administrators in this day and age would be well advised to buttress cheating allegation procedures with sensible regulations, to which competitors are made subject as a condition of entry.

CAN CHEATING BE PREVENTED?

It is not difficult to prevent cheating in top-level events. Four suggestions were made after the events described here:

1. A screen can be placed diagonally across the table, so that each player cannot see his partner, and is also screened from one opponent. Such a screen had sometimes been used in major Italian events, and is known there as the "Franco Board." A trap in the center of the board is raised before the start of play so that the players can see the dummy.

2. A long box, or what the mathematicians would call a prism of square cross-section, can be placed on end on the table with an edge pointing to each player. Each player would then see his two opponents but not his partner. The box would be removed after the opening lead.

3. A large, square lamp shade, of a type sometimes used in card clubs, can be lowered to a point about a foot above the table. This would effectively block each player's view of his partner. It would be necessary to raise the lamp slightly at the start of play.

4. The players can be physically separated. One player from each partnership sits in each of two distinct rooms, with substitutes occupying the vacant seats. An announcer repeats the bids and plays in pairs, over a microphone or telephone connection and the substitutes follow instructions. This drastic solution would be quite cheat-proof except perhaps against short-wave micro-radio. It would have one supplementary advantage: the ethical problems which result from bidding hesitations would virtually disappear.

Whether any such plan should be employed was hotly debated. Expert opinion was divided in America, but the concept was strongly favored in Europe, where the proven cases of high-level cheating had occurred. Some were opposed because they felt these devices would reduce the sporting and friendly spirit in which international contests should be played, and would imply that players might otherwise cheat. Those in favor suggested that some plan was needed which would not only prevent cheating but would also prevent unfounded suspicions of cheating and restore public confidence in the honesty of the world's greatest players.

Screens were the solution adopted in 1975 and they have been used ever since in major championships. The players are in favor of this, partly because it makes cheating very difficult and partly because they can relax: if your partner cannot see you, you do not need to sit poker-faced for fear someone will think you are giving information.

WHY WOULD THEY CHEAT?

This is the most difficult question of all, and it has been left almost to the end of the book. The psychology of cheating has been little explored; it is described as a neurosis, a comfortable catchall term which helps not at all.

Cheating can be regarded as a special case of fraud, which was fully explored by Frank Gibney in his book, *The Operators*. The following is his verdict on a highly respected and popular New York judge who indulged in a variety of illegal financial manipulations, including the forging of stock certificates:

"To this day George Brenner's many friends cannot understand what made him do it. He was not addicted to high living or purposeless spending . . . Yet he represents a classic motive for white collar crime: the desire for power and prestige."

Power and prestige, Reese and Schapiro had in plenty. They dominated British bridge for almost two decades, and were often able to ensure that British international teams included their friends and excluded their enemies. They built a reputation as one of the world's greatest partnerships, and would have received many knowledgeable votes, including mine, for the greatest of all in the first forty years of the game.

The financial motive was of little direct significance, for world champions do not receive cash prizes. But it is worth noting that Reese and Schapiro often won substantial sums in European tournaments, and as we have seen, Reese first came under suspicion when gambling in a London club. Indirectly, Reese's international reputation was of great benefit to him, for it contributed greatly to the sales of his many bridge books. (They would have sold well in any event, for they were among the best of their kind.)

One of the few books which deals specifically with cheating is *Great Scandals of Cheating at Cards* in which John Welcome describes three famous nineteenth-century court cases. In his introduction he writes:

That there are motives which make men cheat, and not for gain, and that they are bound up with the quirks of human character is undeniable. An intense dislike of being beaten is one of them, and this is often coupled with a streak of arrogance which makes defeat even more unacceptable, especially by a despised opponent. Megalomania, too — the feeling that one is set apart from and above one's fellows and must never be touched by failure, however small — has a part in it. A third motive may be triumph of successful deceit; the warm self-congratulatory feeling of having pulled the wool successfully over an opponent's eyes.

There are striking similarities in the characters of the plaintiffs in these three cases ... all of them were proud, arrogant and reserved men, contemptuous of those that they considered beneath them and not slow to show that contempt; all of them had success attend their actions and their lives; each ... appears to have had a strong streak of megalomania running through his character.

All of this description fits the British players. Many of their opponents in England and elsewhere can testify that they were arrogant and contemptuous of those that they considered beneath them. Reese was certainly reserved, while ill-mannered would be a better term for Schapiro, who was no introvert.

A megalomaniac contempt for others would perhaps explain why Reese and Schapiro did not bother to make their codes unbreakable, and did not abandon their habits when they had reached the top of the bridge ladder.

"Two qualities distinguish all such white-collar criminals," remarks Gibney, "immoderation and self-delusion. The first is the same flaw which scars the villains in the fairy tales of the brothers Grimm ... generations of children have privately wondered why the wolf or the goldsmith could not have been content with his first stroke of good fortune, without trying to crowd his luck."

It is difficult for the average bridge enthusiast to believe that anybody would cheat. A game from which endless satisfaction can be derived loses its point if the rules are not obeyed. But there is no doubt that a tiny minority of players do cheat, and presumably they believe that they will not be caught, or that if they are they will be able to talk their way out of trouble.

Reese clearly got considerable satisfaction out of writing his book in his own defense. It recalls an unusual quotation from Publius Terentius Afer, commonly known as Terence, which Reese used to preface another of his books:

"There is a demand nowadays for the man who can make wrong appear right."

SINCE BUENOS AIRES 23

THE FIRST edition of this book faced some roadblocks. The publishers' lawyers asked for supporting evidence, and this was provided. They then stated that if the book was published, there might be a suit. If there was a suit — they did not estimate the chances — they were confident that the suit could be successfully defended. A successful defense might cost $30,000.

One might think that the publishers would reason, in these circumstances, that the accused players might be reluctant to invest money in a losing cause. But because they were afraid of having to win a suit, the publishers withdrew. Very annoying. An old friend came to the rescue and paid for the publication. The publisher was a notional Yarborough Press, which was me.

While the book was being prepared, Reese's lawyers sent a letter to the publishers, hinting at an eventual suit. This probably had an effect. After publication, he made no move to sue. Asked why, he said "I would not get justice in America". Asked whether certain things in the book were true, he said "I haven't read it". This strained credulity.

ON THE INTERNATIONAL SCENE

The international bodies were deadlocked for several years. In April 1967 the European Bridge League instructed its delegates to ask the World Bridge Federation to accept the Foster verdict and reverse its finding of "guilty."

A month later, in Miami, Florida, the World Bridge Federation Executive Committee voted unanimously to reaffirm its original finding of guilty. The unanimous vote, rather surprisingly, included the four European delegates. The Committee also announced that as far as they were concerned the matter was closed, a statement that was open to two interpretations. The European delegates assumed this to mean that the whole affair could now be forgotten, and that the accused players could play again. The delegates from the United States and the rest of the world merely intended to close any further debate on the subject of innocence and guilt. They were not in the least impressed by the report of Sir John Foster and his verdict. The world body also voted to reserve to its full Executive Committee the right to accept or reject applications to play in a world tournament from players "found guilty of irregular practices."

The British Bridge League, with European support, passed a resolution deploring the Miami decision and asked the world body whether a British team including Reese would be acceptable in the 1968 World Team Olympiad. The answer to this question was negative, and this put the Council of the British League in a difficult position. As a protest the British decided not to enter teams in the Olympiad, in spite of the fact that its women's team had a world title to defend.

This inevitably meant that the matter which had been closed in Miami in 1967 had to be reopened in Deauville, France in 1968. The Europeans were sharply divided from the rest of the world on this issue, and there seemed some danger that the World Bridge Federation would split in two. Many of the delegates to the world body simply wanted peace, and a compromise was worked out. The Federation announced that it reaffirmed its original finding of "guilty," but was lifting its ban on the accused players for subsequent world championships. They had, in effect, been suspended for three years.

Tension was high in Deauville. The British players who attended, as spectators, were loyal to the accused pair and were not speaking to me. Most of them switched sides after they read this book, which appeared the following year. An exception was Rixi Markus, who in Deauville saw me playing a deal with Priday, accidentally, in a demonstration of a French product. As a punishment for consorting with the enemy, she poured a glass of water over his head. Rixi was a dynamic and vibrant personality, and she did not speak to me for the next fifteen years. Then she decided after all that I was her best friend. Confusing.

The World Bridge Federation gave way, announcing that the suspension was over. Reese and Schapiro would be allowed to play, but not together. Reese chose to play, with another partner, in the 1970 World Pairs in Stockholm.

A STORM IN BRITAIN

There was peace on the international scene, but a cloud in England, where two prominent personalities, Konstam and Harrison-Gray, died in 1968.

The Buenos Aires scandal had generated three libel suits in England. Two of them were by Reese, and he did not choose to press them when the publishers concerned showed an intention of defending themselves. The third was quite different.

During the summer of 1965, the American *Bridge World* carried some accounts of the Buenos Aires affair and published some of the deals which were being put forward by the prosecution. The editor, Alphonse Moyse Jr., invited his English agent, Rixi Markus, to write him something he could publish about

English reactions to the affair. He wanted an article, but what he received was a series of letters passionately defending the two accused players. He eventually welded together extracts from the letters to form an article.

The article was a remarkable document, especially when one considers that Mrs. Markus was not present in Buenos Aires and therefore had no first-hand knowledge of the events. Her sharpest arrows were hurled at Swimer:

> I have discussed the behavior and action of the British captain and delegates with many great brains, lawyers, psychologists, doctors, and even bridge players.
>
> All the intelligent people have come out with the same answer, when Swimer was told by the trio that Schapiro and Reese used signals, etc., he readily believed that that was so and when he went to watch them he saw what he was told to see.
>
> Had he not thought them guilty he would have told the accusers to go to hell or look for someone else. I like Ralph Swimer and consider him a decent and honorable man, but he was an utter failure in his duties as a captain.
>
> How can I ever play for my country where my captain becomes a party to conspiracy to convict me of a crime?

These intemperate remarks were not well received in some quarters here. If there had been a conspiracy, then Gerber, Becker, Mrs. Hayden and I must have been parties to it.

In England, quite naturally, Swimer began a libel action against Mrs. Markus. She refused to withdraw her observations or apologize, and the wheels of British justice ground slowly on. The case came to court in February 1969.

THE LIBEL HEARING

The nature of the defense to the libel charge was of great importance. Mrs. Markus could have pleaded "justification" and endeavored to prove that what she said was true. She would have had to demonstrate that there had been a conspiracy, and this would have meant reopening the whole cheating issue. Numerous witnesses from both sides of the Atlantic would then have been involved. But the defense of truth was not put forward. For the purposes of the hearing the assumption was that there was no conspiracy, and that Swimer's evidence in Buenos Aires was entirely honest.

Nevertheless, Swimer's conduct in Buenos Aires was a matter of concern to the London court. Here are some extracts from his testimony as reported in the London Times:

> The finding of Not Guilty by an inquiry in London conducted by Sir John Foster Q.C. . . . was a "mistaken verdict," Mr. Ralph Swimer, the team's non-playing captain, told a High Court judge and jury yesterday.
>
> Mr. Swimer said, "I saw them cheating with my own eyes. . . After I had seen several of the finger movements I was completely convinced, because I went out of the room and did not feel very well . . ."
>
> "Are you still absolutely convinced you saw Reese and Schapiro cheating?"
>
> "Absolutely."

When Mrs. Markus was cross-examined, she quoted the Foster verdict, made public in August 1966, to support her statements made a year earlier:

MR. DUNCAN: You had formed the view that there had been a plot?

MRS. MARKUS: Yes, it was proved in the Foster tribunal that the accusations were completely unfounded. Yes, to me it looked like a plot. Like an intention to convict the two players of cheating with very little evidence and not conclusive evidence.

MR. DUNCAN: And you thought Mr. Swimer was a party to that plot?

MRS. MARKUS: He was a tool being used.

MR. DUNCAN: Are you suggesting that Mr. Swimer should have been biased in favor of his team but wasn't?

MRS. MARKUS: Yes.

MR. DUNCAN: Let us not funk it. You are saying Mr. Swimer reported having seen things which in fact he had not seen?

Mrs. Markus said Mr. Swimer was sure that he had seen the players giving signals when he had watched them but it would not have been possible for him to have seen what he claimed.

It was technically impossible for an observer to see whether players were cheating. It required an independent tribunal.

This remarkable statement implies that the Foster Tribunal would have managed quite well without any witnesses. The proceedings would have been much speedier, and the verdict would have been the same.

THE DEFENSE, THE SUMMING UP AND THE VERDICT

Mrs. Markus offered two legal defenses to the libel charge. She claimed "fair comment," a defense which the judge rejected as a matter of law. Mr. Justice Brabin "told the jury that Mrs. Markus's claim of fair comment was not open to her since the words complained of were statements of fact."

The second defense was that Mrs. Markus was not responsible for publication in the magazine, and that the statements were made in a personal letter to the editor. The correspondence between Mrs. Markus and the editor made it quite clear, however, that publication was intended:

> Her letter and an enclosure with it to the editor contained her "honest views" and she did not mind being quoted. I didn't think the editor would find space to publish it all, but I told him he could print what he liked.
>
> She agreed with her counsel, Mr. Peter Bristow, Q.C., that she gave the editor "carte blanche" to use what she had written.

This might seem to dispose of this defense, but the matter had to be decided by the jury.

Mr. Justice Brabin told the jury that it did not matter what happened at the Buenos Aires championships. It was what "flowed" from it — the libel allegation — with which they were concerned . . .

He would first ask the jury to answer three questions on fact:

1. Did Mrs. Markus intend the defamatory words complained of to be published in *Bridge World*?
2. Did Mrs. Markus authorize them to be published?
3. Was publication the natural and probable effect of her behavior?

If the answers were affirmative, subject to any legal argument which might be advanced, he would hold that there had been publication by Mrs. Markus. He would then have to ask the jury a fourth question: "Has the plaintiff proved that the defendant was actuated by malice?"

When Mr. Swimer was told of the cheating allegations, he decided to watch the two players.

"Should he have acted differently?" asked the judge. "Would you, in any sense, criticise a man for saying, 'I'll go and see for myself?' Because seeing might end the matter."

It was fairly clear to observers present that the evidence, the law and the judge in summing up were on Swimer's side. But the jury was not. After a retirement of almost four hours they returned with an announcement that they could not agree. In English law the jury must be unanimous. How the jury was divided remains a secret. The costs of the action totaled some $26,000, to be shared between the two parties to the action unless a further hearing was decided on.

Swimer announced that he would consult his lawyers about whether to start a fresh trial. Mrs. Markus declared: "This has confirmed my belief in God and justice."

AN UNENDING FEUD

The libel case was heard while the British team trials for 1969 were in progress. After the first stage Reese's team was in the lead with Swimer's team in second position.

Before the trials were continued, Reese lodged a complaint with the British Bridge League. He and Flint, his partner, complained of Swimer's repetition in court of his belief in the 1965 cheating. They demanded that Swimer be excluded from the trials. Priday, who has appeared in this book as a former partner of Flint and this author, a teammate of Reese, and an assessor at the London Inquiry, had the responsibility of replying as Chairman of the British Bridge League.

"Everyone obviously deplores the further publicity given to the Buenos Aires incident in the recent libel proceedings, but the council does not consider that this calls for any further action on its part.

"The council can understand your reluctance but not that of any other player in the Trials to play at Mr. Swimer's table and, despite the conditions laid down, the council would agree, if you so wish, that in your match against Mr. Swimer's team you play throughout against Messrs. Brock and Manning."

This did not satisfy the complainants, who withdrew from the trials. "In the subsequent letter announcing his intention to withdraw, Mr. Reese said that Mr. Swimer, protected by privilege in court, had made public mockery of the findings of the inquiry which had cleared them of accusations of cheating."

Two other pairs sympathized with Reese and Flint, and withdrew also. Schapiro stated: "I was invited to play in the trials but I refused because Mr. Swimer would be playing." This suggested that he was willing to emerge from the retirement he announced in 1965.

Swimer's team led the trials into the final day of play, but faltered at the finish.

AND MUCH LATER...

In 1975, the World Bridge Federation introduced bidding screens to world championships. This was pressed by Jaime Ortiz-Patino, who in 1976 became President of the world body, serving with great distinction for a decade. Cheating accusations against Italian players surfaced in 1975 and 1976, details of which are given in my *New York Times Bridge Book*, published by St. Martin's Press in 2002.

Cheating problems have been relatively minor at the world level since 1976, partly because of the screens and partly because the W.B.F. established a Credentials Committee, which could bar players without stating reasons. This had an impact in 1981 when Reese was barred from acting as non-playing captain of the British Bermuda Bowl team. The stated reason was that he had brought the game into disrepute by publishing a pornographic bridge novel two years earlier. However, his co-author, Jeremy Flint, was not similarly disciplined and continued to play in world events.

Reese gave up playing after 1970, at any level, but continued writing. He died in 1996. Schapiro continued to play enthusiastically, in London clubs and British tournaments. He won the Gold Cup, the top British event, for the eleventh time in 1998 when he was 89. In the same year, four years before his death, he won the World Senior Pairs title in Lille, France. This is believed to be the greatest age at which anyone has won a major title in any game or sport. It was a notable climax to a long, successful and controversial career in the game.

Appendices

Hands From Buenos Aires A

The inquiry in London spent many hours discussing hands in painstaking detail. Of thirty-four deals put forward by the prosecution and twenty-two by the defense, many had only a remote bearing on the case. In this Appendix the eight strongest hands for the prosecution will first be presented. Arguments for the defense are by Victor Mollo and are italicized. He selected the eight subsequent hands as the strongest on that side. From the defense standpoint, Mollo provided the following Introduction to this Appendix.

Of course people cheat at bridge. The game mirrors every facet of human nature, and people who are dishonest away from the table do not cease to be so just because they sit down to play. It would be unnatural if it were otherwise. But it would be no less unnatural if the innocent did not on occasion also come under suspicion. For just as wrongdoers often look innocent and thrive, so the innocent at times look surprisingly guilty — and suffer the dire consequences.

Without doubt, the charges against Reese and Schapiro appear formidable. Yet are they not, by their nature, improbable? And in some ways are they not incredible? In one vital respect, that of the hands themselves, they are surely quite impossible. As he examines critically the hands that follow, the reader should apply a twofold test. Picking up the cards held by the accused, he should ask himself: "Would I have made the same bid without illicit information about partner's length in hearts?" If the answer is "Yes," if the bid could have been made in the ordinary way, then be it good or bad, orthodox or eccentric, it does not indicate cheating.

The second question should be: "Would I have made the same bid or play had I known the number of hearts in partner's hand?" If the answer is "No," if a bid is such that a good player would not have made it with foreknowledge of the heart position, then the charge of cheating falls to the ground. A very few hands in this second category should prove decisive in refuting the charges against Reese and Schapiro.

Italy 18
North-South vulnerable.

NORTH
- ♠ Q 10
- ♡ K 10 7
- ◊ 9 8 7 4
- ♣ K J 7 4

WEST
- ♠ J 6 5
- ♡ 6 5
- ◊ J 3 2
- ♣ 10 9 8 6 5

```
     N
  W     E
     S
```

EAST
- ♠ A 9 8 7 2
- ♡ 9 2
- ◊ K Q 10 5
- ♣ A 3

SOUTH
- ♠ K 4 3
- ♡ A Q J 8 4 3
- ◊ A 6
- ♣ Q 2

WEST	NORTH	EAST	SOUTH
Reese	Forquet	Schapiro	Garozzo
		1♠	dbl
pass	2♣	2♡	2NT
all pass			

The five of spades was led, and South made nine tricks. When the hand was replayed, the British pair bid and made the easy heart game, and Great Britain gained 10 IMPs.

ARGUMENT

This psychic bid of two hearts by Schapiro may be unique in the literature of the game; I cannot recall seeing anything like it in the past twenty years. The reason is not difficult to see: in an honest partnership the risks far outweigh the prospects of gain.

From East's angle his partner is likely to be short in spades, since he failed to raise to two spades, a bid that could be desperately weak in this situation and vulnerability. And West is likely to have some length in hearts, since the opponents have not bid the suit. So a very likely result of the psychic bid of two hearts is that West, influenced naturally by the vulnerability, would bid a disastrous four hearts should there be an opposing bid of three notrump.

Reese claimed that he "would have been alive to the possibility that partner's heart bid might not be genuine." Being alive to a slight chance is one thing, but taking the appropriate action is another. And Reese's ESP has never led him into the dismal paths that result from an erroneous assumption that partner's normal bid is psychic.

With illicit knowledge, East's bid has everything to gain and nothing to lose. He knows that the opponents have nine hearts between them and can make a vulnerable game in that suit. (North's response showed positive values in the Neapolitan System.) He knows that his partner will not raise the suit. He knows that his partner knows the bid is psychic. And he knows that he can find a safe haven in two spades or three diamonds: when one side has a good fit the other side will tend to have one also.

For forty-eight hours after this deal was played Forquet eagerly showed this hand to anyone who would look at it. "How can they bid like this?" he demanded. No one could tell him.

ANSWER

Looking at the North-South hands, it seems incredible that any competent pair, let alone world champions, should miss so obvious a contract of four hearts. For once, the Neapolitan pair was caught in the toils of its devious system, but what signal — or magic crystal — could tell Schapiro that this would happen?

If he knew that Reese had only two hearts, he would also know that Garozzo had five (or six). He would expect then a sharp double to expose his psyche, which would have helped, instead of hindering, the opponents.

Turn to Reese. He knows that Garozzo would not make a takeout double of one spade without strength in hearts. If, then, he has four or five hearts himself he will be very wary. With only thirteen hearts around, everyone can't be long in the suit. If, on the other hand, Reese has fewer than four hearts, his urge to sacrifice will be kept within bounds. Either way, there is no danger of landing in four hearts as a sacrifice against three notrump — or anything else.

Schapiro's two hearts may not be oversubtle — and with a doubleton opposite it looks positively fatuous — but it is no more risky than any other psyche at favorable vulnerability.

Italy 127
North-South vulnerable.

NORTH
♠ A K 9 7
♡ Q 9 8 5
◇ A 4
♣ 9 6 3

WEST
♠ Q 5 4
♡ A J 7 3
◇ K 7 5
♣ A K Q

```
        N
   W         E
        S
```

EAST
♠ J 10 8 3 2
♡ 4
◇ J 6 3
♣ 10 8 5 2

SOUTH
♠ 6
♡ K 10 6 2
◇ Q 10 9 8 2
♣ J 7 4

WEST	NORTH	EAST	SOUTH
Reese	Forquet	Schapiro	Garozzo
			pass
1♣	dbl	1♡	2◇
2NT	pass	3♣	all pass

ARGUMENT

Schapiro's one-heart psychic bid with the East hand is a venerable maneuver that has been almost entirely abandoned in serious play. It is usually exposed quite easily by the accepted countermove, a penalty double by the fourth player if he holds four cards in the psychic suit and a few high-card points, so the chance of a profit is usually less than the chance of a loss by misleading partner. However, the Italians were not always adept at handling such situations, and South failed to double — a failure that placed West in difficulty because he had no technical reason to suppose that his partner had psyched.

Reese stated that after the bidding on both sides of him "he was bound to suspect the heart bid." It is true that he could legitimately infer that his partner's hand was extremely weak, but it by no means followed that East did not have length in hearts.

The normal, standard interpretation of one heart is that East has a weak hand with at least five cards in hearts. East's bidding suggested a hand such as:

♠ x   ♡ K 10 x x x   ◇ x x   ♣ x x x x x

In this case the combined hands would have an excellent play for four hearts.

West's failure to support hearts at any stage would be regarded by any experienced tournament committee as clear evidence of an improper understanding. A player may suspect that his partner's bid is psychic, but he must not act on that suspicion until the bidding reveals the situation.

Two minor points made for the defense on this deal are easily answered. West could not afford to double two diamonds and lead hearts, because that inspired action would go far beyond the limits of tolerance that a cheating pair would set for itself. And the knowledge that his partner held four hearts would not particularly discourage East from making the psychic bid. If West's opening bid is a normal minimum, North-South will no doubt be able to make four hearts in spite of the four-one break; and if North-South do reach hearts in the face of the psychic they are likely to misread the trump situation.

ANSWER

If Schapiro knows that Reese has four hearts, why should he seek to deter the Italians from running into an unlucky four-one trump break? Surely he will welcome the prospect. His rather puerile psyche clearly indicates that he knew nothing about the hearts opposite.

If Reese knows that Schapiro has a singleton heart, there is no reason for him to bid at all.[1] He passes (no need to double), happy in the knowledge that ruffs in defense will upset his opponents' calculations.

North's double suggests at least 13 points, probably more. South's free bid at the two-level promises not less than 6. With 19 points himself Reese will naturally suspect any bid made by his partner — in hearts or in anything else.

---

1. Come, come. That would really be a giveaway, far beyond the limits of "tolerance."—
    A.T

U.S. 30
Neither vulnerable

NORTH
♠ A K 8 6 4
♡ 9
◇ K Q J 10 2
♣ J 8

WEST
♠ 10 9 5 3
♡ K J 10 8 6
◇ 9 4
♣ 6 5

EAST
♠ Q J 7
♡ Q 7 4 2
◇ 7 6 3
♣ K 10 4

SOUTH
♠ 2
♡ A 5 3
◇ A 8 5
♣ A Q 9 7 3 2

WEST	NORTH	EAST	SOUTH
Reese	Becker	Schapiro	Hayden
		pass	1♣
1NT	dbl	pass	pass
2◇	2♠	pass	3♣
pass	3◇	pass	3♡
pass	4◇	pass	5♣
pass	6♣	all pass	

ARGUMENT

The strange one notrump overcall is only partly explained in that Reese and Schapiro were using the Gardener notrump overcall, a device used by a few English experts. It is used by English players when holding a hand that in America would be suitable for a preemptive jump overcall: a good six-card suit or a seven-card suit with little or no side strength. The one notrump overcall becomes a two-way bid. It may be a natural strong notrump hand or a weak hand with a long concealed suit. The responder can if he wishes bid two clubs to ask the overcaller to clarify the situation. West's use of the bid in this situation is certainly farfetched, holding a suit of only five cards and a multitude of losers.

Reese admits that "of course some slight risk attaches to the overcall," which is an example of masterly British understatement. The risk is considerable. A frequent result of the overcall will be a doubled partscore by East-West and a loss of

500 or 700 points. This can be demonstrated quite easily by dealing out a series of hands in which South has an opening bid and East does not. With the actual hand, even with the heart fit, the penalty would have been 500. In the event of a misfit things would have been far worse. It is true of course that North-South may have a slam, but in that event they can ignore the psychic and bid the slam anyway, as they in fact did.

Frivolous tactical bids are almost always based on a favorable vulnerability situation, but here North-South were not vulnerable. As it is, the bidding strongly points to illicit knowledge of the heart suit. If West knows that his partner has four hearts the prospects of the one notrump bid greatly improve, the danger of a heavy penalty diminishes, and the chance that the opponents can make a slam increases.

Reese claimed that because he was playing against Becker and Mrs. Hayden for the first time "it was natural that I should attempt a diversion." The logic of this remark is difficult to see; one might think that a player in a crucial international match would concentrate on playing a sound and careful game when his team held a small lead. No other players in Buenos Aires showed the slightest inclination to attempt a risky diversion. But that may not be the same thing as a diversion.

ANSWER

Every psychic or tactical bid involves a risk. The weak notrump, for example, may cost 800 and occasionally 1100 at unfavorable vulnerability. Those who play it believe, however, that it shows a profit on balance. The same applies to the Gardener notrump overcall. As used by Gardener and Rose, it is of the nuisance type not less than two-thirds of the time. The point-count rarely exceeds 5 or 6, and there is usually, though not always, a six-card escape suit. Give Reese the deuce of hearts and his hand would qualify as a textbook example of the Gardener notrump overcall.

Not every hand, however, can come up to the classical requirements. Here the bid was shaded, but it is sound tactics to confuse the opponents at the beginning of the match and hardly surprising that Reese should be willing to take an extra risk. As with preempts, sabotage bids may lead to a loss on any given board, but there is often a profit in the end.

Italy 25
East-West vulnerable.

NORTH
♠ Q 8 4
♡ J 10 4
♦ K Q 5 2
♣ J 6 5

WEST
♠ A K J 10 2
♡ Q 9 7 2
♦ 7 6
♣ 4 3

```
      N
  W       E
      S
```

EAST
♠ 9 7 6
♡ A 8 6 5
♦ A J 9
♣ A 9 7

SOUTH
♠ 5 3
♡ K 3
♦ 10 8 4 3
♣ K Q 10 8 2

WEST	NORTH	EAST	SOUTH
Reese	Forquet	Schapiro	Garozzo
	pass	1♣	pass
1♠	pass	1NT	pass
2NT	pass	3♡	pass
4♡	all pass		

ARGUMENT

East's three-heart bid is quite outside my experience, and I do not believe a parallel could be found anywhere in the records of major matches.

The second-round raise to two notrump in principle requires East to pass or to continue to three notrump. As his hand is a minimum for a vulnerable opening, a pass would seem automatic. It is true that vulnerable games should be bid slightly more often at International Match Points than in rubber bridge. (The possible-gain/possible-loss ratio is 10-6, not 11-6 as Reese states, and game should be bid with a 37 per cent chance. The equivalent figure in rubber bridge is 49 per cent.) But this consideration is known also to West, who could have bid three notrump directly over one notrump if he felt he had the slightest excuse for doing so.

If East does decide to be an optimist, his normal course would be to continue to three notrump. His alternative, quite a possible one with his actual hand, is to bid three spades. This shows three-card spade support and offers West a choice between spades and notrump.

A sensible expert interpretation of three hearts would be: "I have strength, but not necessarily length, in hearts, but I am worried about diamonds for notrump purposes." Yet Reese states sweepingly: "Once East decides to bid on, three hearts is clearly best." He explains that this bid may lead to four spades, because West is given the opportunity to bid three spades.

But for this purpose the devious bid of three hearts is clearly worse than the normal bid of three spades because it gives more away to the opposition without any compensating advantage. The three-heart bid decreases the chance of an opening heart lead and increases the chance of an opening club lead if the final contract is three notrump. The only conceivable advantage of bidding three hearts is that a last-minute heart fit may be uncovered, a possibility that is most unlikely to occur to East without illicit knowledge.

West's raise to two notrump is as significant as East's three-heart bid although not as spectacular. He has three choices: two hearts or three hearts, which describe the distribution but are respectively an underbid and an overbid, or two notrump, which describes the strength at the cost of concealing the distribution from partner and perhaps missing a heart fit.

Reese says that West "would surely favor two hearts if he knew that his partner held four," a highly disingenuous comment. As two hearts is an unconstructive action that may be based on a hand with only 5 or 6 high-card points, West can expect that two hearts will end the auction if his partner has four cards in the suit. Two notrump, on the other hand, gives him the best of both worlds: he can show his strength and invite game in the knowledge that his partner can back into the heart suit if he so desires.

ANSWER

Should Schapiro pass two notrump? With three aces and good middle cards he is clearly worth more than 13 points, and he knows that in the other room the aggressive Italians are not likely to hold back. The decision may be a close one, but the Italians did, in fact, bid four hearts without causing a scandal. Schapiro cannot be crimed, therefore, for bidding on.

What should be his bid? If he calls three notrump the auction comes to an end. If he bids three spades, Reese can call four spades with a five-card suit and three notrump with four spades only. Since this allows two chances and costs nothing, three spades is twice as good as three notrump.

Now consider three hearts. Reese can still bid three spades if he has five spades. If he has not he can still bid three notrump. But he may have four hearts — it is not against the rules — and if so he can bid four hearts. There are now three chances where before there existed one and two respectively. Schapiro's three hearts is, therefore, three times as good as three notrump and half again as good as three spades. And it costs nothing, for partner knows on the bidding that he cannot have more than four hearts.

Turn to Reese. If he knows that Schapiro has four hearts, his rebid should surely be two hearts, not two notrump. This shows five spades by inference but does not pinpoint the high-card strength. The hand might be a weak two-suiter, but it need not be particularly weak, for Reese would not want to bid three hearts with less than 12 points or the equivalent in distribution. Whether two notrump or two hearts is the better bid may be open to question, but Reese's choice of the former suggests that he had no illicit knowledge of Schapiro's four hearts.

The accusers should answer this question: How should Reese and Schapiro reach four hearts? Or is the contract itself evidence of cheating[2]?

Italy 35
East-West vulnerable.

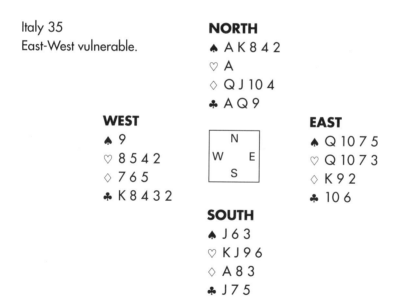

NORTH
♠ A K 8 4 2
♡ A
◇ Q J 10 4
♣ A Q 9

WEST
♠ 9
♡ 8 5 4 2
◇ 7 6 5
♣ K 8 4 3 2

EAST
♠ Q 10 7 5
♡ Q 10 7 3
◇ K 9 2
♣ 10 6

SOUTH
♠ J 6 3
♡ K J 9 6
◇ A 8 3
♣ J 7 5

2. Since he asks I will answer. Reese and Schapiro should miss the borderline contract of four hearts, as most pairs would when using standard methods after the bidding starts one club, one spade, one notrump. It takes an overbid of three hearts by West on the second round to get there honestly. — A.T.

WEST	NORTH	EAST	SOUTH
Forquet	Schapiro	Garozzo	Reese
			pass
pass	1♠	pass	1NT
pass	3NT	all pass	

ARGUMENT

The raise to three notrump is an astonishing bid for a player of international class. From his angle there is not the slightest reason why his partner should not have a hand such as:

$$♠ x x \quad ♡ x x x \quad ◇ K x x x x \quad ♣ K x x$$

With this combination of cards North-South would make six diamonds quite easily but would fail in three notrump after the expected heart lead.

And there are many other hands that South could hold on which the final contract should be four spades or five diamonds, and some on which five clubs or six clubs would be appropriate. Three diamonds leaves open all doors, but three notrump closes them firmly. The chance that three notrump will be the right contract is greatly increased if North knows that his partner has four hearts, and by concealing his distribution he makes it harder for the defenders to find the right opening lead.

The defense admitted that three notrump was an inferior rebid, and Schapiro's explanation was that he bid too quickly — somewhat unlikely in a stock situation that is familiar to all experienced players. The defense pointed out that knowledge of the heart suit would help North to judge the later bidding if he chose the normal bid of three diamonds. While this is no doubt true, it does not seem particularly relevant.

ANSWER

Undoubtedly Schapiro made a poor bid, but what bearing has that on the cheating charges? Give Reese a fourth x in hearts (instead of the third x in clubs) in the example shown, and six diamonds is just as good and three notrump almost as bad, as before. Likewise, despite four hearts in the South hand, four spades might be a far superior contract to three notrump. Conversely, three notrump might be best if South's hearts are K-Q-x or K-J-x or even K-x.

Surely this hand shows nothing either way.

Argentina 30
Neither vulnerable.

NORTH
♠ 9 5 4
♡ A 8 6 5
◇ A 5 4
♣ Q 10 2

WEST
♠ A Q J 7
♡ Q 10 7 4 3
◇ 10 6
♣ K 9

```
      N
  W       E
      S
```

EAST
♠ 10 8 3 2
♡ K 9
◇ Q J 7
♣ A 8 4 3

SOUTH
♠ K 6
♡ J 2
◇ K 9 8 3 2
♣ J 7 6 5

WEST	NORTH	EAST	SOUTH
Rocchi	Schapiro	Attaguile	Reese
		pass	pass
1♠	pass	3♠	pass
4♠	all pass		

ARGUMENT

Schapiro led the heart five, and when West won with the heart queen he played a second heart immediately, no doubt assuming that South held the ace. South got two overruffs — it need have been only one — and beat the contract two tricks.

Reese introduced his defense of Schapiro's astonishing lead with a helpful generalization: "The choice is basically between a trump and one of the plain suits." (One sees that this would not apply if the opening leader were void in trumps.) But players in a world championship are concerned with accurate judgments rather than platitudes, and the defense was virtually limited to a claim that the heart lead "is at least as good as anything else."

If you show this hand to an independent expert — and I have tried this test repeatedly — the choice of lead is almost invariably a trump. If pressed to select another suit, the choice is a club. If pressed further — and most players have to be pressed very hard at this point — the selection is a low diamond. A heart comes far at the bottom of the list, because it offers the greatest risk of losing a trick without compensating gain. But the risk becomes slight if partner is known to have a doubleton heart.

If North does decide, for some strange reason, to underlead an ace, the diamond suit is clearly a better choice than a heart. The greater length in hearts increases the chance that a heart trick will be lost permanently. Another danger of an underlead is that partner will not expect it and may misdefend in consequence — as might have happened here if North had underled his diamond ace. Curiously enough, the British team discussed this precise point en route to Buenos Aires and reached a firm agreement: in no circumstances would any player underlead an ace against a suit contract. Schapiro's memory was not as good as Reese's, but one would have expected him to be able to remember this on the second day of the tournament.

The later play was also significant. West won the first trick with the heart queen over South's jack and led the heart three. Schapiro won and led the heart eight, a play that would have been a losing one if South had held one more heart and the declarer one fewer.

ANSWER

Underleading aces is always unorthodox and sometimes spectacular, but it has been done so often it has became a very ordinary piece of brilliance.

Feeling, perhaps, that a passive lead would give declarer time to develop a side suit — diamonds were rather more likely than hearts since he himself was longer in the major — Schapiro took the risk of leading away from an ace. Declarer played none too well and went down, but the lead in itself was surely not sensational.

In the same championship, Belladonna led away from an ace (the jack from ace-queen-jack against a three-spade contract by Leventritt on Italy v. U.S. Board 36). In his Win at Bridge with Jacoby and Son, Oswald Jacoby recalls leading away from an ace against Ely Culbertson and thereby presenting him with a hopeless slam. Ely himself brought off a coup in a national championship when he sat West with:

♠ A J 6 5 3 2   ♡ A J 10   ♢ 7 5   ♣ A 2

He had opened the bidding with one spade, North had overcalled two clubs, and after a pass from East, South bid three notrump. Culbertson hit on the jack of hearts (yes, hearts!), found partner with Q-9-7-4-2, and beat the contract, which was easily made in the other room.

In a key match against Venezuela at the 1966 South American championships, Zumaran of Uruguay underled an ace against a slam with devastating effect. Two days later Brazil's Amaral played a slam on the assumption that the opening lead was from an ace. With K-x in dummy and J-x in hand he went up with the king at Trick 1! None of these plays gave rise to accusations of cheating. Why then make an exception in the case of Reese and Schapiro?[3]

Italy 48 (hands transposed to make South declarer)
North-South vulnerable.

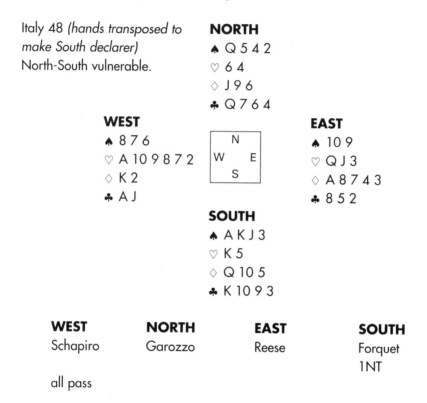

NORTH
♠ Q 5 4 2
♡ 6 4
◇ J 9 6
♣ Q 7 6 4

WEST
♠ 8 7 6
♡ A 10 9 8 7 2
◇ K 2
♣ A J

EAST
♠ 10 9
♡ Q J 3
◇ A 8 7 4 3
♣ 8 5 2

SOUTH
♠ A K J 3
♡ K 5
◇ Q 10 5
♣ K 10 9 3

WEST	NORTH	EAST	SOUTH
Schapiro	Garozzo	Reese	Forquet
			1NT
all pass			

ARGUMENT

West led the heart ten, and East overtook with the jack. South won with the king, and cashed four rounds of spades, ending in the dummy. East discarded the seven and three of diamonds, and West threw the club jack. A club was led to the king, and when West won with the ace the position was this:

---

3. Because the examples are not comparable. The underlead of an ace against a suit contract is indicated when the bidding has marked dummy with the king of the suit and defensive prospects seem poor. Neither factor applied to Schapiro's lead, but it did in the other examples quoted. Culbertson's effort was imaginative, but there is nothing unusual in underleading an ace against notrump. — A.T.

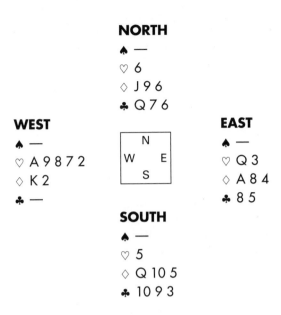

NORTH
♠ —
♡ 6
♢ J 9 6
♣ Q 7 6

WEST
♠ —
♡ A 9 8 7 2
♢ K 2
♣ —

EAST
♠ —
♡ Q 3
♢ A 8 4
♣ 8 5

SOUTH
♠ —
♡ 5
♢ Q 10 5
♣ 10 9 3

East had played high-low in diamonds, so the one card about which West could be completely certain was the diamond ace. He therefore had a completely automatic play of the diamond two, knowing that his partner would return a heart permitting him to claim the remaining tricks. Instead Schapiro laid down the heart ace, which is explicable only if he knew that the declarer had begun with a doubleton heart, and that the queen would fall if South held it.

Reese offers an elaborate chain of reasoning by which Schapiro could have calculated that his partner held the heart queen. It depends on an advanced inference, that East would not discard two diamonds if he held the queen as well as the ace, and on a very careful count of the declarer's points.

But he does not explain why his partner should reject a highly obvious play in favor of one that requires considerable inference and calculation, relies on the accuracy of the opposing bidding (for South might have had 18 points instead of his normal maximum of 17), and loads East unnecessarily with an unblocking duty.

ANSWER

Since Schapiro knew that Reese had the ace of diamonds — and this is not in dispute — he needed no signal to make five heart tricks. He could do that anyway. Perhaps his reasons for playing as he did were complex and devious. Perhaps he was too hasty in drawing inferences from declarer's dummy play. Perhaps he just played badly. But why assume that he made use of a signal that would have been, at best, of academic interest to him?

Turn to Reese. If he knew that Schapiro had six hearts, why did he not make things easy for him by throwing his queen on the last spade? It would have been a good play in any event, for by then Schapiro had parted with the jack of clubs and it was clear that he had at least five hearts. Reese no longer needed the queen, which was, if anything, an encumbrance.

Both Reese and Schapiro might have played differently, and the same reflection could doubtless be made about many players on many hands. But where does cheating come into the picture?

Argentina 131
East-West vulnerable.

NORTH
♠ A Q 4 3
♡ K 10 3
◇ K 10
♣ A K 10 5

WEST
♠ 10 7 6
♡ —
◇ A 9 6 4 3 2
♣ Q 7 4 3

	N	
W		E
	S	

EAST
♠ K J 5
♡ A Q J 6
◇ Q 8 7
♣ J 6 2

SOUTH
♠ 9 8 2
♡ 9 8 7 5 4 2
◇ J 5
♣ 9 8

WEST	NORTH	EAST	SOUTH
Reese	Berisso	Schapiro	Lerner
			pass
pass	1♣	pass	pass
1◇	dbl	pass	1♡
pass	pass	1NT	2♡
pass	pass	2NT	pass
pass	dbl	all pass	

ARGUMENT

West's balancing bid of one diamond was quite remarkable. Any expert not blessed with second sight would pass without hesitation, for several reasons.

First, the odds are that North-South have the balance of power.

Second, East is marked with a fair hand and did not overcall. So he is most unlikely to have more than four hearts and may have fewer. North-South are therefore marked with nine or ten hearts between them and may easily have a lay-down game in that denomination.

Third, it is clear that North-South are in a poor contract and perhaps in a terrible one. East's failure to make a takeout double suggests that he has a few clubs, so North may have only four or five trumps in the combined hands in a club contract instead of nine or ten in a heart contract.

Reese dismisses this hand airily by saying: "West's reopening is natural enough, especially near the end of a match which we were winning by about 200 match points." Which being interpreted means: "I agree I made a bad bid, but we were winning the match and I wasn't bothering." The contention that the British team was not bothering in this final session against Argentina is disposed of elsewhere (see page 158). Certainly the score in the session (68-3 in favor of Britain) does not suggest a team that was not bothering.

ANSWER

Whether Reese's balancing bid is good or bad, it surely has nothing to do with the very ordinary distribution of the heart suit. Since the Argentinians stopped in one club, why should Reese expect them to have a game in hearts — in face of the worst possible trump break? If, in fact, the hand belongs to North-South, spades, not hearts, must look to West to be the dangerous suit. At least, if North and South have eight or nine between them there will be a tolerable split in trumps.

Look at the hearts once more. With a void himself, Reese would tend to place Schapiro with four, his fair share of the suit. Since that was precisely his holding, why should an illicit signal, confirming normal expectancy, cause Reese to do something "quite remarkable"? Why should it cause him to do anything at all?

Surely, if Reese made a risky or lighthearted bid, it was because he could well afford it. Victory for the British, by an overwhelming margin, was assured before the last session began. Higher mathematics apart, there was therefore no need to fight grimly for every match point[4] — and no incentive whatsoever to cheat.

---

4. But see page 158. — A.T

The following eight hands were chosen by Victor Mollo as proof that Reese and Schapiro did not have knowledge of the heart suit. The answers for the prosecution are by the author.

Italy 126
Neither vulnerable.

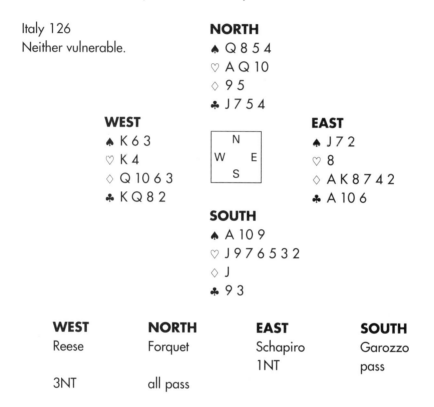

NORTH
♠ Q 8 5 4
♡ A Q 10
◇ 9 5
♣ J 7 5 4

WEST
♠ K 6 3
♡ K 4
◇ Q 10 6 3
♣ K Q 8 2

EAST
♠ J 7 2
♡ 8
◇ A K 8 7 4 2
♣ A 10 6

SOUTH
♠ A 10 9
♡ J 9 7 6 5 3 2
◇ J
♣ 9 3

WEST	NORTH	EAST	SOUTH
Reese	Forquet	Schapiro	Garozzo
		1NT	pass
3NT	all pass		

ARGUMENT

Garozzo opened the deuce of hearts, and the Italians reeled off seven hearts before taking the ace of spades — hardly a good advertisement for illicit heart signals.

Tactical bids are necessarily speculative, but had Schapiro known that Reese had two hearts only, he would not have embarked on this particular speculation. With ten hearts between them the Italians were almost certain to open the suit, wrecking any notrump contract from the start. On the other hand, with three probable tricks in defense, Schapiro had no reason to suppose that the Italians held the balance of power. Why then did he land in an absurd contract that cost Britain 330 points — four down in one room against four diamonds made (130) in the other? What went wrong? There can be but one explanation: Schapiro had no idea that Reese had a doubleton heart. A simple signal would have put him wise, but clearly there was no signal.

ANSWER

This deal would have been a "good advertisement" for illicit signals if South had held the heart ace, which was a 50 per cent chance.

If East knows that his partner has a doubleton heart, the chance is very slight (about one in seven) that the doubleton consists of the king and a card below the queen. Even in that case, and in the very remote chance of an ace-queen doubleton, there is an even chance that it will not matter which hand becomes the declarer in notrump.

By opening one notrump East has a very good chance of shutting the opponents out of their heart fit; as it was, North-South could have made nine tricks in hearts with little high-card strength but were unable to enter the bidding. South will often have a hand on which he can bid one heart after the normal opening of one diamond, but cannot afford to bid at the two-level as there is a greatly increased risk of a penalty double. From East's angle, the chance of preventing North from bidding hearts is also improved by bidding one notrump. West may be able to respond in spades, crowding the bidding further.

This deal could very well have been quoted by the prosecution, because the opening bid of one notrump is quite extraordinary. In any system, a player whose partner opens the bidding with one notrump is entitled to proceed on the assumption that his partner has at least a doubleton in each suit. This is one aspect of the game in which experts are completely rigid in their bidding. In the whole recorded history of the World Championship, from 1953 to 1965, there are only three other cases of opening notrump bids that included a singleton. It is noteworthy that two of the others were by Reese and Schapiro — and in both cases the singleton was a heart. (See pp. 169-171.)

U.S.A. 68
Both vulnerable.

NORTH
♠ 9 3
♡ J 10 8 7 5 4 2
◇ J 8
♣ 10 3

WEST
♠ 6 4
♡ A K 6
◇ 7 5 4 3 2
♣ A K Q

```
    N
W       E
    S
```

EAST
♠ A K 10 8 5 2
♡ —
◇ A 10 9 6
♣ J 9 6

SOUTH
♠ Q J 7
♡ Q 9 3
◇ K Q
♣ 8 7 5 4 2

WEST	NORTH	EAST	SOUTH
Reese	Becker	Schapiro	Hayden
1♣	pass	2♠	pass
3NT	pass	4♠	pass
5♡	pass	5♠	all pass

The diamond king was led, and eleven tricks were made.

ARGUMENT

After his three notrump jump rebid, Reese can have little more to say. He is under no compulsion to bid on, and if he calls five hearts, as a slam try, it can be only because he attaches special importance to his top cards and two controls. Yet one of these controls and 7 of his 16 points face a void. Does Reese know it? Surely not, for duplication of values is always a liability, and to treat it as a slam-going asset would be an affront to the laws of bridge gravity.

The five-heart cuebid carries within itself a further contradiction. It invites a slam and simultaneously deters partner from bidding it, by warning him of duplication in hearts. Intending to accelerate, Reese deliberately applies the brake. It is clear that had Reese known about Schapiro's void in hearts, he would have passed four spades, and had he intended to encourage Schapiro he would have found some other trial bid.

The five-heart bid shows, therefore, that Reese knew nothing of the void, that there was no heart signal and no cheating.

ANSWER

The two-spade jump shift was superlight even by English standards, and one might have expected West to drive the bidding to slam. It would certainly have been excessively cowardly to pass four spades. It is true that he had shown about 15 points by his second-round jump to three notrump, but that bid was far from doing justice to the slam potential of the hand. East could not expect his partner to furnish five cast-iron tricks.

Five hearts seems to be the natural move toward a slam whether or not West has illicit knowledge. If he knows about the void, his three notrump bid has already shown a double heart stopper and given warning of duplication. The subsequent five-heart cuebid indicates that the heart strength will not be wasted but will furnish discards. East would have been able to bid six spades if he had held the spade queen instead of the ten.

The opening bid of one club was distinctly eccentric and makes it most unlikely that East-West will ever be able to reach a diamond contract. (As it was, they could have made six diamonds with a lucky two-two break.) The one-club bid makes more sense if West has illicit knowledge that his opponents have ten hearts. If North becomes the declarer in a heart contract and East has a weak hand, a club lead may be vital and a diamond lead disastrous. And West can reason that he and his partner can survive the hazards of the one-club bid because they start with some distributional information.

U.S.A. 36
Both vulnerable.

NORTH
- ♠ 10 7 2
- ♡ K 8 4
- ◇ A 8 6 4
- ♣ 9 8 5

WEST
- ♠ 4
- ♡ J 6 5 3 2
- ◇ Q 5
- ♣ K Q J 10 4

```
    N
W       E
    S
```

EAST
- ♠ K Q J 9
- ♡ A 10 9 7
- ◇ J 10 9 7 3
- ♣ —

SOUTH
- ♠ A 8 6 5 3
- ♡ Q
- ◇ K 2
- ♣ A 7 6 3 2

WEST	NORTH	EAST	SOUTH
Reese	Becker	Schapiro	Hayden
pass	pass	1♠	pass
1NT	pass	2♡	pass
4♡	all pass		

Lead: ♣A. Score: 100 to North America.

ARGUMENT

Both Schapiro and Schenken opened one spade on the East hand, but many good judges would prefer one heart. Partner could show a four-card spade suit at the one-level or support hearts on a weak hand. The reverse does not apply over one spade, and the red major might be lost altogether.

Admittedly, when he opens one spade, East intends to rebid two hearts, but he may not get the opportunity. With something like:

$$♠ A 10 x \quad ♡ K x x x x \quad ◇ x \quad ♣ J x x x$$

West would raise one spade to two spades and the hand would be played in a partscore. Yet he would be worth three hearts over one heart — an Acol limit raise — and four hearts would be an easy make. In fact, twelve tricks might be there.

Whatever advantage the one-spade opening may have over one heart, it obviously has nothing to commend it if East knows that West has five (or four) hearts. Why, then, if Schapiro received the appropriate signal did he make so inappropriate a bid?

Turn to Reese. If he knows that Schapiro has four hearts why should he make the unnatural response of one notrump? What can he hope to gain by it? Why does he not call two hearts as Leventritt did in the other room? For all Reese knows, North may preempt in diamonds and partner, who could be 4-4-2-3, would have no chance to mention hearts.

What is one to think of heart signals that make it hard to reach so simple a contract in hearts? Is it not apparent that had there really been signals, Schapiro would have opened one heart, not one spade, and Reese would have responded with two hearts, not one notrump?

Curiously enough, this was one of the few exhibits put before the W.B.F. at the outset of the Buenos Aires affair.

ANSWER

This hand was quoted by the prosecution, not the defense, in the London Inquiry. East's rebid of two hearts was distinctly odd and suggested special knowledge. Two diamonds was the natural action, making it possible for the partnership to play in any of the three suits at the level of two.

Without special knowledge, the continued concealment of East's longest suit could easily have led the partnership into the wrong partscore. If West had held three hearts, with a singleton or doubleton in spades, East would regret not bidding his diamonds. And it makes no sense to say that East will show diamonds on the next round, because there is unlikely to be a next round. A two-spade preference bid is possible although not likely, but in that event three diamonds would be construed as a forward-going bid.

It is not in the least difficult to see why East would bid one spade rather than one heart, knowing that West held five cards in the suit.

First, East was in third seat with an 11-point hand, and in such circumstances the opponents are likely to have the balance of power. The lead-directing quality of the bid becomes an important consideration, and in this case East certainly wants a spade lead.

Second, the spade bid may help West to make the right decision on a later round. As it was, Reese eventually had a close decision. With no aces, no high trump honors, and the knowledge of spade strength opposite him he could have contented himself with three hearts and made a profit thereby.

The risk of failing to reach a heart contract as a result of the one-spade bid was completely negligible. Even if West had held the precise hand suggested by the defense, with three spades and five hearts, one of two things would no doubt have happened. Either North-South would have entered the bidding — by no means unlikely with nine clubs between them and more than half the deck in high cards —allowing East-West to alight in hearts eventually; or West would have responded two hearts and been blessed by a "little bit of luck."

West was not running the slightest risk of missing the heart fit by responding one notrump. East's failure to open one heart clearly indicated that he was in a position to bid hearts on the second round. With a 4-4-3-2 hand, the opening bid would surely have been one heart.

The suggestion that "North may preempt in diamonds" after the one notrump response is totally unrealistic. North is vulnerable and passed originally. He could not open with a weak two-bid, so there is not the slightest chance that he can make a preemptive jump the second time round.

U.S.A. 76
North-South vulnerable.

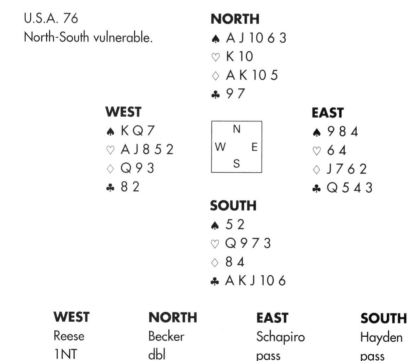

NORTH
♠ A J 10 6 3
♡ K 10
◇ A K 10 5
♣ 9 7

WEST
♠ K Q 7
♡ A J 8 5 2
◇ Q 9 3
♣ 8 2

EAST
♠ 9 8 4
♡ 6 4
◇ J 7 6 2
♣ Q 5 4 3

SOUTH
♠ 5 2
♡ Q 9 7 3
◇ 8 4
♣ A K J 10 6

WEST	NORTH	EAST	SOUTH
Reese	Becker	Schapiro	Hayden
1NT	dbl	pass	pass
2♡	pass	pass	dbl
all pass			

North led the ◇ K. Score: 900 to North America.

ARGUMENT

Reese's rescue attempt into two hearts is incomprehensible — if he knew that Schapiro had a doubleton. The normal expectation would be to find Schapiro with three hearts, and if so, Reese could hope to make two tricks more in hearts than in notrump and maybe even to escape a double. Neither prospect would be a likely one if Schapiro had two hearts only. Reese could not have fared worse in one notrump than he did in two hearts, and he would surely have done better in two diamonds.

It was not to be expected that Schapiro would turn up with a five-card suit, for he would have shown it over Becker's double of one notrump, but if he had a doubleton heart he could not fail to have two four-card suits. Why, then, did not Reese send out an S.O.S. redouble for one of them? Better still, why did he not call two clubs, wait for the inevitable double and then redouble, calling on partner to choose between diamonds and spades?

Had Reese been aware of the heart situation he would doubtless have explored one or other of these possibilities. Or else he might have stayed in one notrump, keeping his hearts concealed. He chose instead to bid two hearts at a cost of 900. Should this be put down to bad luck? Or is this just the sort of bad luck that the alleged signals were expressly designed to prevent, at any rate in hearts? And if this is so, should one not conclude that there were no heart signals?

ANSWER

It does not appear that West lost anything by retreating from one notrump doubled, which would also have cost 900. With a five-two trump fit he could expect to make at least one trick more in the suit contract.

It is quite true that with knowledge of the heart suit West can place his partner with some 4-4-3-2 distribution. It is therefore clear to him that the partnership hands do not have more than seven cards in any suit and hearts should be as good as anything. Two diamonds would probably have played one trick better than hearts turned out to do, but that was unforeseeable.

So the elaborate self-rescuing operation suggested for West, beginning with two clubs, could not have given East anything better than the seven-card fit he got as it was. And there were two very good reasons for not treading such devious paths.

The bidding sequence to reach two diamonds doubled on the actual hand would take East-West far beyond the limits of "tolerance," a factor that Reese would not be disposed to disregard. Suppose the bidding had gone:

WEST	NORTH	EAST	SOUTH
1NT	dbl	pass	pass
2♣	pass	pass	dbl
redbl	pass	2◊	pass
pass	dbl	all pass	

The players and the press would regard West's bidding with incredulity. East's bidding would be entirely consistent with a 3-3-3-4 distribution, in which case the partnership would be playing in a 3-3 fit instead of a 5-3 fit. West's bidding would be a complete giveaway to any subsequent inquiry into the honesty of their methods.

The second consideration is far more important. The immediate bid of two hearts gives West by far his best chance of escaping a heavy penalty. If the North-South hearts had been divided 3-3, neither player would have felt inclined to double. If West retreats to two clubs and then redoubles, he makes it quite clear to the opposition that his side is in trouble, and North-South will have no difficulty in doubling everything thereafter.

Italy 55
Both vulnerable.

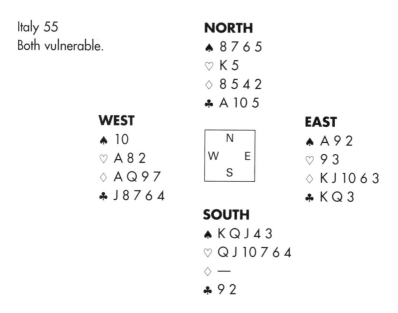

NORTH
♠ 8 7 6 5
♡ K 5
◊ 8 5 4 2
♣ A 10 5

WEST
♠ 10
♡ A 8 2
◊ A Q 9 7
♣ J 8 7 6 4

EAST
♠ A 9 2
♡ 9 3
◊ K J 10 6 3
♣ K Q 3

SOUTH
♠ K Q J 4 3
♡ Q J 10 7 6 4
◊ —
♣ 9 2

WEST	NORTH	EAST	SOUTH
Reese	Forquet	Schapiro	Garozzo
			1♠
pass	2♠	pass	4♠
all pass			

Both Souths, Garozzo and Harrison-Gray, opened one spade, but whereas Avarelli doubled on the West hand, Reese passed. The American Contract Bridge League booklet on the World Championship comments: "West (Reese) might have been more inclined to make a vulnerable takeout double if he had possessed a fourth heart."

Precisely — but not if Reese and Schapiro were using the illicit signals attributed to them, for then Reese would have known that Schapiro could not bid hearts anyway, and in that case, he did not need a fourth heart himself.

Schapiro, too, might have shown more enterprise, but evidently, the same consideration — concern for the hearts — held him back. On the bidding, Reese was marked with one or two spades only and also with something in the way of high cards, since both Garozzo and Forquet, playing Neapolitan, had made strictly limited bids. Schapiro had excellent support for both minors, but he feared to double in case Reese responded in hearts. A three-fingers/three-hearts signal would have set his mind at rest, for if Reese had three hearts, he would have eight or nine cards in clubs and diamonds, a situation tailormade for the "unusual notrump" by Schapiro. In the event, knowing nothing about the hearts, Schapiro passed, and the Italians sailed unopposed into four spades to score 620.

In the other room Avarelli and Belladonna bid up to six diamonds on the East-West cards and very nearly made it. Dummy lost the slam by playing low, automatically, to a club and blocking the suit on the table before the declarer could stop him. But for this curious lapse, Board 55 would have led to the biggest swing in the World Championship, a vulnerable game to the Italians in one room, a vulnerable slam in the other. As it was, despite dummy's help, the British lost 520 (11 IMPs).

Would Reese and Schapiro have allowed themselves to be crowded out of the auction so easily had each player, in turn, known that the other was short in hearts and long, therefore, in the minors? If they cheated, could they possibly have cheated so badly?

ANSWER

This deal is well designed to show the superiority of Italian bidding methods but has little bearing on the subject of illicit signaling.

With the West hand, Avarelli was able to double the opening bid of one spade because the Roman System he used had a unique approach to defensive bidding. Takeout doubles had a maximum of 16 points, but the doubler's hand was not well defined distributionally.

In England and America the West hand was below the standards of the time for a vulnerable takeout double. Experts tend to make marginal doubles with borderline hands containing four hearts because they are afraid of being talked out of a heart game. Reese had no reason to fear being talked out of the heart suit. With illicit knowledge, one would expect a takeout double with this hand if East held five hearts, not two.

West, of course, could not know that his side had any fit in the minor suits because he could not immediately infer anything about his partner's spade length. It is unsound in principle, especially at IMP scoring when vulnerable, to fight the spade suit with the minors. Although it worked out badly here, the normal action for West, with or without signals, is to pass and let North-South get on with it.

It is difficult to imagine that any good player would even consider any action with the East hand after one spade has been raised to two — with or without knowledge of the heart suit. He has a defensive hand, he is vulnerable, and he would be committed to the three-level. Two notrump by East would be a very unusual "unusual notrump" indeed. It would normally show at least five cards in both minor suits, so East's five-three distribution can hardly be called "tailor-made."

The arguments put forward to justify intervention by East suggest some lack of knowledge of the Neapolitan system. East does not know that his partner has at most two spades, for the opening bid of one spade is often made on a four-card suit and is often raised with three trumps. Nor is the limitation on the strength of the North-South hands any great comfort to East. South can have 16 points for his bid, and North could have 10, which would leave West with one. So if East launched into the auction over two spades he could find himself in three diamonds doubled opposite a dummy consisting of one jack and a 3-3-3-4 distribution. He might have some difficulty in explaining the resulting penalty of 1100 or 1400 to his teammates.

Argentina 141
North-South were vulnerable.

NORTH
♠ A Q 7 5
♡ Q 10 2
◇ A 4
♣ A K 3 2

WEST
♠ K 9 3
♡ A J 9 8 6
◇ J 10 6 5
♣ 5

EAST
♠ J 8
♡ K 7 5 4 3
◇ K Q 8 7
♣ 9 8

```
      N
  W       E
      S
```

SOUTH
♠ 10 6 4 2
♡ —
◇ 9 3 2
♣ Q J 10 7 6 4

WEST	NORTH	EAST	SOUTH
Reese	Berisso	Schapiro	Lerner
	1♣	pass	4♣
pass	4◇	pass	5♣
all pass			

The heart four was led. 600 to Argentina.

ARGUMENT

In both rooms, North opened one club, but whereas Attaguile, Argentina's East, over-called with one heart, Schapiro passed. Neither player can be criticized, for it is a bor-derline case, but had Schapiro known that Reese had five hearts, would not that have made all the difference? What would he have risked then by calling one heart? What could he hope to gain by passing?

The Argentinians bid up to three hearts without arousing the least suspicion. The British passed throughout, missing a possible sacrifice in five hearts. At favorable vul-nerability, it would have been worth 300.

Surely Schapiro's pass, understandable in itself, ceases to be so after a heart sig-nal. And if Reese and Schapiro used illicit signals at all, it is reasonable to suppose that they would have made use of them in a marginal situation like this one. The fact that they did not, speaks for itself.

ANSWER

Some players would overcall with the East hand, but the majority, probably, would pass. Reese's published recommendations in this area clearly indicate that he would favor a pass. In *Blueprint for Bidding*, coauthored by Albert Dormer, which is probably the most authoritative work on British bidding methods, he indicates that a non-vulnerable overcall should normally be made only when there is a good expectation of buying the contract for a plus score, or effectively penalizing the opponents. In other words, you should have reason to think that the hand "belongs" to your side.

East's hand does not meet this standard, nor does it qualify under any of the three exceptional cases that Reese suggests: good prospects of a sacrifice (which would apply up to a point if East's major suits were reversed); a strong desire to direct an opening lead; or a wish to crowd the opponents' bidding, which would also apply to a one-spade overcall of one club.

It seems a little farfetched to claim that East must be innocent of cheating because he follows the normal methods of his partnership on this deal. It is quite true that knowledge of the five-five heart fit would increase the chance of a profitable save, but Schapiro might have reasoned that his partner would have a chance to introduce the heart suit. He had no reason, of course, to suppose that the bidding was going to reach the four-level so quickly: South's preemptive jump was a highly improbable development from East's angle. Alternatively, Schapiro may not have reasoned much at all. This deal was played about 1 A.M. at the end of the eighth day of an exhausting tournament, so perhaps he "bid too quickly," which was his own explanation of his action on Italy 35 (see page 211).

Even if East-West could see each other's hands, they probably would not choose to save in five hearts over five clubs. The defense may well take three tricks against five clubs, in which case five hearts would be an expensive phantom. Five clubs reached by the hit-and-miss methods adopted by North-South may be (and was) the wrong contract.

The save would have been worth 100 points to East-West (not 300), so the failure to bid hearts can hardly be considered a disaster.

U.S.A. 74
Both vulnerable.

NORTH
♠ 10 6 2
♡ A Q 8 3
◇ 7 3 2
♣ A J 9

WEST
♠ A 7 4
♡ J 9
◇ K J 10
♣ K 10 7 6 3

```
      N
   W     E
      S
```

EAST
♠ K 5 3
♡ 10 6 5 2
◇ A 9 8 4
♣ 5 2

SOUTH
♠ Q J 9 8
♡ K 7 4
◇ Q 6 5
♣ Q 8 4

WEST	NORTH	EAST	SOUTH
Reese	Becker	Schapiro	Hayden
		pass	pass
1♣	pass	1♡	all pass

Down two. 200 to North America.

ARGUMENT

The normal response to one club on Schapiro's holding is one diamond. Whatever merit there may be in calling one heart, there can be none if partner is known to have a doubleton. Why, then, if signals were exchanged, did Schapiro respond one heart?

If Reese, in turn, knows that Schapiro has four hearts only, he will surely not pass one heart. He has no need to accept as trumps a suit in which he knows the other side to possess numerical superiority.

ANSWER

This deal was discovered by Swimer on Saturday afternoon in Buenos Aires and was reported by me to the World Bridge Federation meeting. It is the only case in which Reese and Schapiro played a heart contract with fewer than seven trumps, and it is remarkable for more than one reason: it requires an explanation by both sides of the argument.

The normal response by East to one club would be one diamond, partly because of the strength of the suits and partly because the bid is more economical. One heart is very odd and becomes odder in the light of a comment made by Reese on another deal. On Italy 23 he held:

$$\spadesuit\ Q\ 8\ 7\ 5 \qquad \heartsuit\ 9\ 4\ 3\ 2 \qquad \diamondsuit\ Q\ J \qquad \clubsuit\ Q\ 8\ 6$$

Schapiro opened in fourth seat with one diamond, and in explaining his decision to respond one spade rather than one heart Reese said: "On a hand so weak for play in a suit contract it is folly, and certainly not my style, to choose a very bad suit." Most experts would say that it is folly, and certainly not the Reese-Schapiro style, to respond one heart on the East hand in U.S.A. 74. What was Schapiro's motive?

If the two players have illicit knowledge of the heart suit there are two possible explanations for this minor debacle.

One is the simple one that someone gave the wrong signal or misread a signal — for it is just as easy to have an accident with the fingers in signaling as it is to have a slip of the tongue in bidding.

The second is that the players got their wires crossed in the manner predicted by S. J. Simon a quarter of a century earlier. It can best be explained by reconstructing the mental processes of the two players:

SCHAPIRO: "I know I can bid one heart, because Terence knows this is a four-two fit and will not pass. This may stop them from leading hearts if we play in notrump."

REESE: "What is my crazy partner up to? He knows this is only a four-two fit, so why does he make the bid? Presumably he has a very strong four-card suit, in which case one heart will be playable. And perhaps North will balance. So I pass."

SCHAPIRO : "Blast!"

Argentina 34
North-South vulnerable.

NORTH
♠ Q 7 6 2
♡ Q J 3
◇ K 10 6
♣ K Q 9

WEST
♠ A K 9 5
♡ A 7 5 2
◇ A Q 8
♣ J 4

```
    N
W       E
    S
```

EAST
♠ 8 3
♡ 10 9 4
◇ 9 7 4 2
♣ A 8 7 2

SOUTH
♠ J 10 4
♡ K 8 6
◇ J 5 3
♣ 10 6 5 3

WEST	NORTH	EAST	SOUTH
Rocchi	Schapiro	Attaguile	Reese
		pass	pass
1♣	pass	1◇	pass
1NT	all pass		

North led the heart jack. 50 to Great Britain.

ARGUMENT

Rocchi's one-club opening and Attaguile's one-diamond response were conventional, and in effect, no genuine suit had been mentioned when Schapiro opened the jack of hearts. Reese played the eight, and declarer, winning with the ace, played back another heart.

This is not a spectacular hand, like Argentina 141[5], but it is no less indicative. The basic technique of card play in notrump contracts centers on the promotion of low cards. Hence the standard lead is "the fourth-highest of the longest suit" — to promote the long cards. Here the long card in hearts belongs to the declarer, Rocchi. Why, then, should Schapiro lead hearts? Obviously, because he is unaware of the position and hoped to find some length in the suit with Reese. Had Reese produced the appropriate three-finger signal, his partner would have known better.

---

5. See page 229.

Turn to Reese. Had he known that Schapiro possessed three hearts only, would he have played the eight on the jack? Note the importance of that card. With the eight out of the way, Rocchi could be certain of setting up his long heart, no matter how the suit was divided. Obviously, Reese knew no more about the heart position than did Schapiro.

There are times when a defender may have a hunch to lead a short suit. Instead of deceiving declarer and helping partner, this may deceive partner and help declarer. It may be a case of bad luck or bad judgment or both. But can such things happen in the heart suit to expert players who exchange illicit heart signals?

ANSWER

It seems a pity to deprive Schapiro of the credit for listening to the opposing bidding and making a well-judged lead. He had recognized a not-infrequent exception to the general principle that requires the defenders to establish a long suit in a notrump contract.

Attaguile and Rocchi were playing the Neapolitan system, so that the bid of one notrump following the strong forcing one-club bid showed a balanced hand with 17-20 points. East's negative response of one diamond showed a maximum of five points and his pass showed that his hand was also balanced. North himself has 13, so he knows that his partner, as well as the dummy, will be very weak. The lead situation is therefore analogous to that of a player with a good hand leading against a two-notrump opening bid that has been passed out.

In these circumstances the vital consideration is not suit establishment but safety. The opening leader must do everything he can to avoid giving an immediate trick to the declarer: he can expect that his partner and dummy will have little part to play in the proceedings. In a sense, North is thrown in before he starts, and the lead of a heart honor is clearly his best chance of avoiding a donation to West. It will cost a trick only if South has no heart honor and if dummy, known to be very weak, produces A-10, K-10, A-9, or K-9.

It is easy to work the more numerous situations in which leads in other suits will surrender a trick. A spade will injure the defense if South has nothing in the suit, or any single honor apart from the ace. A club honor will turn out badly whenever South has no honor in the suit, and also when he has the ten but dummy has the jack.

The location of the heart length is almost irrelevant here. If the suit is divided 4-3-3-3, the thirteenth card can be established regardless of the lead. If declarer has it he will surely be able to develop it in any event; if it is anywhere else, lack of an entry is likely to deprive it of value.

Whether or not South plays the heart eight on the first trick of course makes no difference to the result. The suggestion that he would not play that card if he knew that his partner held only a three-card suit is due to confused thinking. The argument would hold water only if South knew his partner's heart holding, but the converse was not true.

If both players know that their partner knows the heart length, it is clearly right, for two reasons, for South to play the heart eight on the first trick. South wants to indicate that a second heart lead will be safe for North when he gains the lead and has a problem — and there is no chance of misunderstanding about the length. Failure to make the routine play of the eight on the first trick would clearly go beyond the limits of "tolerance."

(N.B. The opening lead of the heart jack was "Rusinow" by partnership agreement. It implied possession of the queen, so South was in the same position as a player whose partner has led the queen using standard methods.)

The Foster Report[1]

We were asked by the British Bridge League to enquire into allegations that Mr. Reese and Mr. Schapiro had cheated by giving finger signals at the World Bridge Championship in Buenos Aires in May 1965.

We agreed to conduct this inquiry in an honorary capacity and have held some thirty sittings which have been spread over approximately some ten months during which fourteen witnesses have been called. The reason for this length of time is very largely (except for the period of the General Election) due to the fact that Counsel for the two persons accused was unable to agree to more frequent hearings owing to pressure of other cases in which he was engaged. We were assisted most expertly and most patiently by the two assessors, Messrs. Priday and Hiron, who commented on and explained the analysis of over fifty hands put forward by both sides.

The reference to us arose out of a report by the World Bridge Federation drawn up at the end of the World Bridge Championship, in which the Federation announced its findings on the allegations of cheating brought by certain members of the American team and Mr. Truscott, *The New York Times* bridge correspondent. The report recorded the fact that the Federation had found the allegations proved. The allegations were that Messrs. Reese and Schapiro had signalled with their fingers the number of hearts in their hands. One finger on the outside of the cards when they were held in the right or left hand denoted one heart, two fingers two hearts, and so on to four fingers. Two fingers splayed indicated five hearts, and three fingers splayed represented six hearts.[2]

The report was referred to the British Bridge League who decided that an independent inquiry should be held. It was agreed with the legal representatives of the two players accused (they were represented by Counsel and solicitors) and with the British Bridge League who were similarly represented, that the case against Messrs. Reese and Schapiro should be presented by the British Bridge League. Accordingly this report is being communicated privately by us to the League, to whom we leave the decision of whether to publish all, or some, or none of the report.

---

1. Footnotes have been added by the author of this book.
2. And four fingers, seven hearts, which was better documented than the three-finger, six-hearts signal. See the Becker-Hayden notes for Deal 114.

The evidence before us can be divided into two classes; the evidence of witnesses who say they saw finger signals exchanged and the technical evidence as to the bidding and sometimes (but much less often) as to the play of the hands.[3]

The conduct of the proceedings by the World Bridge Federation was most unsatisfactory.[4] The allegations were first investigated before the Appeals Committee, then by the Executive Committee. Mr. Butler, who is Chairman of the British Bridge League, was Chairman of the Appeals Committee at which Mr. Swimer, the non-playing captain of the English team, also attended.

The evidence before the Appeals Committee was mainly concerned with the direct evidence of signals being exchanged. Mr. Swimer and Mr. Butler read from their notes as to the number of fingers shown by Mr. Reese and Mr. Schapiro in front of their cards. Mr. Swimer gave evidence that he had watched the pair and that there was an exact correspondence between the number of fingers shown and the holding of hearts in 19 hands, while Mr. Butler's evidence, confined to watching 9 of the hands which Mr. Swimer had observed, was that there was correspondence in some 5 or 6 hands.[5] Similar evidence was given by these gentlemen to us.

Mr. Truscott was reported by Mr. Butler (to the Appeals Committee) as having observed signals and came to the conclusion that they represented heart holdings.[6] Mr. Truscott had told Mr. Butler that in a number of cases the bidding had suggested that the pair knew the distribution of the heart suit. Mr. Truscott had shown Mr. Butler and Mr. Swimer a number of hands which, according to Mr. Truscott, "indicated that this pair had never played a heart contract if it was unsuitable." Mr. Butler and Mr. Swimer had agreed that in some cases the bidding looked suspicious. Mr. Truscott also gave evidence to us on the same lines but was on this occasion much less positive about his "indirect" evidence, i.e. his analysis of the bidding.[7]

---

3. These two classes of evidence do not cover all the ground. They exclude, for example, the negative evidence, that no finger movements were visible when the players played with other partners, and the confession by Schapiro to which Swimer testified.
4. See Chapter 9.
5. Not a very accurate comment, since it implies a degree of non-correspondence. See pp. 55-56.
6. This *is* what Butler reported, but it is a rather misleading condensation of the observation and decoding process. As Butler did not fully absorb this part of my account to him, it is not surprising.
7. I was slightly less positive, for a good and objective reason. When I spoke to Butler and Swimer, I had found no bad heart fits played or good heart fits missed. I had not seen U.S.A. 74, which we then discovered, and Argentina 141 had not been played at that time.

Mr. Becker of the American team told the Appeals Committee that he had noticed finger signals during the play and that his partner, Mrs. Hayden, had also noticed signals. Both these players gave evidence at the hearings before us in great detail to the same effect.

Mr. Reese was called in before the Appeals Committee and denied the charge. He asked to see the evidence and Mr. Truscott was called in with his analysis of the hands which he had previously shown to Mr. Butler and Mr. Swimer.[8] Mr. Reese did not agree that the bidding had been unnatural or had suggested knowledge of the heart suit.

Mr. Schapiro when summoned before the Committee denied the charge and said it was absurd.

In the afternoon of the same day, Sunday May 25, 1965, there was a meeting of the World Bridge Federation Executive Committee at which Mr. Butler and Mr. Swimer repeated the evidence they had given before the Appeals Committee. Mr. Reese and Mr. Schapiro were called in and told of the detailed check of the hands observed, both by Mr. Butler and Mr. Swimer. After they withdrew, the charges were held proved.

We say that the proceedings at the Appeals Committee, and at the review by the Executive Committee, were unsatisfactory for the following reasons:

Mr. Butler was Chairman of the Appeals Committee yet his evidence was of the greatest importance. Mr. Swimer, who was also a witness, was nevertheless present throughout the sitting of the Appeals Committee.[9]

The Appeals Committee did not seek all the available evidence, some of which was disclosed in Mr. Butler's testimony. Neither Mrs. Hayden or Mr. Kehela, the American deputy-Captain, were called in to give evidence.[10] Mrs. Hayden's evidence in particular was of great importance as she had taken notes and had played against Messrs. Reese and Schapiro, both in the sessions where observations had taken place and before.[11]

The two players were not, in our opinion, given sufficient opportunity of defending themselves. The main defense against the direct evidence was a denial but it was very important that this direct evidence should be tested as soon as possible to examine whether any errors or self-persuasion had occurred and the

---

8. In this the Report accepts Reese's version of the events without question. In fact, I was present when he was called in, and he had heard a substantial body of the direct evidence against him when I was asked to go through some hands — and was cut short in the middle.

9. See page 138.

10. The fact that Kehela had any evidence to give was unknown to the officials.

11. What Mrs. Hayden had to say was put forward by Becker, Gerber and myself. And to object to a verdict because it could have been reinforced by other evidence seems to be a curious attitude.

opportunities and positions for observations should have been closely examined as near the time for observation occurred as possible. This was not done. Nor was the technical evidence examined, except very perfunctorily. [9]

The evidence at our hearings of the experts who came from various countries, was that if there is any cheating it is always revealed in the bidding and play.[12] Mr. de Hérédia (a professional tournament director), Mr. Ortiz-Patino, Mr. Flint and Mr. Konstam were quite categorical that if a pair cheated, then this could be detected in the record of their bidding and playing the cards.

The evidence about the bidding and play did not support the allegations of cheating.[13] There were hands where Messrs. Reese and Schapiro had cards which, using conventional methods, would have justified a bid in hearts yet they either failed to find the suit at all or failed to bid high enough.

In U.S. 74, Mr. Reese left his partner in a One Heart contract when Mr. Schapiro had four hearts to the ten and Mr. Reese had jack and another, instead of calling One No Trump, which would have been a better contract in any case, and certainly better with the knowledge of the heart holding.[14]

In Italy 56, Mr. Reese, playing against Three Diamonds, failed to make the ace of hearts after winning with the king when his partner had a singleton in hearts.[15]

---

12. These were all experts for the defense. The prosecution witnesses would have given a very different answer on this point. Even one of the defense witnesses was cautious: "The analysis of the cards would create a suspicion or presumption," was as far as Franklin was prepared to go.

13. See Chapter 16.

14. See pages 231-232.

15. Mollo did not regard this hand worthy of inclusion in his selected eight. The deal was:

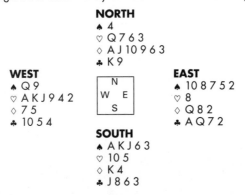

NORTH
♠ 4
♡ Q 7 6 3
◇ A J 10 9 6 3
♣ K 9

WEST
♠ Q 9
♡ A K J 9 4 2
◇ 7 5
♣ 10 5 4

EAST
♠ 10 8 7 5 2
♡ 8
◇ Q 8 2
♣ A Q 7 2

SOUTH
♠ A K J 6 3
♡ 10 5
◇ K 4
♣ J 8 6 3

North played in three diamonds after Reese, West, had opened the bidding with one heart. After winning the first heart trick Reese shifted to a club and the declarer was eventually able to discard all his hearts and made his contract. The defense contended that Reese would have cashed the second heart winner if he had known the lead was a singleton, but the need for this was not easy to foresee.

In Argentina 141, they had ten hearts between them yet never found the suit.[16]

Obviously categorical evidence from several prominent players in International Bridge to the effect that they saw Mr. Reese and Mr. Schapiro signal by changing fingers on the back of their cards raises a strong suspicion that the allegations were well founded. Against that must be set a number of considerations: the crudity of the signals,[17] especially when one finger was shown, or when the fingers were splayed, with two or three fingers to show five or six hearts; the concoction of a code to communicate information which is not as valuable as other information which could have been communicated less crudely and more economically in the number of signals.[18] Six different positions of the hands were required for the code.[19] At some of the sessions in which they were alleged to be cheating, there was no point in their doing so since Great Britain could not win the tournament and in the last session at which observation took place, Great Britain was defeating the Argentinians anyway.[20]

There is the further fact that Mr. Reese and Mr. Schapiro were on bad terms before the tournament at Buenos Aires; that Mr. Reese had written a letter to the British Bridge League asking not to play with Mr. Schapiro and that the two players had a row at Buenos Aires.[21]

As indicated above, the play and bidding of the hands did not disclose any cheating.[22] It was argued that players of the calibre of Mr. Reese and Mr. Schapiro would be so skillful as not to use the information so as to excite suspicion,[23] but this would not account for the negative part of this matter, namely that Mr. Reese and Mr. Schapiro played worse than their usual form in Buenos Aires[24] and often failed to achieve a contract which they should have established if they had been playing non-cheating conventional methods and which they could not have failed to have reached if they had foreknowledge of the hearts. In other words, when there was a legitimate choice, if these two had been cheating, they would have called a contract which they would have been justified in calling on their style of

---

16. See page 229.
17. See page 162.
18. See page 161.
19. This should be seven — all numbers of hearts from one through seven.
20. See page 158.
21. See page 91-92.
22. See Chapter 16 and Appendix A.
23. See page 131.
24. See pp. 156-157.

play and which a knowledge of hearts holding in partner's hand indicated clearly?[25]

It is with reference to the "direct" evidence of observation that we have most reason to regret the procedure adopted at Buenos Aires and by the British Captain. What should have happened, in our view, when the Captain was informed of the suspicions, is that the players should have been watched either by the Tournament Director[26] or by neutral persons (in this case neither United States, British, Italian or Argentine nationals)[27] appointed by the Federation for this task, which would probably have been delegated to the Tournament Director or his subordinates. Obviously the object should have been to obtain independent corroboration of the accusation. Allegations of cheating are made fairly frequently and, as we were told, without real basis, in International Bridge.[28] The corroboration sought and obtained was that of Mr. Butler and the English Captain. Mr. Butler's evidence is, we think, not clear corroboration[29] and Mr. Swimer was a witness whose powers of observation and recollection were marred by difficult relations with the two players.[30] At the end of his evidence he gave entirely fresh evidence that Mr. Schapiro had confessed to him and that he, Mr. Swimer, had told Mr. Schapiro to deny the allegations. Mr. Schapiro had, according to Mr. Swimer, said that "that evil man Reese" had forced him to cheat because Mr. Schapiro would not play the Little Major.[31] We do not believe that Mr. Schapiro would consent to cheat because he was unwilling to play the Little Major or that Mr. Schapiro would have chosen the English Captain to whom to confess as their relationship was distant and to an extent antagonistic.[32] We cannot understand why, if this confession took place, Mr. Swimer never reported it at Buenos Aires or told solicitor or Counsel[33] for the British Bridge League, who called him as a witness.

---

25. See Chapter 16.
26. In the special circumstances in Buenos Aires his appearance would have been a conspicuous tip-off to the two players. See pp. 74-75.
27. There were no such neutrals. See page 75.
28. As far as I know, the total is eight in the 40-year history of the game to 1965. Five of these were made against Reese and Schapiro, in 1949, 1952, 1955, 1960, and 1965. See Chapter 12.
29. Why not? His observations fitted the code very closely. See pp. 55-56.
30. See page 182.
31. See page 181.
32. See page 182.
33. A careless suggestion for a Queen's Counsel. In English law the Counsel may not have any direct contact with a witness before the hearing takes place.

As we said, the direct evidence is bound to raise suspicion. If accepted[34] the odds against the observed fingers corresponding in so many cases to the number of hearts held were so astronomical (running into million-to-one) that the only conclusion would have been that the two players were cheating.

Mrs. Hayden gave evidence before us, as did Mr. Becker and Mr. Truscott, that she had observed the players and noticed that Mr. Reese and Mr. Schapiro were making finger signals simultaneously. Later she, Mr. Becker and Mr. Truscott had "discovered," on checking with the hand records available, that the fingers corresponded with the heart holding. The notes which she produced to us were not before the Appeals Committee, since Mrs. Hayden was not called by them.[35]

Mr. Truscott, who went to watch after being told of their suspicions by Mr. Becker and Mrs. Hayden, also gave evidence to the same effect. In his case he told us he took no notes because he thought it might excite suspicion.[36]

Mr. Kehela, the Vice-Captain and Coach of the United States team, states that he had come to the conclusion that the two players accused were not cheating. Mr. Kehela told us that he had watched some nine or ten hands; that while he was watching he was convinced that the pair were cheating; that this conviction was not due to what he saw but because he believed what he was told. Later, after looking at a record of the hands, he had come to the conclusion that Mr. Reese and Mr. Schapiro had not been cheating[37] since the hands showed no evidence of such cheating. He decided that the correspondence in fingers and hearts holdings which he had observed was coincidental, i.e. not due to cheating. The other hands which he watched, the number of fingers shown and the number of hearts held did not tally. At the time he had watched the play he was not concerned to see if the pair were cheating since he had believed what he had been told, namely, that Mr. Reese and Mr. Schapiro were exchanging signals and he was at that time only interested in seeing how they were cheating, a fact about which he was already convinced. It was only afterwards, he told us, that he realized from the bidding and play that there had been no cheating.

The effect of a finding of cheating is just as serious for those accused as a finding of guilt of a crime. The standard of proof required in a criminal court to return a verdict is that the jury or court should be satisfied beyond a reasonable

---

34. The direct evidence was not accepted. The implication is that Swimer, Becker, Mrs. Hayden, Truscott, and perhaps Butler gave false testimony. In effect Sir John is saying, "The direct evidence proves guilty, so we must reject it in order to find them not guilty."

35. The copy in my possession was available to the Appeals Committee — not that they paid much attention to it.

36. This was a minor reason. The main reason was shock at what I saw.

37. This exaggerates what Kehela later told me he said to the Inquiry, which did not keep a transcript of his testimony. See Chapter 6.

doubt. We think that the same standard should be applied here and that the indirect or technical evidence raises such a doubt. There was no sign of cheating in the bidding or play of the cards.[38] In fact the bidding and play were in instances such that it would appear that the pair could not be cheating. They failed to find contracts or failed to make bids which a foreknowledge of the heart holding would have enabled them to achieve without raising suspicion. Mr. Reese and Mr. Schapiro played badly in Buenos Aires,[39] below their form and certainly no better than the other British pair[40] against whom there were no accusations of cheating.

The indirect evidence is of importance in considering the findings of guilt before the Appeals Committee and the Executive Committee. When Reese "asked to see the evidence . . . Mr. Truscott was called in with his analysis which he had previously shown to Mr. Butler and Mr. Swimer."

Clearly the Appeals Committee attached importance to this "indirect" evidence,[41] but unfortunately the "analysis" of Mr. Truscott was superficial having regard to all the hands played by Mr. Reese and Mr. Schapiro.[42] Mr. Butler had reported that Mr. Truscott had told him that "a number of hands" had "indicated that this pair had never played a heart contract without a fit and had avoided a heart contract if the fit was unsuitable." This is not true.[43] The 8 hands produced to Mr. Butler by Mr. Truscott were Italy 22, 23, 25, 26, 34 and 117 and USA 30 and 36.[44] Mr. Truscott told us "I did not find at that time any hands which[45] the play-

---

38. A sweeping statement open to plenty of doubt. See Chapter 10 and Appendix A.
39. But see pp. 156-157.
40. There were four other players playing in a variety of partnerships — a fact that might have been known after a year of testimony.
41. The degree of importance attached by the Appeals Committee to this subject was very slight. Several responsible people criticized me for introducing hands into the evidence at all, on the ground that nothing could be proved by them and a clear-cut issue would be confused.
42. I fail to see how I could have done more than I did. At 4 A.M. on Saturday I went through five of the ten sessions played by Reese and Schapiro up to dinner time on Friday night — all that were available to me. On Saturday afternoon Swimer and I went through three or four more sessions, so almost all the ground was covered.
43. It certainly is true. There was only one hand in Buenos Aires — U.S. 74 shown on pp. 231-232 — in which Reese and Schapiro played a heart contract with fewer than seven trumps. This was discovered by Swimer after I had reported to Butler, and was mentioned by me to the committee on Sunday.
44. Not at all. These were the eight deals mentioned to Reese in the Sunday meeting. I gave Butler and Swimer a list of eighteen deals, and I have my original typewritten notes to prove it. The others were: Italy 20, 35, 39, 41, 54, 57, 58; U.S. 31, 37, 39 and 42. This makes a total of nineteen, because Foster has Italy 34 when, presumably, he means 35.
45. I am sure I did not insult the relative pronoun in this way.

ers had failed to locate a good fit in the heart suit or in which they had arrived at an unsatisfactory contract in the heart suit."[46] Later he said "it seemed to me they were locating the heart suit with great consistency." It was wrong of the Appeals Committee to rely on the small sample of eight hands produced by Mr. Truscott[47] without considering the overall picture. We had a very full analysis, lasting over twenty-two days, of all the hands that might have a bearing on these allegations and we had clear evidence that neither the bidding nor the play of the hands revealed any foreknowledge of the hearts.[48] If evidence of this sort had been before the Appeals Committee they might well have come to a different conclusion.

The other matter which raises a reasonable doubt in our minds is the evidence of Mr. Kehela referred to in detail above.[49] Mr. Kehela both observed the play and after studying the bidding he came to the conclusion that the pair were not cheating. We therefore think that the direct evidence as to the exchange of finger signals, strong as it is, cannot be accepted because of the reasonable doubt which we feel on these two grounds.

We find that Messrs. Reese and Schapiro were not guilty of cheating at the tournament in question.

JOHN FOSTER

BOURNE

4 August 1966

---

46 Note that the only hand that could belong in the "failure to locate" category is Argentina 141, which had not been played when Swimer and I did our analysis.

47. They didn't.

48. See Chapter 16.

49. See Chapter 6.

The World Bridge Federation Report[1]

THE MINUTES OF THE BUENOS AIRES MEETINGS,
WORLD BRIDGE FEDERATION APPEALS COMMITTEE

Buenos Aires   Sunday 25.5.65

Chairman:

> G. L. Butler

Present:

> C. Solomon (President W.B.F.)
> W. von Zedtwitz
> Robin MacNab

In attendance:

> R. Swimer (British Captain)[2]

The Chairman said he had called the meeting because of certain irregularities alleged to have been committed by the British pair: Reese and Schapiro.

He had been consulted by Swimer the previous afternoon and had had a conference with him and A. Truscott. Truscott reported that as a result of information he had received he had examined a number of hands played by Reese and Schapiro.[3] In a number of cases the bidding had suggested that the pair knew the distribution of the heart suit. He (Truscott) had been told by B. Jay Becker and his partner, Mrs. Hayden, that on Monday, Becker, when playing against the British pair had noticed that they held their cards in a peculiar way showing a varying number of fingers in front. He had watched them again on Wednesday[4] when he was not playing and had told Mrs. Hayden that he thought the number of fingers showing in front indicated certain holdings, but he could not discover any code.

---

1. With footnotes added by the author of this book.
2. Gerber states that he was present throughout.
3. The cart before the horse. Examination of hands was an afterthought, after the finger signals had been observed, recorded and decoded.
4. Nothing happened on Wednesday. The author of the Report (Butler) may mean Friday, when four people watched.

He had subsequently told his Captain, J. Gerber, who after watching this pair had asked Truscott to see if he could discover any relationship between the number of fingers showing and the holding of the heart suit.[5] Gerber had noticed that when one finger was in front one heart was held, when two fingers were showed three or four hearts. Both players were using these signals and in every case he had noticed the signs corresponded. Truscott had told the Chairman that he had studied the hand records early on Saturday morning and at 4 A.M. he had in his opinion broken the code.[6]

He showed a number of hands to him and to Swimer which indicated that this pair had never played a heart contract without a fit and had avoided a heart contract if the fit was unsuitable. He (the chairman) and Swimer had gone through these hands[7] and found one where they had played a one heart contract with a 4-2 fit but agreed that in some cases the bidding looked suspicious.

Truscott had said that they held their cards always in the left hand when they were alleged to be using the signals.[8] Swimer and he (Butler) agreed to watch the pair. On the Saturday, for part of the match, Reese had played with another partner and no signals were seen by Swimer who was observing him.[9] In the last session Swimer had watched for about ten hands and he had watched for the remaining ten hands while Reese and Schapiro were paired together.[10] Afterwards they had met and each said he felt quite sick because the signals fitted the code.

The hand records were not yet available and in some cases it had not been proved that the heart holdings fitted the signals. Frequently the cards were thrown in when there had been a number of tricks played and it had not been possible to prove that Schapiro had in fact held the hearts he had signaled. Both he and Swimer in turn had been sitting by the side of Reese and in every case but one, which he would refer to later, Reese's signals had fitted the heart holding.

He therefore summoned the Appeal Committee for this urgent matter and had invited Swimer to be present.

Swimer gave evidence of the same kind, and said that he could not discover how they differentiated between two and five hearts. He produced his notes made at the table and against each hand he had marked the heart signals. He had not

---

5. This is quite inaccurate. Gerber had not asked me to do anything, nor had he noticed anything about the heart suit.
6. No mention of Becker and Mrs. Hayden, who did much more than I did.
7. Not "these hands," obviously. Swimer went through other hands that I did not have.
8. I said nothing about left hand or right hand, and neither did anyone else to my knowledge.
9. Swimer watched Schapiro, not Reese.
10. Swimer watched another nine deals after Butler had taken the official seat.

checked them with the hand records but in all cases which he had been able to see the hands played out the code fitted.

The chairman produced his own notes of hands 126 to 134 of the match against Argentina. On two occasions (127 and 131) Reese had signaled four hearts but had had none. On 131 he had held his cards as usual but during the bidding he had lowered his left hand to the table and it might be that this was the signal for a void. He had not noticed anything about 127. Reese might or might not have lowered his hand after holding it up.

On hand 130 his vision had been obscured by a spectator and he could not see exactly. He thought Reese had signalled three hearts but in fact held two.

On some occasions he had not been able to check Schapiro's holding against the signals.

Both players throughout held their cards in their left hand.

It was decided to call in B. Jay Becker who repeated what the Chairman had said in his statement. He said he had no wish to damage Reese and Schapiro but could not let the matter pass. He said his partner, Mrs. Hayden, was so upset that she played very badly on the Thursday against the British pair.

John Gerber was called in[11] and his evidence coincided with the Chairman's statement. In his view the signal for five cards was two fingers spread and for two cards was two fingers together. The Chairman interposed to point out that as he himself had been at the side of Reese, seeing the faces of the cards he could not see how the fingers were held, spread or unspread, on the backs, but spread fingers could account for 129 and 132 when Reese had held five hearts and had had two fingers on the backs of the cards.

It was decided to call in Schapiro and Reese.

Schapiro came in first and the Chairman said it was alleged that by finger signals they were communicating their heart holdings to each other. When asked if he had anything to say he made a blank denial and said the charge was absurd.[12]

Reese was called in and also denied the charge. He asked to see the evidence and Truscott was called in[13] with his analysis which he had previously shown to the Chairman and Swimer. Reese did not agree that their bidding had been unnatural or had suggested their knowledge of the heart suit.

---

11. He says he was there all the time.
12. MacNab has a different recollection. He says that Schapiro's first reaction was to ask "Where's Terence?" He was a man in need of support from the stronger member of the partnership.
13. I was there already, and again this emphasizes the technical evidence when the important thing was the observations and notes.

The various members of the press were aware that an investigation was being conducted and sent in to ask for a statement. It was discussed that the following might be published: "A protest has been made against Reese and Schapiro and until the Appeal Committee has resolved the matter the pair will not play."

It was subsequently decided to issue no statement.

Von Zedtwitz said that he would have to leave for America but would hold himself at the disposal of the Committee as long as possible. He had learned of the protest and had seen a few hands on the Saturday and the signals fitted the heart holding.[14]

After further discussion it was unanimously agreed that the evidence was very strong and that a meeting of the World Bridge Federation Executive should be called after lunch. The meeting then ended after three and a half hours.

WORLD BRIDGE FEDERATION EXECUTIVE MEETING
Sunday

Present: C. Solomon (President), R. MacNab, G. L. Butler, C. A. Perroux, the Argentina representative Dr. Labougle, W. von Zedtwitz, General A. Gruenther (Hon. President); T. Hammerich (Venezuela) with the British Captain, R. Swimer, in attendance.[15]

The President gave a full report of the morning's proceedings of the Appeal Committee, after which the hand record sheets of the Argentine match the previous evening were produced.

R. Swimer called out from his notes the heart holdings indicated by the code and these were checked against the hand records. These were as follows (R - Reese; S - Schapiro):

135	3R	4S
136	4R	4S
137	3R	2S
138	3R	2S
139	1R	4S
140	3R	3S
141	2R (=5)	2S (=5)
142	4R	3S
143	4R	2S
144	3R	2S

14. Von Zedtwitz watched on Friday night.

15. Gerber was also in attendance. And Hammerich's initial is J.

In every case the holdings coincided. Mr. Butler then read out from his notes the signals he had seen. His record was not complete as he had been partly unsighted. In 127 Schapiro had signaled with three fingers but had in fact six hearts and Reese (as stated in the earlier proceedings) had shown four fingers but had no hearts. The remaining hands were:

128	R4	S3
129	R2 (=5)	S4
130	R2 or 3	S4
131	R4 (but had lowered his hand perhaps to show more.)	
132	R2 (=5)	S2
133	R3	
134	R4	S3

A long discussion followed and Mr. MacNab proposed to call the pair in together for a further investigation. This was carried unanimously.

Reese and Schapiro then appeared and were told of the detailed check of hands 128 to 144. The checkings were repeated before them and it was stressed that neither Swimer nor Butler had had any opportunity of consulting the hand record sheets.

After Reese and Schapiro had withdrawn there was a lengthy discussion. Both Butler and Swimer said that they had never suspected this pair before and were dumbfounded when they had been given the code by Truscott.

Mr. Solomon said that at the end of the Olympiad in 1960 in Turin,[16] alleged irregularities had been reported to the Director. H. Franklin of England had undertaken to report these to Mr. Butler, Chairman of the British League. Mr. Butler said that Mr. Franklin had not done so and this was news to him. General Gruenther said he had been greatly impressed by the checking of the heart suit from the notes produced by the British Captain and Mr. Butler. Three or four examples could well be coincidences but when in nineteen successive hands the signals coincided he was convinced.

Other members of the committee expressed the same views and complimented Messrs. Butler and Swimer on their impartiality in most trying circumstances.

As time was passing Mr. Swimer said that until the matter was settled neither

---

16. Butler's draft minutes read "1964 in New York." He had not understood which Olympiad Solomon was referring to.

player could be allowed to play in the match against America now proceeding. If the allegations were proved Great Britain would, if they won, concede the match to America.

Mr. Butler said that it would also be proper to cede the match, already won, to Argentine but no statement could be issued about the American match until the result was known for it would spoil the interest of spectators if Great Britain stopped playing before the match was settled. Great Britain was leading but the match was not yet won.

It was eventually put to the vote that the pair was guilty of illegally conveying signals.

This was carried unanimously with the exception of C. A. Perroux, who abstained. Von Zedtwitz said that the pair should be suspended for a year.

It was then decided that no statement to the press would be made until the end of the match against America. Mr. Butler said that it might be proper for Great Britain to withdraw, if they were ahead, two or three boards from the end. This proposal was not carried further.

Various forms of wording for the official statement were then discussed. It was proposed to issue the following:

"Certain irregularities have been reported. The Appeal Committee fully investigated the matter and later convened a meeting of the World Bridge Federation who found that the British pair, T. J. Reese[17] and B. Schapiro, were guilty of using illegal signals.

"During the meeting the British Captain was present and he announced that this pair would take no further part in the tournament."

This was signed by C. Solomon and Geoffrey L. Butler, Chairman of the Appeal Committee.

Reese and Schapiro were then called in and were told the findings of the Committee. Reese said he thought the verdict was absurd but that if the Committee had so decided they could do nothing other than what they had done. He asked if further steps would be taken and was told that the matter would be referred to the British Bridge League. He also said that he thought the Committee should have produced more convincing evidence that they had gained as a result of using these alleged signals. All the hands should be gone through for evidence that their bidding had been affected by their knowledge of the heart distribution. He also said if they wanted to cheat there were many cleverer ways than the one alleged here. He was told that the Committee was not saying that, in fact, they had benefited but was convinced they had used signals. Possibly the code was a new

17. Should be J. T. Reese.

one, not used before, and was felt to be enough to give them such an advantage as would be obtained by a chess player who was given a knight or a bishop. Mr. Reese had an inventive mind as was proved by his instigating the Little Major, and it could be that this concealed code about the heart suit was his invention to give them a practical advantage which in fact they might not, as the play went, have derived. They had not been found guilty of winning illegally but of signalling illegally. It was also pointed out that the last session against the Argentine had been won by 68 to 3.

Mr. Reese said he knew they were being watched and saw Mr. Butler take notes on Saturday night. When asked if he intended to withdraw from the International scene he said he would probably do so as accusations of this kind, and earlier, made it impossible to play any further. This should not be taken as an admission of guilt.

Mr. Schapiro said that before he knew of the proceedings he had announced that he would not play again in International bridge.

The pair then withdrew and an alternative statement was prepared. This would be released at the end of the Tournament. The President said he thought it was incorrect now to put the onus on the British Bridge League. The Committee adjourned until half past midnight.

Mr. Solomon said that in the interim, he, with Mr. Butler, had seen Mr. Reese and showed him the proposed statement in which their names were mentioned. He (Reese) said that he had no objection on his own account but if Schapiro's name were mentioned it would be disastrous for him. He asked if reference could not be made more indirectly to "two players of the British team." Mr. Solomon had pointed out that this would be unfair to the other four members whose names might be under suspicion but he would consider the matter.

Finally Mr. Solomon had hit upon the following wording:

"Certain irregularities having been reported, the Appeals Committee fully investigated the matter and later convened a meeting of the Executive Committee of the World Bridge Federation. The Captain of the British team was present.

"As a result of this meeting the Captain of the British Squad decided to play only K. Konstam, M. Harrison-Gray, A. Rose and J. Flint in the remaining sessions and very sportingly conceded the matches with the United States and Argentina. A report of the proceedings will be sent to the British Bridge League."

This was approved and signed by Solomon and Butler. Members of the press were called in and given the statement. Some members asked for further particulars and whether they could mention finger signals. The president said the statement made no reference to signals and that he would add nothing to the statement.